INSTITUTE FOR RESEARCH ON
TEACHING INFORMATION CENTER
238 Erickson Hall

Organizing an Anarchy

Organizing an Anarchy

Lee Sproull
Stephen Weiner
David Wolf

Belief, Bureaucracy, and
Politics in the National
Institute of Education

The University of Chicago Press
Chicago and London

The University of Chicago Press, Chicago 60637
The University of Chicago Press, Ltd., London

© 1978 by The University of Chicago
All rights reserved. Published 1978
Printed in the United States of America
82 81 80 79 78   987654321

Lee Sproull is assistant professor of social
science, Carnegie-Mellon University.
Stephen Weiner is associate dean of the
Graduate School of Public Policy,
University of California, Berkeley. David
Wolf is assistant dean of college
development, Los Angeles Mission College.

Library of Congress Cataloging in Publication Data

Sproull, Lee.
    Organizing an anarchy.

    Includes bibliographical references and index.
    1. National Institute of Education. 2. Bureaucracy.
I. Weiner, Stephen, joint author. II. Wolf, David,
1942–   joint author. III. Title.
LB2806.5.S68   379   77–15411
ISBN 0–226–76992–5

To Bob Sproull, Pat Weiner, and
Ruth Wolf

Contents

Foreword

Students of public organizations have a reputation for extracting interesting ideas from the fine detail of careful case studies. For examples, consider Philip Selznick's treatment of the Tennessee Valley Authority, Arthur Maass's examination of the Corps of Engineers, Roberta Wohlstetter's analysis of the United States military at Pearl Harbor, Herbert Kaufman's portrait of the Forest Service, or Graham Allison's reconstruction of decision-making during the Cuban missile crisis. Each study combines attention to the confusion of real events with a willingness to speculate about the nature of things.

This book is a continuation of that tradition. It is both a careful history of a specific agency over a limited period of time and a contribution to organization theory. The subject is the National Institute of Education as it tried to survive birth. As the authors demonstrate, birth is the assertion of uniqueness by which the chicken honors the egg. The creation of the National Institute of Education was one effort in a long history of efforts. The institute inherited perplexities, diagnoses, expectations, solutions, people, programs, friends, and enemies from its ancestry. It celebrated the possibility of a new life; but it was conceived in the usual way, born innocent, and lost its virginity in a Senate subcommittee.

For students of organizations, NIE was a natural experiment in organizational development. It was a compounding of four processes in the birth and early history of an organization: The first was the political process of securing and maintaining support. The second was the bureaucratic process of establishing procedures, structure, personnel, and priorities. The third was the personal process of negotiating and furthering reputations and careers. The fourth was the symbolic process of developing meanings, interpretations of events, and beliefs.

In examining each of these processes and the way each formed the context for the others, yet proceeded independently of them, Lee Sproull, Stephen Weiner, and David Wolf outline a general view of organizational development. They suggest ideas for understanding organizations in which objectives, technologies, beliefs, actions, and outcomes are ambiguous and only loosely connected to each other.

Although the study is relevant to many aspects of behavior by such organizations, it seems to me particularly useful in illuminating three things:

1. The authors provide clarification, elaboration, and qualification to familiar modern complaints about planning and organizing as instruments of bureaucratic action. They show how an organization dedicated to rational procedures, excellence, and the use of intelligence came to be indecisive, incompetent, and disorganized.

2. They examine the way beliefs were formed, diffused, and reinforced in a world of ordinary ambiguity. A national capital is a city of librarians and bookkeepers made dramatic in newspapers. The drama affects diaries of librarians and bookkeepers and the stories of observers, but does not much affect libraries or ledgers. The authors see NIE as a prosaic world often reported in poetic diaries and stories.

3. They exhibit a sense for the basic elements of tragedy in organizational life. The players played their parts as they were written. Other people might have done better, but those people were not interested. Other strategies might have avoided some of the specific disasters that befell the agency, but some were arbitrary acts of an indifferent fate. What happened was not foreordained, but neither was it very responsive to intentional human control.

Without compromising the generality of such observations, the authors also describe a specific governmental agency and a specific set of historical circumstances. The National Institute of Education was established in 1972 to further research and development in education. The time and focus dictated an environment, and the authors explicate the numerous ways in which that environment made a difference. Watergate, conflict between Congress and president, a declining political status for education, doubts about the efficacy of social research, a history of attitudes about the Office of Education, and a file of existing commitments defined a milieu for the organization that is unlikely to be duplicated in detail. It is history with history's limitations and charms.

The birth of NIE provided a lucky opportunity for translating organizational experience into understanding through research. The timing was right, the organization exceptional, the patience and perceptiveness of the authors impressive. This book is the result. It is written by professionals. It tells a story in the terms in which it took place, reporting events rather than inferences, and imposing order gently. The claims are modest and the conclusions conservative.

It is also sympathetic. Sproull, Weiner, and Wolf write organizational biography with the simple honesty of affectionate friends, recording human imperfections and failures without surprise, and without implication for human worth or human will. As a result, I suspect their study will be appreciated not only by social scientists of education, government, and organizations, but also by anyone who has ever lived and dreamed in those refineries of disillusion.

James G. March
Stanford University

Preface

In 1973 we made an innocent decision. We decided to collaborate on a study of the National Institute of Education (NIE) as an exemplar of implementing government policy through a new bureaucratic mechanism. The task seemed straightforward and not too time-consuming. We were wrong on both counts. Establishing a reasonable history of what had happened in a new bureaucracy and forming some satisfying theory to account for events proved to be a mysterious and challenging process.

Our joint venture is traceable to two factors. First, each of us had worked for the federal government in Washington, D. C. Sproull had been a member of the NIE Planning Unit and had worked for the Rand Corporation in Washington. Weiner had been a congressional staff member and had worked for the National Advisory Commission on Civil Disorders. Wolf had been one of NIE's first staff members and was employed by the institute throughout its first year. In Washington we had each observed the initiation of new bureaucratic programs. Our experience had been that they almost always fell victim to disillusion and left a mixed and controversial record behind them. We shared an interest in understanding the life cycle of new policy ideas and their bureaucratic embodiments.

The second factor in our collaboration was our common work and study at the Stanford Graduate School of Education. Each of us had been drawn to studies of organization decision-making and to that domain's most creative theorist, Professor James G. March. During the course of our research on NIE, we spent many long evenings with Jim March. We brought problems and he brought wine. Somehow they both disappeared.

Our study draws upon several sources of data. First, over a two-year period we interviewed all senior NIE officials plus a wide range of institute staff. In some cases we conducted multiple interviews with the same informant. In addition we drew upon supplementary interviews with top NIE officials provided by Susan McCarthy, staff historian for the institute (the list of interviewees is contained in Appendix 1). Second, we examined a large number of documents from the files of the NIE Planning Unit and the institute itself, public testimony and debate in the United States Congress, and articles of relevance from both the popular and the educational press (a full listing of the major documentary sources is included in the bibliography). Third, we administered a questionnaire to the professional staff of the institute in June 1974 (N = 288, response rate = 86%). Questionnaire responses were analyzed by computer at Stanford University. Finally, our comprehension was enriched by a number of informal conversations with current and former members of the institute staff.

We also sought to tap two other resources, but with less success. During the early months of 1974 we searched for careful descriptions of the internal dynamics of other new public bureaucracies. We found only a small literature, of highly uneven quality. In the early months we were aided by reading Philip Selznick's (1949) *TVA and the Grassroots*; Herbert Simon's (1953) "Birth of an Organization"; and Stephen Strickland's (1972) *Politics, Science, and Dread Disease*. However, most of the books and articles we identified yielded little more than recitations of dates and names—organizational histories that went little beyond the detail and insight of routine newspaper coverage. Toward the end of our work, Donald P. Warwick's (1975) *Theory of Public Bureaucracy*, a study of attempted reorganizations in a section of the United States State Department, came to our attention and was useful. However, Warwick also reported that his search for comparable materials on other executive department organizations had gone largely unrewarded.

With the assistance of William Richards of the Stanford Communications Department, we conducted a computerized network analysis of work-related and social interconnections within the NIE staff in an attempt to understand more fully the relationship between organization structure and bureaucratic communication. The data for this analysis were collected as a part of our larger questionnaire in June 1974. Although the network analysis technique is both powerful and ingenious, in our case it produced little insight that was not already available from interviews and organization charts. Perhaps this is a finding of interest in its own right.

Our data collection activities began in January 1973 and ended in November 1974. Our study says virtually nothing about events after the end of data collection. But, the curious reader might be interested to know that Congress renewed the life of the institute for another three years by legislation enacted in late 1976.

Bureaucrats are more accustomed to commissioning studies than to being the subjects of them. Fortunately we encountered some unconventional bureaucrats who consistently supported and encouraged us in our examination. Thomas K. Glennan, Jr., the institute's first director, gave us virtually unrestricted access to the organization and a considerable amount of his time in personal conversation. Emerson Elliott, deputy director, and Bernard Martin, associate director for planning and management, generously gave us access to their thoughts and their files. Glennan, Elliott, and Martin reviewed an earlier draft of this manuscript. Their comments improved the factual accuracy of the book; of course they are not responsible for, nor do they necessarily share, our interpretation of those facts. Our efforts throughout the institute, whether in the form of interviews or of questionnaires, were met with cooperation and candor. Elisabeth Hansot and Susan McCarthy of the institute staff were particularly generous in sharing their impressive knowledge with us and never laughing at our silly questions.

Our work benefited from a critical review by our colleagues at Stanford University. Allen Campell, John Curry, Carla Edlefson, Sue Estler, Margret Floden, Jane Hannaway, Helga Hernes, Ray Leavit, and Jay Schoenau were tactful yet demanding reviewers. Dan Weiler, of the Rand Corporation, made many helpful suggestions, and the resulting improvements to our work are greater than we should admit.

Our research was supported financially by the Spencer Foundation. Lee Sproull was supported during the latter portion of the study by the Stanford–National Institute of Mental Health Organization Research Training Program. Stephen Weiner received support during the early stages of the work from the Center for the Advanced Study of the Behavioral Sciences. Our friends and sponsors are, of course, exempt from any blame that might ensue from their encouragement.

Organizing an Anarchy

List of Acronyms

AASA	American Association of School Administrators
AERA	American Education Research Association
ASPE	Assistant Secretary for Planning and Management, HEW
CEDaR	Council on Educational Development and Research
CRP	Cooperative Research Program, OE
ERIC	Educational Resources Information Center
FIS	Field Initiated Studies, NIE
GAO	Government Accounting Office
HEW	Department of Health, Education, and Welfare
NASA	National Aeronautics and Space Administration
NCEC	National Center for Education Communication
NCEC	National Committee for Educational Change
NCER	National Council on Educational Research
NCERD	National Center for Educational Research and Development
NDEA	National Defense Education Act
NIE	National Institute of Education
NIH	National Institutes of Health
NSF	National Science Foundation
OE	Office of Education
OECD	Organization for Economic Cooperation and Development
OEO	Office of Economic Opportunity
OMB	Office of Management and Budget
OPM	Office of Planning and Management, NIE
ORES	Office of Research and Exploratory Studies, NIE
OST	Office of Science and Technology
PPBS	Program Planning and Budgeting System
PSAC	President's Science Advisory Committee
R&D	Research and Development
SDC	System Development Corporation
USGPO	United States Government Printing Office

Introduction

A simple theory underlies much of the rhetoric, and some of the practice, in the creation and management of public agencies. The theory holds that it is both possible and appropriate to establish clear, coherent goals for the agency's work. It is then possible to select strategies that will maximize the probable attainment of those goals. Once the selected strategies have been implemented, so the theory goes, substantive success or failure will follow. Success or failure will then lead to appropriate changes in the agency's resources—changes consistent with the public welfare. This theory has been labeled the "rational model" of decision-making or management (see March and Simon 1958; Cyert and March 1963; Allison 1971; Steinbruner 1974).[1] Of course it is possible that the initial set of goals will have to be modified or that the first strategies will go awry. But, by comparing the agency's successes or failures with the original goals, the agency managers can determine what corrections are necessary. This process of comparing and modifying is usually called "learning." And, like "rational" decision-making, "learning" is viewed with great favor by managers and those who evaluate them.

These models, which visualize organizations as a series of tight connections between a small number of fairly stable elements, inevitably oversimplify how bureaucracies actually function. In the case of new organizations or ones operating in areas of complex political policy, we suspect they are substantially wrong. Establishing clear, coherent goals requires either a unitary decision-maker or consensus among a stable group of decision-makers. Selecting appropriate strategies to achieve goals requires that the organization possess a fairly clear and well-defined technology, that is, the capacity to identify or develop courses of action that have the intended impact upon the problems the organization seeks to solve. Implementing those strategies requires that the decision-maker be able to translate his or her intentions into organization action. Evaluating their success requires that there be a clear connection between organization action and outcome; the manager and evaluator must be confident that their strategy has been implemented and that what happened was what they intended to happen. Finally, for a manager to "learn" from this cycle, all the above requirements must be met and, in addition, the manager must be sure that the rewards or punishments received from the outside world are in fact in response to the actions of the organization. None of these requirements is likely to be met very often in a political bureaucracy or one endeavoring to make social policy in a value-laden field.

These organizations can be better described by a different set of characteristics. A new bureaucracy inherits a context and a technology. Both have profound implications for a sensible theory of decision-making and management for such organizations. The context is composed of the general social and political attitudes of the times. Events in a particular bureaucracy tend to be heavily influenced by a flow of political, economic, social, and personal action. Thus they cannot be adequately understood in terms of that organization alone. To understand the organization, one must understand the context. This is the most ancient of historical cliches, but one that is easily ignored in examining organization life.

The context also includes a set of expectations for the new agency. These expectations are influenced by a history of failure or success in the field in which the organization will work. They are also influenced by current attitudes about the priority and relevance of the organization's intended work. Additionally, the set of expectations inherited by the new bureaucracy is influenced by the act of creation itself, which is often accompanied by heroic claims for the new agency's capabilities.[2] Debates on the creation of new bureaucracies are systematically biased against the recognition that a new bureaucracy inherits a history that may have bedeviled its predecessors.

Further, the new organization is subject to pressures from conflicting external groups. If the bureaucracy is created within a complicated authority structure, such as the federal government, it is subject to requirements, rewards, and penalties stemming from a number of legislative, executive, and judicial overseers, who are rarely of one mind. It is accompanied by a community of constituents who are united in the desire for more attention and resources from the patron agency but divided over how those goods should be apportioned.

A bureaucracy functioning in the domain of social policy faces an additional set of uncertainties. In order to establish and maintain supporting political coalitions in a value-laden field, organization goals must be couched in fairly vague terms. But, in addition, even if the organization could specify its goals, it is likely it would not know how to achieve them. Policy decisions in the social sector must rely primarily upon knowledge developed within the social sciences, fields characterized by weak and competing theories. Thus the technology available to the organization in the pursuit of its goals is often unclear.

If the above characterization is at all reasonable—if there is a class of organizations with an unpredictable environment, ambiguous goals, and unclear technology—the simple theories of rational management are inappropriate and misleading. We believe an alternative theory—a theory of organized anarchies—both better describes how these organizations function and leads to more interesting predictions about managerial behavior.[3] An organized anarchy is characterized by ambiguous goals, unclear technology, and fluid participation. In organized anarchies it is usually the case that if goals are measurable, they are not widely agreed to; if they are acceptable to all parties, they are neither measurable nor operational. An unclear technology is one in which there is only a low probability of identifying or developing courses of action that have an intended impact upon a previously specified problem. And fluid participation recognizes that people both inside and outside an organization have limited resources of time and energy. Their attention to particular issues within the organization is neither continuous nor stable. We believe these three factors characterize most new government organizations, irrespective of their mission, and most agencies operating in social policy domains, irrespective of their age. The theory of organized anarchies, which visualizes organizations as a series of loose connections among a large number of changing elements, suggests that decisions can be only partially explained as outcomes determined by rational intentions. In order for there to be a decision, there must exist the occasion for a decision. In a public bureaucracy there are only a limited number of such occasions—the annual budget preparation and the hiring of new personnel, for example. When such occasions are viewed over time, it becomes evident that different problems are considered relevant to the decision at various times. The meaning of the decision to be made changes as different problems enter and leave the decision arena. These entrances and exits are as much a function of uncontrolled external events and the emotional state of the decision-makers as they are of a rational analysis of goals.

Unlike the rational model behavior, in an organized anarchy the search for solutions is not necessarily contingent upon the identification of a problem. Solutions exist independent of problems, and problems may be created in order to provide opportunities for the application of previously discovered solutions. Participants both inside and outside the organization vary in the amount of time and attention they can devote to individual decisions. These variations arise both from differences in personal dedication and from competing attention demands. At any point in time, the definitions of both problems and solutions are at least partially dependent upon the mix of participants in the process.

In an organized anarchy, the process of decision-making serves functions other than the production of decisions. It aids both individual participants and the organization as a whole to arrive at socially generated interpretations of what they are doing. Further, participating in decision-making forums is a pleasurable activity. It helps identify and certify who is important within the organization.

Learning in an organized anarchy is not a straightforward process. It is likely that success will be defined by a creative interpretation—on the part of people both inside and outside the organization—of ambiguous experience. The lessons will be heavily influenced by simple indexes or symbolic acts. Translating what the managers have "learned" into a new round of organization action may be difficult. In the absence of unambiguous organization goals, subunit or individual goals will predominate. In the absence of a reliable technology, there will be a heavy reliance on standard operating procedures and simple decision rules.

In summary, the theory of decision-making and learning in an organized anarchy emphasizes the limited capacity of human beings to rationally resolve intricate and vague problems; the heavy influence of context upon organizational processes; the power of simple rules or symbolic acts for action and the evaluation of action; and the ascendancy of social mechanisms and individual preconceptions over deductive standards in the process of organization learning. None of this is to say that organized anarchies are "bad" organizations or that decision-making in them leads to "bad" decisions. Far from it. Some of the most interesting and socially productive organizations in our society—for example, universities—have more in common with organized anarchies than with rational organizations. However, if the managers in these organizations believe in and act on the basis of a rational model, complications will surely arise. Making decisions, implementing decisions, and learning from the consequences of those decisions will all become especially problematic.

This book is about what happens when people try to organize and manage a loosely connected set of ambiguous goals, unclear technologies, and fluid participants. It tries to answer several questions:

How does context affect organization decision-making and action?

What happens when models of rational decision-making are applied in organized anarchies?

In what ways are managerial intentions related to organization actions?

How are external assessments of organization actions related to those actions?

What does management learn from those external assessments?

How are beliefs and subsequent behavior changed as a result of those assessments?

The empirical focus of our study is the National Institute of Education (NIE), an agency created within the United States Department of Health, Education, and Welfare in 1972 to support research and development in education. The birth and early years of NIE provided an excellent opportunity to study the organizing of an anarchy. Its goals were certainly ambiguous.

As defined in its authorizing legislation, NIE was to "seek to improve education" through

Helping solve or alleviate the problems and achieve the objectives of American education.

Advancing the practice of education as an art, science, and profession.

Strengthening the scientific and technological foundations on which education rests.

Building a vigorous and effective educational research and development system.

Its technology was unclear. Education research and development has long been judged the weakest of the social science R&D efforts. And it was characterized by a high degree of fluid participation. There were three sets of planners before the agency was established; none came to run the new agency. There were two sets of key congressional actors; the legislators who authorized the creation of NIE had practically nothing to do with providing funds for it. And those who worked inside the agency had so many issues to attend to that their attention to any one issue was sporadic.

We have studied the early history of the institute with an eye toward three things: First, we have tried to portray the detail of the genesis and early events of NIE. As much as possible, we have tried to reconstruct some major elements of what was happening to and within NIE during this period. Second, we have tried to speculate about the fundamental processes involved, processes characteristic of the class of organizations to which NIE belongs. Third, we have tried to draw implications from the NIE story for public policy and organizational leadership. The first three chapters of our work present the prehistory of the institute, establishing the context of history and expectations in which the agency took form. The fourth chapter considers the new organization's relationship to its environment, principally the congressional appropriations committees. These first four chapters, part 1, comprise the major elements of a political history of the institute's creation and its first two years of existence. Some of those familiar with the history of the institute—particularly some of those who work in Washington, D. C.—might argue that once the political tale is told, the story is over. We disagree. A purely political analysis is inadequate because it fails to probe the process through which NIE tried to translate high expectations into reality; the anarchic conditions that emerged; the conflict between managerial theories of decision-making and the reality of the bureaucratic world; the process of managerial learning growing from three consecutive years of congressional slashes in the agency's budget requests; and the difficulties that arose when the institute attempted to change its fate. Part 2 focuses on these issues in the context of the bureaucratic development of NIE. Chapters 5 and 6 detail the major factors involved in staffing the agency and establishing its programs. Chapter 7 analyzes the process of creating an organization structure, and chapter 8 describes the decision processes in developing budgets, creating a planning process, and organizing a research agenda. Chapter 9 analyzes the changing belief structure within the agency. And chapter 10 attempts to synthesize some of the major themes emerging from our work in speculating on two general sets of issues:

What can be expected from federal efforts in education research and development?

What should organization policymakers and managers keep in mind when creating and organizing a new agency?

Intensive study of a single organization has its theoretical and methodological dangers. It is easy to be so captivated by unique events and actors that the resulting explanation has no value for any other organization. But we believe the advantages of a careful case study outweigh the disadvantages. A case study provides a developmental perspective on an organization that a cross-sectional analysis of many organizations can never offer. Even longitudinal studies of large numbers of organizations are not very satisfactory in this respect, because they are so complicated to design and expensive to run that the questions they ask are often not very interesting. A case study also encourages the analysis of contextual effects on an organization and permits the identification of many kinds of variables and the analysis of interactions among them. We believe that organization actions are the result of a complicated set of interactions among diverse factors; our study permits us to investigate these interactions. We have tried to guard against writing only a history of a single organization by framing our questions in general terms at the beginning of each chapter and reflecting on significant generalizable features at the end of each chapter as well as in chapter 10. Further, we conclude with policy, managerial, and research implications that emerge from the perspective we develop in our analysis of the NIE story.

Part One   Historical and
                     Political Context

One	Models of Success, Models of Failure: The Impetus for NIE

Introduction

New organizations are created for a reason. There is the expectation that they will do something. Often, at least one of the reasons for creation is to remedy the perceived failures of the new organization's predecessor. In addition, new organizations are created with at least an implicit model of how they will function—often this model is provided by another, successful organization. Initial expectations of what an agency will do and how it will do it have a major impact on a new bureaucracy. Such expectations comprise a major element of the context within which the new organization will exist. They also provide initial guides for action to the first managers of the new organization and function as evaluative criteria for people interested in its "success."

NIE was created for a number of reasons, which we explore in this chapter. Certainly one of the major ones was the perceived failure of another organization, the research and development unit in the United States Office of Education (OE). The analysis of OE's shortcomings led directly to aspirations for the new agency. But those expectations also derived from an admiration of the past success of the federal agencies that support R&D in the natural sciences and a belief that those agencies and the work they supported could provide models for NIE.

In this chapter we examine the model of federal support for science R&D, the history of education R&D within the Office of Education, and the genesis of the NIE proposal.[1] This analysis should allow us to answer several questions important for understanding any new organization.

Whose interests are served by the creation of the new organization?

How clear are the expectations for the new organization?

How appropriate are they?

What is the new agency's inheritance in terms of past success or failure? technology? constituents?

Models of Success, Models of Failure Chronology

1945

Vannevar Bush proposes creation of the National Science Foundation

1950

President Truman signs legislation creating the National Science Foundation

1951

President Truman establishes the President's Science Advisory Committee

1954

Congress authorizes the Cooperative Research Program within the United States Office of Education

1957

Sputnik I is launched, spurring increase in United States research support

1964

OE funds nine R&D centers. President Johnson's Task Force on Education, chaired by John Gardner, proposes Regional Education Laboratories

1965

Congress approves initiation of Regional Education Laboratories and ERIC as part of the Elementary and Secondary Education Act.

OE is reorganized and consolidates research function in the Bureau of Research

1966

Twenty separate regional laboratories under development by OE; Secretary Gardner commissions an inquiry into laboratory development

Coleman et al. report on equality of educational opportunity released

1967

Two congressional committees issue stinging criticism of OE research administration

1969

Bureau of Research is reorganized as National Center for Educational Research and Development

Westinghouse evaluation of Head Start released; White House Working Group on new initiatives in education formed

1970

President Nixon proposes creation of the National Insititue of Education

Scientific R&D: The Model for Education

For most individuals with an interest in improving education R&D, the model provided by federal support of science R&D has proved compelling, beguiling, and perhaps misleading. The attraction is certainly understandable. The natural sciences R&D effort, whose federal sponsorship is embodied in such agencies as the National Science Foundation (NSF) and the National Institutes of Health (NIH),[2] has enjoyed high prestige and substantial financial support in this country; has expanded theoretical understanding and created new technologies; and has led to a mutually beneficial relationship between the federal government and the scientific community. But the model is not unflawed. Federal support of science R&D has not been without its lean years and congressional detractors.[3] Furthermore, its applicability to education is problematic. Although it is impossible to provide here more than the briefest sketch of the character of the federal role in science R&D, it is important to do that much, because NIE would be deliberately modeled after agencies such as NSF and NIH. Furthermore, many of the people who participated in the planning for or early work of NIE had been associated with NSF or NIH—either as contractors or as staff. Their expectations for NIE would be shaped by their earlier experiences with these agencies.

Federal support of science R&D grew rapidly during and after World War II.[4] In 1945 Vannevar Bush, first chairman of the National Defense Research Committee and the Office of Scientific Research and Development, called for a new government agency "to promote the flow of new scientific knowledge and the development of scientific talent in our youth" (Bush 1945, p. 4). He envisioned that the new agency would provide support for medical research, natural sciences research, and national defense research and would provide scientific policy advice for the president and Congress. This new agency—established five years later as the National Science Foundation—was to be characterized by independence, stability, and high status:

1. It should have stability of funds so that long-range programs may be undertaken.
2. It should recognize that freedom of inquiry must be preserved.
3. It should leave internal control of policy, personnel, and the method and scope of research to the institutions in which it is carried on.
4. It should be fully responsible to the President and through him to the Congress. [Bush 1945, p. 3]

The full scope of the Bush conception was never to be realized (Bush 1970, p. 5). During the five-year delay between the Bush recommendation and the initial authorization and funding of NSF, other sources of R&D support were formalized and expanded. The Department of Defense, for example, established the Office of Naval Research, with expenditures in 1949 of nearly $20 million for 1,200 projects in 200 institutions that involved nearly 3,000 scientists and 2,500 graduate students. By 1951, NIH was spending approximately $30 million a year for health research (Penick et al. 1972, pp. 24–26). Thus, by the time NSF was established its originally proposed research domain of natural science, health, and defense had been reduced by two-thirds. Additionally, its policy-advising function had been foregone out of fear of alienating those with vested interests in the location or funding levels of federal contracts (Lomask 1976, p. 92). This was hardly the situation Bush had envisioned.

The period from 1950 to 1957 was a fairly lean one for science R&D. The President's Science Advisory Committee (PSAC), established by President Truman in 1951, was languishing. Early funding for NSF was fairly modest. In 1952 its budget was $3.5 million; by 1957 it had grown to $40 million. While this rate of growth is handsome—a tenfold increase in five years, the absolute magnitude is not large by federal standards.

The launching of *Sputnik I* in 1957 provided a major impetus for the ascendance of United States science R&D in the 1960s. President Eisenhower reactivated PSAC and appointed a special science adviser. Funds for NSF grew from $50 million in 1958 to $480 million in 1966. President Kennedy created the National Aeronautics and Space Administration and established the Office of Science and Technology (OST) to coordinate science activities throughout the government and to provide the policy advice NSF had previously eschewed.

The second half of the sixties saw the R&D star setting once again. Urban decay and pervasive inequities in the distribution of education and other social services were "discovered." But there was no analogue to the Manhattan Project in atomic energy to mobilize the research community around social problems. NSF and NIH increased their funding of R&D in the social sciences, but the social scientists seemed to produce only studies, not solutions. Legislators began demanding results for the millions of dollars they were appropriating year after year. Some university communities began rejecting defense-related contracts, and war protests on campuses did nothing to endear the universities to either President Johnson or President Nixon. By the time President Johnson left office, the cordial and mutually beneficial relationships between science and government envisioned by Vannevar Bush and nurtured during the early sixties were severely strained.[5] With President Nixon's abolition of the position of science advisor, PSAC, and the OST in 1973, the R&D star was low in the sky.

Scientists are trained to believe that knowledge, in and of itself, is good and more knowledge is better. But scientists who believe that Congress holds the same view and evaluates research support programs according to academic criteria suffer from political naivete. Historically, the federal government has tended to support those research and development activities that appeared to have the potential to solve immediate problems. In the field of education, for example, concern for the development of trained manpower for the national defense promoted increased funding for science curriculum development in the late 1950s and early 1960s. A desire to alleviate social inequities and quell urban unrest spurred funding for research and development on compensatory education in the mid-1960s. Improving education, as education, has never been a pressing concern for the federal government; any attention it has received has been the consequence of a belief that education was a means to desirable ends. By the end of the 1960s, it was clear that education could not cure the host of social problems originally thought to be within its healing powers. And it was also clear that seeking more money for education R&D would not meet with great success. In 1970 an appropriations subcommittee chairman told those seeking an increase in R&D funds for the Office of Education:

> Since the Russians fired Sputnik there has been no horizon to research of all sorts and kinds. And it's just too bad that you fellows should come in at the tail end of this thing after a generation of research being the word, and the thing. Now you come limping in at the end of the thing all steamed up about research after everybody else is beginning to slacken. It is just a burden you are going to have. [House Appropriations Subcommittee 1970, p. 826]

Even had scientific R&D not been losing favor in Congress and the White House and even had education not been losing its position of domestic importance, it is not clear that attempting to model the support of education R&D after that of science R&D would have been a good idea. The conventional model of scientific R&D and its support by the federal government are founded on two cornerstones, neither of which may be appropriate for education. One cornerstone consists of assumptions about the nature of scientific knowledge, the other of assumptions about the nature of the institutions that produce and utilize it. The scientific model assumes that it is possible to isolate phenomena of interest, to subject them to examination under known conditions and accepted "laws of nature," and to predict their behavior under deliberately varied conditions. In the crudest, or linear, model of R&D, this process begins in the basic research laboratories. Once the basic researchers can confidently predict the behavior of the phenomena of interest, then the developers can build on that knowledge to create products or procedures that can then be provided to consumers. Most scientists themselves would argue that this model erroneously oversimplifies the process of R&D.[6] Yet it does capture the fact that stable institutions exist whose primary purpose is to perform one or more of these activities. And it reflects the assumption that knowledge can be effectively transferred among these institutions.

Complications arise when this model is applied to education. First, education research largely rests on knowledge in the social sciences. The theoretical base of the social sciences is far weaker than that of the natural sciences, and the ability to produce interventions in the social system that will have significant and predictable consequences is similarly weak. Further, communication and knowledge transfer within the education research community is erratic and unreliable. This community cuts across a number of traditional academic disciplines and is represented in a large variety of institutions including universities, the government, nonprofit institutions, and for-profit companies. Thus its members often have primary identification with a discipline or an institution, not with education research. Some of the most significant research contributions to education have been made by individual scholars working in small-scale projects only loosely coupled to the mainstream of education research.[7] Historically, there have been few institutions that undertook development projects in education other than commercial publishers and teachers themselves. These development efforts were rarely explicitly linked to the findings of past research. The new development organizations, whose creation was sponsored by the Office of Education, were less than a decade old in the early 1970s, and many of them failed to survive even that long. The dissemination function in education is highly informal and idiosyncratic. Again, apart from educational publishers, there is almost no institution that undertakes to spread educational ideas and practices on a person-to-person basis. Local conditions of education practice vary, and new ideas are inevitably adapted to those local conditions. This process of local adaptation has rarely been recognized as worthy of study by researchers and developers. Thus, the community of teachers and administrators has had little contact and no tradition of cooperation with researchers and developers in education. Finally, serious and independent evaluations of local education practice are rarely carried out. When they are, the evaluations quickly become mired in controversy over what objectives schooling should be serving.

In summary, the education system is characterized by a weak knowledge base, substantial political constraints, and poor communication both within the research and the practitioner communities and between the two. All of these factors render the applicability of the scientific model of research and development to education quite problematic and probably misleading.

In the early 1970s no domestic programs had high priority in the Nixon administration; improving education certainly did not. Federal support of scientific R&D was not flourishing; nor was it clear that the scientific model was particularly appropriate for education. Given these conditions, the times seemed inauspicious for beginning a new R&D agency for education.

Education R&D and the United States Office of Education

The history of R&D within the Office of Education created a complicated inheritance for NIE.[8] From its inception through the early 1960s, OE's basic research funding produced little strong theoretical work. In the mid-sixties its support of three major development initiatives produced disappointing results, according to a growing cadre of critics. It developed a reputation for mismanagement and shoddy administration. Furthermore, it was unable to forge a unified corps of political constituents who could be counted upon to provide strong congressional support. The "legacy of failure" created by OE would be a major factor both in the decision to create NIE and in the problems it would face in its early years.

During the first half of the twentieth century, most of the activity formally labeled "educational research" in the United States was undertaken in schools or colleges of education on an unsystematic, individual, part-time, and intermittently funded basis (OECD 1971, p. 298). During this period, the performance of education R&D was characterized by intellectual fragmentation and its sponsorship, by organizational stagnation. The first improvement in the support of education R&D within the Office of Education came in 1954 with the establishment of the Cooperative Research Program (CRP). Proposed by Eisenhower in 1953, the CRP would both fund a modest amount of university and college research and prohibit OE from running its own internal research program so that OE staff size would not increase unduly. During its early years the CRP was a small program with an initial budget authorization in 1956 of $1 million. Through the CRP, OE channeled funds to individuals and small groups of investigators, primarily in schools of education, for projects largely of the researchers' choice. By the beginning of the 1960s the managers of the program and relevant federal policymakers had reached three conclusions: the CRP had led to some improvement in educational research; the research was still "fragmented, non-cumulative, and inconclusive"; and the research did not translate quickly into visible improvements in educational practice.

These conclusions led to the development of three major initiatives to upgrade OE's R&D activities in the mid-sixties.[9] All borrowed heavily from the pattern established for federal support of R&D in the natural sciences. The first was the establishment of R&D centers that could conceive, initiate, and carry through comprehensive programmatic work directed toward solving educational problems. The second was the creation of educational laboratories, which would move research into "the field" (see Appendix 2 for a listing of R&D centers and laboratories). And the third was the creation of an information system to disseminate the results of OE-sponsored R&D.

Envisioned as analogous to the federally sponsored scientific laboratories (such as Argonne National Laboratory or Oak Ridge National Laboratory), the university-based R&D centers were to provide the critical mass of researchers and dollars considered necessary to overcome the shortcomings of the previous CRP effort. But problems plagued the creation and early years of the centers. They were to be the means for insuring that education R&D was responsive to federally identified needs; yet no federal master plan of identified priorities existed at the time of their creation. Thus federal program officers deciding which center proposals to fund had no substantive guidance on which to base their decisions. Each of the nine centers initially funded in 1964 had a different focus—ranging from urban education to higher education management. The "system" of centers seemed incomplete and unsystematic.

Within each center there were difficulties associated with creating a "critical mass." Throughout the first several years of the centers, many small, unrelated projects, each directed by a single faculty member, were funded and then persisted. Institutional constraints in the university setting, such as faculty department affiliation and tenure policies, slowed the development of program-oriented units. Because of uncertainties about OE budgets, centers were unable to plan programs for more than one year ahead with any degree of specificity. Finally, even after some of the centers had created reasonably complex research programs, they and their OE associates discovered they were ill-equipped to carry development beyond the prototype stage.

In 1964 President Johnson's Task Force on Education, chaired by John Gardner, recommended the creation of the Regional Education Laboratories. The laboratories were intended to tie research and development activities more closely to educational practice by creating new curricula and instructional methods based on the latest research findings. They were to reduce fragmentation of effort and to eliminate piecemeal curriculum reform, intermittent production of new hardware, and disorganized attempts to improve methodology. Their work was to be complementary to, and in some cases overlapping with, the efforts of the R&D centers (OECD 1971, p. 299). Governing boards of the laboratories were to be composed of representatives of state departments of education, colleges and universities, private and public schools, and industrial and cultural organizations.

The Gardner Task Force had visualized the laboratories as few in number but high in excellence. They were to be created with great care. However, the OE implementation of the laboratories program was driven primarily by political considerations. OE program staff believed that they had to create the laboratories while the iron was hot. As one top OE official declared:

> We knew damn well that history goes by and you'll never get more [money from Congress] for labs. You can't grow gradually. [Reported in Boyan, August 1974]

OE acted quickly. By February 1966, ten months after the enabling legislation was signed, the first eleven contracts had been negotiated, and by

September 1966, twenty separate Regional Education Laboratories had either developmental or operational contracts from OE (Hannaway 1974, p. 10). Further, the laboratories were distributed around the nation with an eye toward "political realities." This was not the sort of operation envisioned by the Gardner Task Force.

OE administration of the laboratories program got off to a rocky start. The OE offices responsible for its administration were initially allocated twenty personnel positions; yet in their early crucial months of operation only eight positions were filled. Two years passed before a division chief for the laboratories program was appointed. Staff turnover was high. Hostility soon developed between the Bureau of Research in OE and the personnel staffing the laboratories and R&D centers. The laboratories personnel were unhappy with OE's administration of their program. The R&D centers personnel were unhappy that the growth of the laboratories was being financed, in part, at the expense of the existing R&D centers. The critical reaction to the rapid, seemingly chaotic organization of the laboratories was swift. Nineteen months after the enabling legislation had been signed, and before all the laboratories were in operation, the secretary of HEW commissioned a special consultant to provide him with "trustworthy information to determine action with respect to the new laboratories" (Chase 1971, p. 2). Ironically, the secretary of HEW then in need of information was John Gardner, the man whose task force had recommended the creation of the laboratories not two years earlier.

By the mid-sixties OE realized that teachers and school administrators seemed to be wholly unaware of the studies conducted with CRP funds. In response, OE launched the third major initiative, the Educational Resources Information Center (ERIC). Patterned after the Clearinghouse for Federal Scientific and Technical Information, ERIC was an information-retrieval system to acquire, abstract, index, store, retrieve, and disseminate "exemplary information and research." Twenty clearinghouses were eventually established to screen documents for inclusion in the ERIC computer files. All OE-sponsored research reports were automatically included. Because ERIC indexed only unpublished literature, the *Current Index to Journals in Education* was also created, modeled on scientific abstracting services such as *Chemical Abstracts*.

Like the laboratories and centers, ERIC and its adjuncts were judged by some to be a disappointment. School professionals, by and large, did not know what was in the ERIC system, did not know how to gain access to it, and were discouraged from using it because most ERIC facilities were on university campuses rather than on school sites. When teachers and administrators did find a reference in ERIC to a report or document that appeared to meet their needs, their written request for copies often met with delays. When the material did arrive, it was often of doubtful relevance or quality (Greenwood and Weiler 1972).

Financial Support for Education R&D

While funding for education R&D in the United States is huge by world standards, advocates of additional funding use some simple statistics through which they justify further expenditures. They point out that spending for education R&D is less than 0.3% of the total expenditures for education in the nation. And they note that federal spending for education R&D is only 1.25% of the total federal investment in research and development. Between 1950 and 1970 the federal government spent more than $14 billion in health R&D and more than $7 billion in agriculture R&D, but less than $1 billion in education R&D (Levien 1971, pp. 5–6).

After the passage of the Cooperative Research Act of 1954, several other pieces of legislation were enacted that added to the responsibilities and budgets of the Bureau of Research in OE (appropriations for each of these programs from inception through fiscal year 1970 are shown in table 1.1). The major increase—from $19.3 million to $100.5 million—occurred during the two-year period from 1964 to 1966. Two major factors contributed to this increase: lobbying by special interest groups and the general optimism about education in the mid-sixties.

The vocational education lobby and the lobby for education of the handicapped vigorously supported increases in funds for education R&D. The vocational education lobby helped secure passage of the Vocational Education Act of 1963, during a period of rising unemployment, then mobilized behind research appropriations for OE in fiscal years 1965 and 1966. However, after 1966, the vocational education lobby became disenchanted with the nature of OE's research program and pressed increasingly for funds to be given directly to the states, a shift in attitude reflected in the course of appropriations for OE's vocational education research program in the late 1960s. The lobby for education of the handicapped, in addition to promoting a separate OE bureau for these concerns, successfully exerted pressure for increases in research appropriations for education of the handicapped.

The single largest increase during this two-year period was the massive jump in CRP funds, largely spurred by the Gardner Task Force, aggressive OE research bureaucrats, and the commissioner of education, who capitalized on the optimism associated with the drafting and the passage of the Elementary and Secondary Education Act of 1965.

The appropriations for CRP continued to increase from 1967 to 1970, but much less spectacularly. Congress reduced presidential requests for education R&D by $2.5 million in 1966 and in 1969 slashed the administration's request by $52 million. By fiscal 1970, the president's own Office of Management and Budget was exercising discipline over education R&D requests from HEW, as we shall discuss in more detail later in this chapter.[10]

Table 1.1

Appropriations for Research and
Training, United States Office
of Education, 1857–70
(In Thousands of Dollars)

Year	Cooperative Research	NDEA–Title VI	NDEA–Title VII	Vocational Research	Library Research	Handicapped Research	Totals
1970	113,900*	2,500	—c	1,100	—e	18,000	135,500
1970	88,900**	2,500	—c	1,100	—e	18,000	110,500
1969	76,077	—a	—b	11,375	—d	15,000	102,452
1968	66,467	3,000	4,400	13,550	3,550	11,000	101,967
1967	70,000	3,100	4,400	10,000	3,550	8,100	99,150
1966	70,000	2,800	4,000	17,750	—	6,000	100,500
1965	15,800	2,250	4,963	11,850	—	2,000	36,863
1964	11,500	1,800	5,000	—	—	1,000	19,300
1963	6,985	1,800	5,000	—	—	—	13,785
1962	5,000	2,000	4,755	—	—	—	11,755
1961	3,357	2,000	4,700	—	—	—	10,057
1960	3,200	4,000	3,000	—	—	—	10,200
1959	2,700	2,500	1,600	—	—	—	6,800
1958	2,300	—	—	—	—	—	2,300
1957	1,000	—	—	—	—	—	1,000

Source: Boyan 1969, p. 5.
*"Nixon" budget request.
**"Johnson" budget request.

aAppropriation included in Cooperative Research in the amount of $2,465,000.
bAppropriation included in Cooperative Research in the amount of $4,200,000.
cLegislation authorization discontinued.
dAppropriation included in Cooperative Research in the amount of $3,000,000.
eAppropriation included in Cooperative Research in the amount of $2,200,000.

Contending Constituencies

No strong cohesive political force stands behind education research and development to lobby for the growth of federal spending in this field. The elements for a large education R&D lobby exist, but they tend to pull against one another rather than in concert. Six separate groups are readily identifiable. The first are the state and local school districts who are the intended targets of much of the research and whose own participation in conducting research is increasing. The second are the social scientists in the academic disciplines. This group has long felt more cordial toward NSF and NIH than toward OE. The third are the "educational statesmen," a small, prestigious group represented by organizations such as the National Academy of Education (OECD 1971, pp. 286–87). The fourth are the education researchers in schools of education, long the performers of most education research and the recipients of most early CRP funds. The fifth are the staffs of the laboratories and centers. (Although the laboratories and R&D centers have connections with all four of the foregoing groups, they perceive themselves to be, and act as, a separate entity.)[11] The sixth group comprises the myriad organizations attracted by the growth in federal spending on social problems in the 1960s. In education, one part of this group consists of publishing firms competing in the large market for educational materials. Another portion is made up of contract research organizations such as the Educational Testing Service, the American Institute of Research, Stanford Research Institute, the Rand Corporation, Abt Associates, Mathematica, Inc., and others.

Although there is a modicum of cooperation among these six groups and, indeed, their memberships overlap, their differing interests inevitably lead to continuing conflict. The major disagreements center on problem definition, dissemination measures, and the relative importance of practical versus theoretical problems.

Although state and local education agencies control more than 90% of the operating expenditures of elementary and secondary schools, support for education research and development is dominated by the federal government. Before the expansion of the federal effort, local practitioners had been influential in defining the research problems addressed at schools of education. The expansion of OE and NSF efforts meant that researchers in the social science disciplines gained ascendancy in problem definition. This shift meant that R&D increasingly emphasized thorough long-range study; the collection of empirical evidence; an attempt to find generalizable solutions rather than ones that responded primarily to local problems; specialization of R&D roles; and the creation of new organization structures, such as the laboratories and R&D centers, to institutionalize information-seeking and change processes (Sieber 1974, p. 493).

This strategy viewed the consumer—in this case, the local educator—as a rational, information-processing agent eager and willing to read, listen to, digest, and implement the conclusions of research. The appropriate dissemination measures, as exemplified by the ERIC system, were one-way (researcher to practitioner) and largely impersonal (Sieber 1974, p. 498). In this "linear" conceptualization of research and development, the experiences and views of teachers were implicitly discounted in favor of concepts developed by researchers away from the classroom (OECD 1971, p. 272). Practitioners who wanted education R&D to solve their specific local problems found themselves ill at ease with many of these developments. As a result, there has been little demand from this sector for an increased supply of research and development. And the political fact is that the number of teachers and administrators exceeds the number of researchers by approximately 200 to 1.

A second split within the potential R&D community is between practitioners and their allies in some schools of education, on the one side, and the "discipline-based" natural and social scientists on the other. Two phenomena exemplify this split. First, on many university campuses there is a prejudice against schools of education; their past work, often supported by early CRP funds, is viewed by some academics in the disciplines as flimsy and of little importance (Cronbach and Suppes 1969, p. 224). Second, academicians and school practitioners have historically contested for control of major educational associations. In recent times the practitioners have clearly wrested such control for themselves, the example of the National Education Association being most prominent (Dershimer and Iannaccone 1973, pp. 116–17). This 1.4-million-member organization has lobbied ceaselessly for increased federal spending in education at the local level, but it has not pushed vigorously for increased research funds.

The conflict between discipline-based academics and school practitioners is also evidenced in the continuing debate over whether "research" or "development" should receive major priority. Proponents of basic research, including most representatives of the academic disciplines, have argued that an enthusiasm for "products" and immediate impact is unwise because the underlying knowledge base is weak. Supporters of development and dissemination have vigorously defended their position by noting that promising activities should be promoted even if the reasons why they work are not well understood (Sieber 1974, p. 489).

The research versus development split was underscored by the management of OE's newly enlarged R&D programs in the mid-sixties. At that time the OE commissioner of education hired a research engineer from Westinghouse Learning Corporation as the first associate commissioner for research. The associate commissioner actively encouraged the entry of private

industry into educational research and development, with divisive consequences for the research coalition.

> First, new recruits, such as engineers, systems specialists and behavioral
> scientists with industrial and military orientation have entered the educa-
> tional research community. The second effect has been that increased
> specialization has driven researchers and practitioners further apart. The
> third effect has been to sharpen differences between scholars and prob-
> lem-oriented clients. [Dershimer and Iannaccone 1973, p. 119]

The conflicts were exacerbated by the fact that although many constituencies were attracted to education R&D in the 1960s, they found themselves
together in a field characterized by slow growth after the initial explosion in
funding linked to the passage of the Elementary and Secondary Education
Act in 1965. Although higher-education institutions continued to receive by
far the largest proportion of federal education R&D funding, between 1969
and 1971 the university share grew by only 8%, while nonprofit institutions
(including laboratories) grew by 38% and for-profit institutions increased
their share by 200% (Sieber 1974, p. 486). The struggle over shares of a stable
supply of dollars and the absence of magic cures for educational ills did
nothing to contribute to healing internal division and creating unity within
the potential lobbies for research and development funding in education.

OE Administration and Management

Not only was the OE R&D effort undersupported by constituent groups
and sometimes judged to be of dubious technical merit, but also it was only a
small portion of an agency plagued by administrative and management
troubles.[12] Perpetually understaffed, the Bureau of Research found it difficult
to monitor its large collection of projects. The 1967 Special Subcommittee on
Education, chaired by Congresswoman Edith Green (D–Oregon), was highly
critical of staff shortages.

> In the Bureau of Research for example, overall staff cuts were recom-
> mended, based on the administrative view of its function as being that of
> merely funding or disapproving research proposals. Shortages in this area
> are dramatically illustrated by the fact that some research staff members are
> monitoring as many as 172 separate research projects, and that all research
> planning and liaison with other Federal research components is being done
> by a unit consisting of three people. [House Special Subcommittee on
> Education 1967, p. 48]

Even when job candidates could be found, the policy of allowing no one
except the OE Personnel Office to approve any job application meant that
hiring was an excruciatingly slow process. The Green subcommittee found

that it took five months to process a job application, "even for relatively simple actions, such as transferral within [OE], from the field, or from other Federal agencies to the Office"(p. 44).

Hiring people was not the only problem; keeping them was also difficult. Leadership turnover was high. OE had six commissioners of education from 1962 to 1971 (including two acting commissioners). During that time there were eight associate commissioners for research (including three acting associate commissioners). The director of OE's dissemination programs reported that between July 1965 and August 1972 he had been directed by eight different immediate supervisors (Burchinal 1973, pp. 120–21).

. All OE bureaus had to put up with frustrating delays and inadequacies in simple administrative matters (House Special Subcommittee on Education 1967, pp. 752–53). The Green subcommittee staff discovered that it took from six months to a year to procure typewriters and books for OE personnel. OE consultants, a number of whom reviewed proposals for the Bureau of Research, experienced six-month delays in reimbursement for expenses. The office's internal payroll system was characterized by six weeks' delay, on the average, for correcting payroll mistakes. Office space was inadequate. Although each individual administrative problem was minor, their combination produced a sense of administrative chaos.

Managing research and evaluation contracts and grants was particularly troublesome. In 1967 the Bureau of Research was responsible for more than 1,150 contracts and grants. There was no centralized management information system to help the staff keep track of them. The Green subcommittee discovered a number of cases in which multiple awards had been made to a single individual. "Sixty individuals are principal investigators on two projects; eight have their name on three projects; two on four projects, and one individual has his name on eight projects" (House Special Subcommittee on Education 1967, p. 232). Four years later OE was still criticized for its monitoring procedures. It had established a computerized project information system, but an audit by the General Accounting Office (1971) concluded that more effective monitoring procedures were necessary. They discovered there were no written guidelines for project monitors, despite the fact that these monitors were responsible for authorizing the payment of millions of dollars to contractors. In an analysis of a random sample of evaluation and study contracts (from all of OE, not just the Bureau of Research), it was discovered that in 50% of the cases the project monitor had never visited the site where the contract was being carried out. Office files on these projects were often vague and muddled. "Reports [from contractors] were too sketchy to keep the project monitor informed as to progress of the work" (General Accounting Office 1971, p. 22). One of the primary reasons monitoring was so difficult was that contractual work arrangements were often poorly specified. When neither OE nor the contractor had a clear idea of the work to be performed, monitoring "progress" was difficult. Often, if the scope of work for a contract was revised by OE and the contractor, these revisions were never stipulated in writing (General Accounting Office 1971, p. 2).

All these administrative problems and deficiencies contributed to the difficulties in running a creditable R&D program inside the Office of Education. In many instances the R&D program was the hapless victim of other parts of the OE bureaucracy, and it had little recourse. Yet many of the education R&D critics persisted in blaming OE's research managers for the lack of progress and pressuring them for better performance.

Pressure for Reform

In the second half of the sixties, the OE Bureau of Research found itself reorganized by the commissioner of education, in fierce competition with other OE bureaus for tightening resources, buffeted mercilessly by external reviews, and pressured by Congress to show results. The substantial increase for research and development funds in fiscal year 1966, along with the passage of the Elementary and Secondary Education Act, led to a full-scale reorganization of OE on 1 July 1965. In part the reorganization was intended to meet past criticisms concerning the lack of tangible impact of research and development (Hannaway 1974, p. 6). It brought all research programs, which previously had been distributed among six bureaus, into the Bureau of Research. After the 1965 reorganization, the Bureau of Research was one of fifteen separate bureaus and offices that reported to the deputy commissioner of education and thence to the commissioner. Although research activities had been consolidated, R&D still did not enjoy a powerful or prestigious position within the agency. In describing the position of the Bureau of Research, one commissioner of education noted:

> You are still dealing with one bureau within an office [OE] that contains some 15 different bureaus. No matter how able a man may be, his visibility with the community we are serving is necessarily kept to a minimum. He reports to the Commissioner of Education perhaps through two or three layers of necessary governmental arrangements. [Marland in House Select Subcommittee 1971, p. 123]

The bureaucratic layers muffling the research program extended beyond OE (see fig. 1.1).[13] Within HEW the Bureau of Research was subject to policy review by the assistant secretary for planning and evaluation (ASPE), by the HEW budget analysts, and by staff assistants to the HEW secretary. In the Executive Office of the President, the research budget had to win approval from the Bureau of the Budget (renamed the Office of Management and Budget in 1970). Additionally, all education research activities were monitored by the Office of Science and Technology and its President's Science

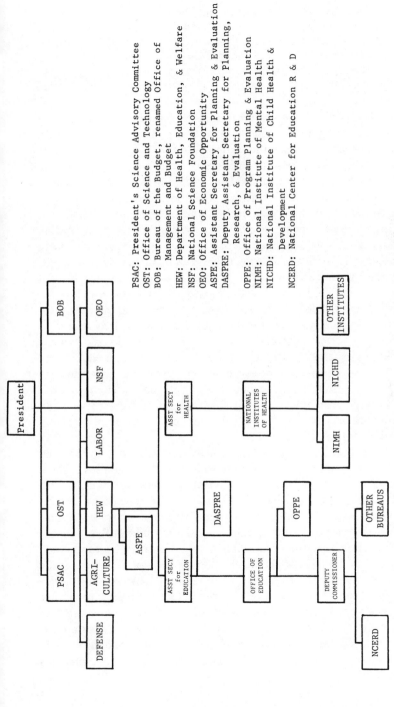

PSAC: President's Science Advisory Committee
OST: Office of Science and Technology
BOB: Bureau of the Budget, renamed Office of
      Management and Budget
HEW: Department of Health, Education, & Welfare
NSF: National Science Foundation
OEO: Office of Economic Opportunity
ASPE: Assistant Secretary for Planning & Evaluation
DASPRE: Deputy Assistant Secretary for Planning,
        Research, & Evaluation
OPPE: Office of Program Planning & Evaluation
NIMH: National Institute of Mental Health
NICHD: National Institute of Child Health &
       Development
NCERD: National Center for Education R & D

Figure 1.1. Main lines of authority in federal education R&D policies, 1969.
Adapted from Organization for Economic Cooperation and Development, *Education R&D in the United States*, in House Select Subcommittee on Education, *Hearings
on the Establishment of the National Institute of Education*, 92d Cong, 1st sess., 1971,
p. 282.

Advisory Committee. A former director of OE's research operation lamented:

> The number of these [outside] people and their participation in policy decision-making appear to be increasing daily. Moreover, they do not hesitate to exercise veto power over [research] programs. The multiplication of people who have authority to change programs but who leave others to face the often negative consequences of their actions is one of the most severe morale problems of government. [Gallagher, cited in Sieber 1974, p. 496]

In the early days of the Nixon administration the degree of staff monitoring of the OE research program became so great that representatives of OMB, OST, and ASPE became known as the "Unholy Trinity." The Unholy Trinity, which included three men who would later occupy top posts in NIE, made life miserable for the Bureau of Research. The warfare between the Bureau of Research and its antagonists arose for several reasons. First, many of the staff review roles were filled by men with backgrounds in the natural sciences or economics, men who believed in the efficacy of "scientific" R&D. As a group, they shared a disdain for "educationists" in the Bureau of Research and in schools of education. There was a strong belief within OMB, OST, and ASPE that the Bureau of Research was run, not very competently, by and for traditional education researchers with no involvement of the broader academic community. Second, the staff agencies were under pressure to produce policy recommendations for their superiors. When they turned to the past products of education R&D in the hopes that they could guide policy, they found little assistance. With less money to spend on major educational programs, there was increased pressure in the Nixon administration to demonstrate that research, which was much less costly than service programs, could lead to important breakthroughs. The Bureau of Research did not deliver such breakthroughs. Third, with the publication of the results from the nationwide survey on equality of educational opportunity (Coleman et al. 1966) and the resulting doubts about the effectiveness of schools in reducing social and economic inequality, the bloom was off the education rose. There was no longer the simple belief in Washington that either schools or educational research would inevitably lead to a better society. And there was dismay among federal policy analysts that the Coleman et al. study—originated by Congress rather than by researchers and supported by OE's National Center for Educational Statistics rather than by the Bureau of Research—had apparently contributed more to the debate about education than had all the multitudinous studies commissioned by the Bureau of Research. Fourth, with a growing disillusionment about the various Great Society programs, Washington analysts had become enamored with "social experimentation" as a means to discover better policy for the future. The strategy of experimentation required a concentration of resources in a few well-defined and carefully planned endeavors. The Bureau of Research seemed ill equipped to play this role. Finally, the oversight agencies also complained that the Bureau of Research was unable to plan properly. Policy analysts at the upper levels of HEW and in the Executive Office of the President wanted the Bureau of Research to write "objectives"—to display a grasp of the policy issues in education then facing the executive branch. In effect, the staff reviewers wanted the bureau to tell a convincing story as justification for the money it sought, and they wanted their own intellectual biases to appear in that story. The analysts found that directors of the Bureau of Research simply could not tell any convincing story.

Congress had also grown impatient with education research and development by the end of the 1960s. Congressmen wanted to see the benefits of the increased expenditures they had approved a few years earlier. They wanted to know whether education R&D had produced benefits that could be seen, weighed, or felt. And the OE research bureaucrats felt compelled to create expectations greater than they could achieve in an effort to satisfy Congress (OECD 1971, p. 281).

In 1969 Congressman Augustus Hawkins (D–California) exemplified the prevailing congressional view in his complaint to James Gallagher, then the new head of OE's research operation:

> I am reminded of a young kid I saw recently that showed some displeasure and I asked what was wrong; he said, "it is too much jive, man, but very little juice." I am wondering if this is a lot of jive we are getting and not practical results. . . . I hope the record will indicate in 1973, some of us will still be in Congress, and we will not have the same testimony that "next year, or the year after," it is going to be completed and "expect results," because I have been hearing it for 15 years. [House General Subcommittee on Education 1969, pp. 188–91]

It was clear that Congress worked on a shorter time cycle than did researchers. While research might require a minimum of five to ten years, and often longer, to begin making progress on a specific educational problem, the legislative and executive branches of the federal government were demanding results within three to four years after the major increase in funds for education R&D. And promises of future progress did not substitute for results. Congress vented its frustration on OE's 1971 appropriation bill shortly after President Nixon proposed the creation of NIE in early 1970. Congress cut funds for researcher training by 68.5% from the previous year; general research was reduced by 33.5% and dissemination funds were trimmed by 28.5%.

Between 1967 and 1969 the increasing frustration over education R&D led to ten studies of federal efforts in the field.[14] The first of these was conducted by the staff of the Research and Technical Programs Subcommittee of the House Committee on Government Operations, who declared, "The kindest consensus [concerning the status of educational research and development] seems to be that it is 'varied' " (House Committee on Government Operations 1967). A special study of education research was conducted by OE at the request of the Bureau of the Budget. Its recommendation, hardly surprising, was that funding for research be increased. The Office of Program Planning and Evaluation in OE conducted a study similar to that requested by the Bureau of the Budget. Their study expressed the need for the Bureau of Research "to establish a consistent set of objectives in close cooperation with the research community" (Gideonse 1970, p. 240). We have earlier referred to the study released in 1967 by the Special House Subcommittee on Education headed by Congresswoman Edith Green. It emphasized the need for coordination among OE service programs, the research units, and the broader research community.

ASPE also conducted a review of HEW's education research and development activities at the request of the Bureau of the Budget. Again, the need for "defining" and "focusing" the bureau's role was stressed. As noted earlier, another study focused on the Regional Education Laboratories program at the request of the HEW secretary.

During 1969 a Panel on Educational Research and Development was established by the President's Science Advisory Committee. Its report expressed concern about the Bureau of Research's inability to state precisely the major educational problems it was trying to help solve. Other studies were sponsored by the Committee for Economic Development, a private group of citizens concerned with public affairs, and by the National Academy of Education. The latter work declared:

> The number of persons in educational research is inadequate. To discuss their quality and productivity is to strike an even more depressing note. Quality is hard to document, but there is remarkably wide agreement that many persons trained for educational research are unproductive, and that many of those charged with doing research are not qualified for their tasks. [Cronbach and Suppes 1969, p. 211]

By 1969 the Bureau of the Budget was slashing Bureau of Research budget requests, and in part was justifying their actions by referring to opinions expressed in the outside studies. The then director of the Bureau of Research recalled:

> Of particular relevance ... appeared to be [the Bureau of the Budget's] concerns about the [OE] Bureau's ability to state precisely the major educational problems it was trying to help solve and its ability to sponsor "good people"[15] in the conduct of unsolicited, basic research. Two special studies of Bureau activity, one performed by the Assistant Secretary for Planning in HEW and one conducted by a subcommittee of educational R&D of the President's Science Advisory Committee, were alluded to as supportive of the views of the Bureau of the Budget examiners on these scores. [Boyan 1969, p. 12]

The Unholy Trinity of ASPE, OMB, and OST was beginning to wreak a heavy toll on the fortunes of the Bureau of Research. The bureau had to find a way out of its troubles.

The Search for a Solution

By the late 1960s the profound political and bureaucratic vulnerability of the Bureau of Research had been amply demonstrated. Lack of support from the practitioner community meant the bureau could not demonstrate the constituency backing that would have pleased Congress. Alienation from the discipline-based academicians meant it could display little research done by "good people" to placate the Unholy Trinity. Understaffed and unable even to keep up with the documents churned out by its own laboratories and centers, the bureau was caught up in a web of uncoordinated and sometimes conflicting initiatives arising from many offices within the executive branch and Congress.

Executive staff officers and congressmen had addressed a series of questions to the Bureau of Research: What are your priorities? What significant problems are you trying to solve? What time-frame is necessary for solving these problems? What evidence will you accept that you are moving toward solution of these problems? These were predictable questions, but the Bureau of Research was largely unable to produce satisfactory answers. From the bureau's perspective, the inability to produce answers was attributable to the fact that education R&D was an insufficiently developed enterprise and to the fact that they were constantly subjected to cross pressures from both within and without the government. The staff review agencies tended toward a somewhat simpler answer: the Bureau of Research was incompetent.

In a final effort at self-preservation, the bureau unashamedly began to model its behavior after the Department of Defense, which had established a reputation for a "mission-orientation"—an ability to set targets and meet them.[16] No longer was the bureau content with allowing researchers to do whatever they chose to do through funding researcher-initiated proposals. It sharply reduced the number of grants for researcher-initiated proposals and began using the Request for Proposal procedure to "procure" research, much as the Department of Defense uses Requests for Proposals to procure submarine parts or a new training manual. Requests for Proposals vary in their degree of specificity but, as OE used them, many went so far as to stipulate sampling design, questionnaire topics, scheduling of project phases, and other features of research design that traditionally had been the prerogatives of the researchers (Sieber 1974, p. 484). As the bureau moved away from "basic research" and toward "development," cutting its budget for basic research by one-half between 1969 and 1972, the pattern of its awards began to approximate closely the Department of Defense patterns. By fiscal year 1970, only 8% of OE's research funds went for activities labeled "basic research," with 31% allocated for "applied research" and 61% for "development." This pattern closely resembled that of the Department of Defense but was dramatically different from those of other HEW agencies such as NIH, which continued to devote one-third of their budgets to basic research (Sieber 1974, pp. 483–84). If Congress wanted results, then the bureau was engaged in a headlong drive to produce—or procure—them.

The adoption of the Defense Department model failed to rescue the Bureau of Research, however. The emphasis on development ignored the fact that "product ideas" did not rest on the solid knowledge base underlying development projects in the physical sciences. OE's centralized formulation of problems and research design completed the alienation of the discipline-based researchers. And, at least in the short run, it did not improve practitioner support (Dershimer and Iannaccone 1973, p. 119).

By 1969 the Unholy Trinity had concluded that new leadership was required if the Bureau of Research was to be reformed. Working in conjunction with the new commissioner of education, James Allen, they helped inspire the reorganization of the Bureau of Research into the National Center for Educational Research and Development (NCERD). This reorganization gave James Gallagher, the respected former head of research for the handicapped and then deputy assistant secretary for planning, research, and evaluation, responsibility for OE's foundering research enterprise.

The Unholy Trinity had high hopes that Gallagher would be able to rescue the faltering R&D effort. When he appeared for his first Bureau of the Budget review session on NCERD's budget, those present assumed he would announce a redirection of NCERD's activities. Instead, Gallagher attacked the Bureau of the Budget for its "harassment" of NCERD. One senior budget official angrily walked out after Gallagher's remarks; OE's critics were disappointed and chagrined. Gallagher, and with him the fledgling NCERD, had completely fallen from the good graces of the Unholy Trinity. So it was that, by the end of 1969, key representatives of the Bureau of the Budget (soon to become OMB), OST, and ASPE had reluctantly concluded that education research was beyond salvation as long as it was controlled by OE. Within a few months, the Unholy Trinity would become key actors in designing the proposal for a new National Institute of Education.

The NIE Proposal

Throughout 1969 President Nixon had been struggling with education lobbies over their demands for increased funding for the various forms of federal aid to education. The struggle had resulted in presidential vetoes of appropriations bills for education, vetoes that were bitterly resisted by national education groups. The White House staff was in the market for ideas that would ameliorate the ill will of the education lobbies and create a distinctive Nixon program in education—without committing the administration to vast new expenditures (O'Keefe 1974). To this end, the White House created a Working Group on new initiatives in elementary and secondary education chaired by Edward Morgan, on the staff of John Ehrlichman, chief aide to President Nixon. This committee was composed of many of the members of the informal club who had been critical of federal education R&D efforts.[17]

Daniel Moynihan, head of the Domestic Council, shaped the Working Group's view of the essential issues to be confronted in establishing new educational policy.[18] Aside from respecting fiscal constraints and recognizing the need for a new "Nixonian" policy, there were three major tenets in Moynihan's position. The first point was that the educational programs of the Great Society were not working well. The Coleman et al. study (1966), the Westinghouse study of the Head Start preschool program (1969), and evaluations of compensatory education programs funded by Title I of the Elementary and Secondary Education Act were cited as supporting evidence. Second, Moynihan asserted that research cast doubt on the effectiveness of compensatory education programs even in the best of circumstances. The effects of family background, ethnic heritage, social class, and peer group influences seemed to leave little margin for the possible effectiveness of compensatory schooling. Third, the conventional remedy of more money for education seemed suspect. Moynihan believed that the education establishment had to concern itself with educational outputs and not solely with more money.

As Moynihan's deputy, Chester Finn, recalled:

> Mankind had arrived at one of those moments in history when no one, least of all government, quite knows what to do; one of those moments when it begins to appear that everything you thought was true isn't true, but you have no truth to substitute for it. Social science had, in a sense, outdistanced public policy. . . .

> As the Working Group reasoned, if what presently goes on in the nation's schools, insofar as we are able to measure it, has little effect on student learning, then we had better find out what does have an effect and how to alter it. [Finn 1974, pp. 234, 240]

More and better research in education seemed to be the answer. Members of the Unholy Trinity argued persuasively that the Office of Education would never be able to improve its research activities. And thus, in the fall of 1969, the Working Group decided that a new federal research agency for education was needed. The idea appeared even more promising after someone recalled that Nixon had proposed a "National Institute for the Educational Future" during the 1968 campaign. Although it was by no means the first time such an idea had been advanced, under its previous sponsors proposals for an education research agency had languished.[19] But now the idea seemed very attractive. It promised an inexpensive solution to the president's immediate political problems; it appeared to be a logical next step to reform education research and development in view of the Unholy Trinity's frustrations with the year-old NCERD; and it was substantively attractive to Moynihan, who believed in the constructive potential of basic research in education.

In his 3 March 1970 message on education reform, President Nixon proposed the creation of a National Institute of Education:

> We must stop pretending that we understand the mystery of the learning process, or that we are significantly applying science and technology to the techniques of teaching—when we spend less than one-half of one percent of our educational budget on research, compared with 5% of our health budget and 10% of defense.
>
> We must stop congratulating ourselves for spending nearly as much money on education as does the entire rest of the world—$65 billion a year on all levels—when we are not getting as much as we should out of the dollars we spend. . . .
>
> Therefore, I propose that the Congress create a National Institute of Education as a focus for educational research and experimentation in the United States. When fully developed, the Institute would be an important element in the nation's educational system, overseeing the annual expenditure of as much as a quarter of a billion dollars.

The president's message set in motion two largely independent processes that would culminate two years later in the creation of the institute. The first was a planning process conducted within the executive branch, described in chapter 2. The second was the legislative process in Congress, described in chapter 3.

Conclusion

Out of frustration with the failure of OE and belief in the power of scientific research, the NIE proposal was born. Its architects were few in number and weak in political power. But their advocacy of a new, independent, and prestigious scientific agency in the field of education became congruent with the requirements of a president in late 1969. That conjunction would lead to the creation of a new agency.

It is interesting to note the lessons that were *not* learned from the OE experience by those who called for an NIE. No one, at any rate no one outside NCERD, concluded that NCERD needed more money, status, and patience from its critics. No one concluded that the model of scientific R&D and its support by the federal government were inappropriate for education. People came to the conclusion that it was easier to create a new organization than to reform an old one. When goals and technology are unclear, this may commonly be the case. Indeed, it may be true that, given sufficient resources, the actual creation of a new organization is not overwhelmingly difficult. But if the goals are still ambiguous and the technology is still unclear, the new organization will be hardly more likely to "succeed" than the old one. Belief in success is easy to sustain in the early days of an organized anarchy. But, over time, the realization grows that the act of creation did not make any of the really hard problems easier to solve. Nevertheless, in late 1969, with the president and history on their side, the creators of the NIE proposal were ready for the step that was self-evidently important to them. It was time to plan.

Two　　　　　　　　　Creating the Institute:
　　　　　　　　　　　　The Planning Process

Introduction

In an agency with well-specified goals and a clear technology for achieving those goals, planning is possible. It is called scheduling. It is also possible to plan in, or for, an organized anarchy. But the connection between those plans and any subsequent action on the part of the agency is tenuous. Unlike most new government agencies, NIE was preceded by a lengthy planning period. From April 1970 to June 1972, when NIE was authorized by Congress, various government consultants developed plans for the new agency. Because there is no well-developed "theory" of planning, because there were few planning models to imitate, and because NIE planners aspired to create an agency different from all that had gone before, the planning period was characterized by ambiguity and uncertainty as well as by optimism and enthusiasm.

The Planning Process Chronology
1970

March	Nixon delivers message on education reform proposing NIE
April	Levien begins work on Preliminary Plan for NIE
November	Levien completes draft of Preliminary Plan
December	Marland named commissioner of education
	Levien not asked to continue his work
	Silberman named associate commissioner of NCERD

1971

January	Planning Unit Steering Committee formed
	(Bills to establish NIE introduced in House and Senate)
February	Levien report published
	Marland chooses OE programs to be transferred to NIE
	(Congressional hearings on NIE begin)
May	Planning Unit officially announced
	Silberman named head of Planning Unit
August	Cody hired
	(Senate passes bill containing NIE provisions)

September	Planning Unit moves out of OE offices
	Planning Unit begins work on year-end report
November	(House passes bill containing NIE provisions)
December	Year-end report completed

1972

January	Year-end report criticized
	Program planning teams organized
March	(Conference committee convenes on bill containing NIE provisions)
April	Team reports completed
May	Elliott arrives
	(Senate passes conference bill containing NIE provisions)
	Elliott takes charge
	Kooi leaves
	Silberman announces he will leave
	NIE legislation signed into law by President Nixon

In examining the history of NIE's planning years, it is helpful to recognize that "planning" is more than generating schedules and blueprints for organization and action. Planning serves as a lightning rod for both friends and enemies of the proposed agency. It creates a locus for the expression of self-interest; people can "plan themselves into" the new agency. Planning certifies who is important. Because OE had been so severely criticized for not attracting "good people," the kinds of people consulted and employed by the NIE planners would be seen as a clue to how different NIE would be from OE. Planning also certifies *what* is important. Decisions about what to plan and what not to plan would be seen as a clue to what the NIE planners considered important for the new agency. Further, the process of planning demonstrates a style of analysis and decision-making. If the audience is impressed with the style, it is less likely to quarrel with the content. Finally, to announce that an agency is being planned endows the concept of that agency with an aura of judiciousness and rationality. The "plan" itself becomes a symbolic reassurance that good faith and sound minds stand behind the proposal.

During the course of NIE's planning years, four separate models of the purpose and process of planning were evident: planning as politics; planning as symbolism; planning as generating alternatives; planning as early action. Each model had its adherents among both the planners and those evaluating the plans. Because the NIE planners had such an ambitious and ambiguous mandate, all the planning models may have been appropriate. Understanding what the planners actually did—whom they hired, what questions they asked and how they answered them, how tightly or loosely their activities were coupled to the legislative process and to the various communities interested in NIE—will allow us to explore the consequences of each of the models.

In this chapter, we examine the twenty-six month planning period with an eye to several questions:

What did the planners actually do?

How were their activities intended to affect the new agency?

How were these activities assessed by external reviewers?

What was the impact of the planning period?

The Levien Report

Remembering with regret and distaste how the OE regional laboratories had developed "while no one was watching," several members of the White House group that created the NIE proposal lobbied vigorously for an opportunity to keep "the larger community" involved in the NIE planning. When James Allen, the commissioner of education, asked the White House group to recommend someone to direct the planning effort, they suggested a man whose career combined dual interests in education and organization design—Roger Levien of the Rand Corporation.[1] Levien fit nicely the "good people" model of which the Unholy Trinity was fond. With an undergraduate degree from Swarthmore and a Ph.D. in engineering from MIT, he had first-rate education credentials. At Rand in the late 1960s he had designed the National Institute for Information Systems and the International Institute for Applied Systems Analysis. By 1970 he was codirector of the education research program at Rand and had completed a study on computers in instruction for the National Science Foundation and another on computers in higher education for the Carnegie Commission. Within a month after Nixon announced the NIE proposal, Levien had been interviewed by the Working Group staff and hired to design a preliminary plan for NIE (Mays 21 March 1974; Levien 21 March 1974).

For six months Levien, with his one-man staff and two consultants, based in a small office in the OE building, interviewed dozens of people "in education and research whose experience has provided them with knowledge and insight about the issues being considered" (Levien 1971, p. 17). Levien characterized this effort as a political one—a process of engaging in the planning of the new agency all the major constituents for education R&D so they would contribute to its design, lobby for its creation, and support it after its authorization. Believing it was important to establish quickly that NIE would be different from OE, he was careful to draw up lists of prestigious consultants in research and development. The Unholy Trinity, weary of what they perceived to be the parochial nature of OE's consultants, took one look at Levien's lists and said "This is more like it" (Levien 21 March 1974). But Levien did not ignore the traditional OE consultants. Using OE's own lists, he also endeavored to see the head of every major education interest group, explain the plan, and listen to suggestions.

Table 2.1   Affiliation of Those Consulted by
                                           Levien during the Preparation
                                           of the NIE Plan

Institutional Affiliation	Number	% of Total
Higher education	57	41.6%
Schools of education	(26)	
Outside schools of education	(31)	
Education associations	23	16.8
State departments of education	8	5.8
Local school superintendents	4	2.9
Foundations	5	3.7
Laboratories and R&D centers	5	3.7
Other	35	25.5
Total	137	100%

Note: Levien also interviewed government   Source: Compiled from Levien 1971.
personnel in the White House, OST, OMB,
ASPE, all major bureaus in OE, NIH,
OEO, NSF, and the National Bureau
of Standards.

Levien's final report synthesized the recommendations from all the people interviewed, "to convey the essence of those discussions, drawing them together, and framing a coherent, reasonably detailed picture of what the NIE might become" (1971, p. 18). A look at the kinds of people Levien interviewed conveys the genealogy of his final product (see table 2.1). They represent a wide range of organizations and interests. It seems unlikely that the executive secretary of the American Vocational Association, the chairman of the Corporation of MIT, the Wisconsin state superintendent of schools, and a professor of English at Amherst, for example, would share a common picture of the major purposes of a federal education R&D agency. Given that the Levien report "synthesizes" the design recommendations from such disparate perspectives, two features of the design are easily predictable. It must embody the assumption that R&D can indeed improve education, and it must present a multifaceted view of what the agency should do.

Levien's analysis led him to frame the principal objective of NIE in comprehensive terms: "To improve and reform education through research and development." He targeted three areas for improvement and reform: "increased equality of educational opportunity, higher quality of education, and more effective use of educational resources" (p. 62). In discussing strategies for achieving these goals, Levien advocated a multiple strategy of problem-solving, improving practice, long-term knowledge building, and improving the educational R&D system (p. 23).[2] Using this formulation, one would find it difficult to imagine activities that would not be appropriate for the agency.

Many of the features of Levien's design were intended to overcome shortcomings in OE's R&D activities. Levien had identified five widely agreed-upon deficiencies: lack of funds; lack of bureaucratic status and power; lack of program continuity and focus; lack of high-quality personnel; and lack of linkages among research, development, and practice. To remedy these deficiencies, Levien proposed five specific features for NIE. The first was bureaucratic status "comparable to that of such R&D agencies as the National Institutes of Health, National Science Foundation, and National Bureau of Standards." The second was "active advisory councils" to assure linkage between research and practice and to provide program stability. "An internal R&D activity" would guarantee that NIE's programs would have the benefit of the latest research. "A flexible personnel system, modeled on those in other federal R&D agencies, such as NSF and NIH," would allow NIE to attract competent staff for all positions. And "authority to carry over unexpended funds from one year to the next" would allow NIE to develop stable, long-term funding patterns for multiyear programs (Levien 1971, pp. 8–9).

In October 1970, Levien presented a preliminary draft of his report to HEW. In November he conducted briefings throughout the government and circulated copies of the draft to more than 450 individuals "in education and R&D representing a wide range of interests" (p. 17). Revisions were guided by the comments of more than 150 people who responded to the draft, and the final report, *National Institute of Education: Preliminary Plan for the Proposed Institute*, was published in February 1971. In comparison with many government planning documents, it was an impressive work. Its organization and management recommendations were supported by citations from the literature on the management of R&D, together with an analysis of R&D agencies such as NSF and NIH. Its programmatic suggestions were given weight by the fact that nearly 300 people in the field had been consulted about them. And, finally, that this was so ingenuously a *preliminary* plan disarmed any potential pragmatic criticism.[3]

One witness in the NIE congressional hearings held after the publication of the Levien report pointed out that funding just one of the Levien suggested problem-solving activities would require $125 million of new money for three to five years (Gallagher 1971). But most readers of the report were not troubled by the absence of specific implementation suggestions; they were impressed by the comprehensive and intellectually satisfying nature of the plan.

The Planning Unit

With the appointment of Sidney P. Marland as commissioner of education in December 1970, Roger Levien's planning days came to an end. Marland asserts that the question of control of the planning process was self-evident; "the only natural place for it to be" was inside the Office of Education (Marland, 22 March 1974). Perhaps Marland was afraid Levien would not be an easy man to control; perhaps he did not like the fact that Levien appeared to be sponsored by the Unholy Trinity, or that he had been hired by Marland's predecessor; perhaps he was intimidated by Levien's intellectuality or felt that because Levien was not an "educationist" he could not really understand the problems NIE would face. In any case, Marland did not ask Levien to continue his planning efforts. This produced mixed reactions among those interested in NIE. Those who had been impressed by the Levien report and believed that OE was incapable of reforming itself were afraid the future of the new agency was in jeopardy. Those who believed NIE should be designed by people with experience in education were pleased.

In December 1970 Marland appointed Harry Silberman associate commissioner of education for the National Center for Educational Research and Development (NCERD), successor to the OE Bureau of Research. Silberman, a gentle, soft-spoken man, had impressed Marland with his "proven track record in educational R&D" (Marland, 22 March 1974). Silberman came to NCERD from System Development Corporation (SDC), a California contract research organization, where he had been director of the Education Systems Division. There, in addition to applying systems analysis techniques to educational problems, he had been one of the codevelopers of the Southwest Regional Laboratory, one of the OE-funded educational laboratories. At SDC Silberman had built a reputation for management competence and for solid work in computer-assisted instruction and in educational planning and development (Marland, 22 March 1974). If Levien represented a pure example of a "good person," Silberman was more problematic. He had a doctorate from a good school—UCLA, but it was in education. He worked for a reputable R&D organization, but in the education division. He was associated with one of the more respected regional laboratories, but none of the laboratories was considered first rate by the Unholy Trinity. The OE critics took a wait-and-see attitude toward Silberman.

Marland hired Silberman as associate commissioner for NCERD because that spot was empty. He believed he had no authority to hire him as director of a planning unit for an agency not yet approved by Congress. But once Silberman was on the OE payroll, Marland was able to relieve him of his NCERD duties and establish an NIE Planning Unit task force for him to head (Marland, 22 March 1974).[4]

Marland and Silberman both stressed the ad hoc, unauthorized nature of the Planning Unit. Marland, who characterizes the typical government response to the idea of a new agency as "don't think about it until it is authorized," believed a certain amount of groundwork could be laid for NIE even before its authorization. He believed the purpose of the Planning Unit was to "sensitize Washington that the NIE idea was growing." He also believed the Planning Unit could build an "options list" that would be useful to the first director. He hoped the Planning Unit could sensitize the research community as well as Congress to the issues and problems NIE would address and involve the research community in the development of the options list. Marland did not believe, however, that the Planning Unit should have "actually designed the new agency." That was to be the job of the first director, and "it would have been wrong for Silberman and the Planning Unit to do his job for him" (Marland, 22 March 1974). The Planning Unit was intended to "sensitize," not "prescribe."

Silberman also employed a medical metaphor to describe his view of the purpose of the Planning Unit. He saw the major function of the Planning Unit as "midwifing the new agency, protecting its birth so it wouldn't be stillborn" (Silberman, 28 February 1974). This process had two major components. One was listening to interest groups describe provisions they would like to see in the new agency, thereby diverting these people from going to congressmen to try to get their interests specifically written into the legislation. Several groups "threatened to kill the NIE bill" if their interests were not satisfied. Silberman patiently listened to all of them. The second element in the midwifing process was providing a supportive environment for the new agency by building a core group of people both inside and outside the government who had been thinking about the problems and features of educational R&D and who had something interesting to say about them (Silberman, 28 February 1974).

The NIE Planning Unit was established with a very ambitious mandate. According to a memorandum sent to HEW Secretary Richardson on 20 January 1971 by one of his deputy assistant secretaries, the Planning Unit, then being established, was to:

A. Further define the purpose of NIE (objectives, priorities, scope) and outline procedures for renewal of objectives and continuous planning of programs.
B. Assess existing and projected R&D programs in education and coordinate NIE planning with them.
C. Develop specific program plans and schedules for NIE.
D. Develop specific start-up plans and schedules for NIE.
[Cross, 20 January 1971]

At the time this memorandum was written, passage of the NIE legislation was expected sometime during the summer of 1971; therefore, the time budgeted for the Planning Unit to accomplish the above tasks was five months. Note that the second two Planning Unit objectives as described by HEW were much more specific than Marland's "sensitizing" or Silberman's "midwifing" conceptions.

Silberman decided that the Planning Unit should use the three Levien priority areas to organize its own new program planning. This focus would provide an opportunity for continuity from the Levien period to the Planning Unit period. These priority areas were clearly important in both political and social terms. They had been endorsed, implicitly at least, by "the wide range of respected individuals" consulted by Levien; and they were broad enough to provide an umbrella for a wide variety of activities.

From April to October 1971, most of the Planning Unit work was loosely directed. In spite of the fact that he had nominally been relieved of his NCERD responsibilities, Silberman felt compelled to spend most of every day working on NCERD problems until October, when the Planning Unit, which had until that time been housed in NCERD offices in the OE building, moved into its own quarters in another building. During these months Beverly Kooi, Silberman's unofficial deputy, thus bore much of the responsibility for the daily operations of the Planning Unit. Kooi had worked with Silberman at SDC before coming to Washington. Her view of the purpose of the Planning Unit differed from that of Marland and Silberman. She went to Washington "to make decisions" (Kooi, 28 February 1974). As a result, much of her Planning Unit work had an air of finality about it that was unsettling to people who believed the Planning Unit should be laying out options, not making decisions.

Outside Assistance

During 1971 members of the Planning Unit were not the only people involved in planning for the new agency. In January 1971 an interagency steering committee for the Planning Unit was formed through the combined efforts of John Mays from OST, who had been on the staff of the White House group that created the NIE proposal, and members of ASPE in HEW. Mays was anxious that NIE planning insure that the agency would be able to attract superior academic researchers. The staff of ASPE shared this interest but also had a more political concern. They were not happy that the planning effort was located within OE; they feared that decisions might be made over which they would have little influence (Mays, 22 March 1974; Silberman, 28 February 1974). Out of these concerns grew the impetus for a steering committee. In addition to Mays from OST, membership included senior officials from HEW, OMB, and OE.[5]

Silberman was less than delighted with the Steering Committee. Because the committee met only intermittently, had no formal responsibility for the Planning Unit, and had little involvement in its daily operations, its advice seemed impractical and its criticisms unrealistic. Silberman thought ASPE's concern over being left out of decisions was unfounded; he believed he had no decision authority and thought ASPE was being paranoid. Furthermore, members of the Steering Committee disagreed among themselves over what the Planning Unit should be doing. As a consequence its advice often seemed inconsistent and contradictory. Finally, and probably most annoying to Silberman, when committee members could not attend meetings the junior staff sent in their place seemed arrogant and condescending. Silberman had no patience with inexperienced "hotshots" who, as he perceived it, were trading on their bosses' authority. He viewed the steering committee experience as symbolic of much of what was wrong with the lowly position of education R&D inside OE.

John Mays influenced the NIE planning in a number of ways. Mays, who had been trained as a physical chemist at Columbia University and had worked at Bell Laboratories from 1952 to 1960, came to Washington in 1960 to direct the NSF curriculum development programs in physical sciences and mathematics. In 1966 he moved to OST and became assistant to the director for education and education R&D programs. At NSF and OST Mays viewed with distress what he considered to be the second-rate work sponsored by OE and the second-rate management exhibited by the OE staff. Unimpressed by the work in most schools of education, he believed that education R&D could be improved by following the NSF model. Mays wanted to involve the best minds in the country—in his view almost always to be found in the best universities in the country—in education R&D. He believed that if he could interest top social scientists in education their research would then lead to major new theoretical insights. Their involvement in development programs, similar to the use of scientists in the NSF precollege curriculum development programs, would lead to more effective programs for the field. Mays was determined that university scholars should be involved in the early NIE planning both so that the planning could benefit from their ideas and so that the academicians would feel well-disposed toward the new agency.

To guarantee this involvement, Mays volunteered to organize a series of meetings to be cosponsored by OST and the Planning Unit. Mays lavished attention on the planning of those meetings, painstakingly fashioning the invitation lists to include illustrious scholars from all over the country.[6] After each two-day meeting, the chairman prepared a paper based on suggestions from the participants, which was then circulated among other members of the discipline and which was to be incorporated by Planning Unit personnel in their problem analyses. All the papers emphasized a basic research agenda and tended to ignore development, field experimentation, and social engineering. This was natural, given the interests and expertise of the meeting participants. However, the Planning Unit, focusing on major problem areas rather than on basic research, did not incorporate many of the research proposals in its work.

The Fall of 1971

By the fall of 1971 those who had taken a wait-and-see attitude toward Silberman and the Planning Unit were not sure they liked what they saw. The senior staff and consultant rosters were filling up with "educationists." All the senior staff had been trained in schools of education; no one had a scholarly research reputation; none had any federal planning or management experience; none had any Washington political experience. All the major consulting contracts, with the exception of a small R&D management contract with Rand, were with schools of education. In addition, the Planning Unit seemed to be snarled in the OE bureaucracy. Silberman was spending most of his time on NCERD problems. Even when he attended to the Planning Unit he had to report to Marland through a deputy commissioner rather than directly. Furthermore, Planning Unit presentations to Washington groups interested in NIE, such as the AERA executive committee, were judged vague and insubstantial. And, finally, program planning for the three Levien problem areas seemed fragmented and not rigorous. To the critics of OE, the Planning Unit gave the impression that in spite of all their efforts NIE might turn out to be less than the sparkling gem of rationality they had envisioned.

By September 1971 both Silberman and Marland were receiving heavy criticism from those who felt the Planning Unit had been captured by OE and the educationists. Marland reports that it had been his intention all along to separate the Planning Unit from OE "as quickly as possible" (Marland, 22 March 1974). He altered the lines of communication so that Silberman would report to him directly, and he encouraged Silberman to move the Planning Unit out of the OE building and into its own quarters. Silberman turned all NCERD activities over to his deputy and, with the move into new offices in October 1971, began devoting his full time to the Planning Unit.

Silberman asked Bill Rabinowitz, a faculty member at the Pennsylvania State University School of Education, which had a Planning Unit contract, to coordinate the program-planning activities. In an attempt to impose some coherence Rabinowitz circulated guidelines to all the consultants and planners involved in program planning. The guidelines asked each planner or consultant to

—define the major educational problems in the area under his or her consideration

—examine past and current R&D efforts addressed to these problems, and

—suggest promising new lines of R&D work which the Institute might consider. [NIE Planning Unit, January 1972]

Rabinowitz, who still had his own teaching responsibilities at Pennsylvania State University, was not able to spend full time managing the planning effort; consequently each planner and consultant group continued to work independently.

A group from the University of Illinois School of Education had been asked to work on the problem area "Improving Education for the Disadvantaged." They spent October and November 1971 crisscrossing the country, interviewing dozens of people they felt could contribute to the planning process but who never would have appeared on one of Levien's consultant lists or on the OE list of interest groups. The Illinois group had devised a plan for using NIE technical support for local education problem-solving activities, based loosely on the OEO Community Action Plan model, and they used a description of this plan as a basis for encouraging poor people to talk about what they believed federal R&D efforts could and could not do for them. The interview transcripts were gathered in a three-inch-thick bundle of papers held together with a rubber band. Several members of the Planning Unit, including Silberman, read them all and found them fascinating, but did not know what to do with them. The Illinois proposal for providing NIE technical assistance for local education problem-solving was poorly received for several reasons. It did not look like a plan for research and development; it was not backed up by an analytic design that would insure implementation or lead to cumulative knowledge about problem-solving; it did not describe alternative approaches to local problem solving; and, perhaps most important, it sounded too much like an OEO social action plan at a time when both OEO and federally sponsored social action interventions were under attack.

In order to produce the program plan for "Improving Resource Use in Education," Beverly Kooi had hired three groups of academic consultants to write papers for her. Kooi was unable to provide much specific guidance to any of these groups—she had other Planning Unit responsibilities and could not spend much time with them. Further, she had never designed a large federal R&D program and she was not an economist. When the papers came in they provided useful theoretical background, but they did not describe a coherent set of R&D activities that could be funded by the federal government (Bowman 1971; Benson 1971; Singell 1971).

The consultant assigned to "Improving the Quality of Education" preferred to work alone. He drew on his own reading and experience as director of an elementary-school mathematics curriculum project as background for his paper and did not provide a rigorous analytic justification for the project ideas he wanted to propose.

The culmination of 1971 Planning Unit activities was a year-end report to Commissioner Marland and the Planning Unit Steering Committee (NIE Planning Unit, January 1972). Most of the activity in the last three months of 1971 was directed to fashioning this report, which contained sections on new program initiatives, organization structure, transfer programs, and administrative issues. This document captured much of the Planning Unit style of operation and thinking on key issues.

The Year-End Report

All the commissioned papers and program-planning outlines were received by the Planning Unit by 1 December 1971. The month of December was devoted to an attempt to synthesize all of them into a single comprehensive program plan, describing all suggested new NIE initiatives for the 1973 fiscal year. Silberman, Kooi, Rabinowitz, and two Planning Unit staff members first read all the commissioned papers and culled ideas they found particularly attractive. These program suggestions, or ideas that might be developed into program suggestions, were then evaluated against two pragmatic criteria: How well-developed were they? (There were some interesting ideas in "Improving the Quality of Education" outlines, but most of them were so sketchy it would have taken three months to begin to develop them. Kooi, on the other hand, was already well along in describing two new initiatives in her problem area, and so they were chosen to be included in the final list.) As a group, how comprehensive were they? (The first December list included no initiatives on postsecondary education, and it was decided that that omission had to be corrected. Similarly, there was no initiative using technology, and such an initiative seemed necessary.) By mid-December the culling and hole-filling process had produced eight initiatives.

These initiatives were only loosely related, at best, to earlier suggestions for NIE work (see table 2.2 for proposed R&D initiatives). The White House working group had proposed initiatives that were described in Nixon's speech. During the spring of 1971, congressional hearings on the proposed NIE had yielded a number of suggested program initiatives (the hearings are described in chap. 3). The Planning Unit did not draw upon earlier suggestions in developing its comprehensive program plan. Only two ideas advanced by the Planning Unit had also been mentioned in earlier proposals—programs for preschool children and education technology. (Note also that by this time the Planning Unit had abandoned the Levien terminology of the three major problem areas.)

In two days of nonstop meetings the Planning Unit staff and Rabinowitz developed the outline of a conceptual framework to link all the initiatives in a sensible way.[7] Rabinowitz rewrote the descriptions of the initiatives to include variables from the conceptual framework, and that concluded the new program planning activity for the Planning Unit interim report. Note that the Planning Unit began with program ideas and then attempted to create a conceptual framework for them. This process was later reversed by

Table 2.2   Program Initiatives Proposed for
                                                 NIE during the Planning Period
                                                 by Various Sources

Nixon: President's message on education reform, March 1970
  New measures of learning
  Compensatory education
  Reading
  Television and learning
  Experimental schools
  Early learning

Levien: Preliminary Plan for NIE, February 1971
  Improving education of the disadvantaged
  Improving the quality of education
  Improving the effectiveness of resource use in education

Congressional witnesses: House hearings on proposed NIE, February–June 1971
  Equality of educational opportunity
  Setting standards for education practice—NIE as a "consumer's union"
  Dissemination of ideas—linking research to practice
  Reducing the cost of education
  Learning more about the affective impact of schooling
  Career education and work-study
  Development of education technology
  Early childhood learning
  Economics of higher education
  Longitudinal studies of schooling impact
  Promotion of alternatives in schooling
  School-community relations
  Childhood nutrition
  In-service training for teachers
  Form, structure, and timing of schooling
  Materials development and the evaluation of textbooks
  Libraries and information science

NIE Planning Unit: Year-end report, January 1972
  Adjusting inequities in education spending—state fiscal equalization plans
  Providing education services for poorly served clients—experimental programs for preschool
    children and old people
  Fostering community involvement in education through community vouchers—similar to
    the OEO voucher plan, except vouchers would go to community groups instead of to
    individuals
  Alternative voting techniques—experimenting with multiple choice and preference ranking
    ballots for local school elections
  Unbundling higher education—experimental effort at separating into discrete "industries"
    various higher education services such as credentialing and instruction
  Stimulating greater use of technology in education—analyzing and funding promising
    developments in education technology, for example, providing social services via cable
    television
  Development of theme schools—alternative demonstration schools based on "educationally
    relevant themes"
  Using community resources to increase the authenticity of learning experiences—
    development of local community-centered curriculum

NIE, which attempted first to define the framework, then to deduce programs from it (see chap. 8, "The Paradigm Search").

The development of a comprehensive program plan was not the only work under way during the last three months of 1971. Wilmer Cody, the former Chapel Hill, North Carolina, superintendent of schools who had been hired by Silberman in September 1971, was responsible for organization planning. He used a Rand survey of federal R&D agency organization plans for background information (Wirt et al. 1972) and spent considerable time talking with Silberman and Kooi. His contribution to the year-end report referred the reader to the Rand reviews but did not itself discuss alternative organization designs, instead presenting a single design in some detail. There are at least two reasons why Cody presented a single design. One is referred to in the report itself: OMB and HEW were pressing the Planning Unit for specific NIE budget projections; they could be provided most easily within the context of one specific organization structure (Interim Report, p. 7). The second reason is that Silberman, Kooi, and Cody honestly believed their proposed design was the best one; presenting it as only one of several alternatives would be merely "playing games" (Silberman, 28 February 1974).[8]

The issue of transferring OE R&D programs and personnel was also addressed in the Planning Unit year-end report, in a section written by Beverly Kooi. Kooi indicated that approximately $100 million of the projected $125-million 1973 NIE budget would probably be absorbed by programs that would be transferred from OE. She then described the criteria by which OE programs were chosen for transfer. "If [an OE] program's basic task is to create new knowledge or solutions, its budget is slated for transfer to NIE. If the program's basic thrust is to assist education consumers using the tools we already possess, its budget will remain in OE" (NIE Planning Unit, January 1972, p. 108).[9] Kooi estimated that at least 267 current contracts and grants would be transferred (p. 108). She reported that a program-by-program evaluation had been planned for the spring of 1972 for all transferring programs, the results of which "would be used in making recommendations for program changes" (p. 116).

The final section of the year-end report described some management changes being considered for the transferring programs and some tentative plans for the placement of OE personnel then operating the programs slated for transfer. The transfer of personnel was acknowledged to be "complex and important," complicated by three conditions identified by Kooi: OE personnel "feel a natural propriety" toward their programs; the Civil Service Commission "has regulations that govern positions associated with transfer of programs"; and the government employee's union "is extremely interested" in protecting the rights of current government employees. Kooi offered a solution to these issues. She proposed to identify all personnel positions being transferred with each OE program, to interview the OE person currently occupying the position, then to write a job description for each position that would specifically either include or exclude the current OE occupant. "These definitions [of personnel positions] must be clear enough to show how closely the NIE mission can or cannot be met by any existing staff or new applicant for each position" (p. 128). This plan was to insure that NIE would receive only those OE personnel it found appropriate.

The Planning Unit Interim Report was sent to Commissioner Marland during the first week of 1972. Every member of the Steering Committee also received a copy, as did a small number of other federal government staff members interested in education. Both Silberman and Kooi were pleased with the Interim Report (Silberman, 28 February 1974; Kooi, 28 February 1974). They believed that implementation of its key features—focusing problem-solving initiatives on important system variables, organizing by management style, and separating evaluation activities from program activities—would significantly improve the conduct of educational R&D in this country.

Other people did not view the Interim Report so positively. Marland would not accept the OE personnel transfer plan. He believed that if it were implemented it would siphon off all the better OE personnel and leave OE with the less desirable ones. Members of ASPE believed that separating the program evaluation function from the program managing function would stifle the development of creative, responsible program managers. A more sweeping criticism of the Interim Report was that it seemed to be closing off options for the first director rather than expanding them. It was viewed as a "selling job" for a particular organization and set of programs rather than as an analysis of all feasible alternatives (Timpane, 24 January 1972).

A February 1972 memorandum to HEW Secretary Richardson from the assistant secretary for planning and evaluation listed the major Planning Unit responsibilities, evaluated progress on them to date, and described planning tasks to be undertaken during the spring of 1972 designed to remedy some of the perceived deficiencies in the earlier planning. The assessment was negative; the proposed remedies were ambitious.

> Program plans—"unsatisfactory. . . . the Planning Unit initially viewed its tasks as that of defining in detail a single research program for the Institute. This orientation did not lead either to a comprehensive planning effort or to an analysis of alternative programs for the Institute in terms of their feasibility, their potential impact on significant educational problems, their cost . . ."[p. 1]

> Organization design plans—"the particular design advocated by the Planning Unit has several critical shortcomings."[p. 2]

> Professional staff recruitment—"progressed very little."[p. 3]

Definition of NIE's relationship to other organizations such as OE and state and local education agencies—"progressed very little."[p. 4]

Analysis of administrative requirements—"relatively unsatisfactory to date."[p. 5] [Lynn, 4 February 1972]

The last three Planning Unit functions described in the ASPE memorandum had been given little attention by the Planning Unit. Professional recruitment had been the responsibility of a young psychologist who thought she had been hired by Silberman to do research. When she arrived at the Planning Unit in July 1971, Silberman asked her to take "temporary" charge of Planning Unit personnel work and professional recruitment. Although knowing little about either, she accepted because she was assured it would be a temporary assignment and she could soon move into the research and program planning area (Brainard, 26 March 1974). She remained the only Planning Unit person working on personnel and professional recruitment issues until June 1972. The ASPE memorandum pointed out that no analysis of the major categories of personnel required by NIE had been undertaken, nor had the characteristics of the several positions directly beneath the director been described. It acknowledged that until a director was chosen it would be impossible to begin actively recruiting staff, but it described activities that should be undertaken during the spring of 1972. ASPE staff and OST staff were to work with the Planning Unit to analyze personnel categories, develop staff selection criteria, and list potential candidates for each category.

Because the person responsible for defining NIE's relationship to other education agencies was interested in the issue of dissemination, he focused his work on defining those relationships in terms of NIE's dissemination capability. In addition to reflecting only one facet of NIE's relationships with other organizations, this view of NIE's dissemination role directly contradicted ASPE's view.[10] ASPE (and Marland) wanted the dissemination function to remain within the Office of Education. The Planning Unit was content to have unglamorous dissemination efforts such as ERIC remain within OE but believed NIE developers would have to "market" their own products if they were to be successful.[11] The ASPE memorandum described the spring 1972 tasks as "analysis of alternative NIE–OE dissemination functions; staffing and administrative implications of major options" (p. 5). These were to be carried out cooperatively by the Planning Unit, ASPE staff, and OE staff.

From September to December 1971, the person responsible for NIE administrative planning had spent much of his time on administrative details connected with the Planning Unit itself. He was responsible for moving the Planning Unit out of the OE building and into its new quarters, hiring secretaries, and keeping track of Planning Unit expenditures. Nevertheless, he was also responsible for NIE administrative planning and, according to the ASPE evaluation, failed miserably. He did not address "a wide range of 'nitty-gritty' problems concerning transfer of OE programs and personnel to NIE, contracting procedures, a Management Information System, physical plant, personnel policies, etc." (p. 5). According to the ASPE memorandum, the spring planning activities for administration would include an "analysis of NIE's administrative requirements, description of administrative options, procedural recommendations and staff implications" (p. 5). These activities were to be performed by the Planning Unit in cooperation with staff from the Office of the Assistant Secretary for Administration in HEW.

The two functions on which the Planning Unit had spent most of its time during the fall of 1971—organization planning and new program planning—were to be revised significantly during the spring planning period, according to the ASPE memorandum. The Planning Unit was, in effect, to do no more organization planning; instead, the Rand Corporation, in collaboration with ASPE consultants, would continue its Planning-Unit-funded work on its analysis of R&D agency organization design options. Upon completion of the analysis, Rand, ASPE, and the Planning Unit would issue a joint report on the Rand/ASPE work. Wilmer Cody was to be the Planning Unit representative in these activities.

New program planning was to be more comprehensive and analytic. Joan Bissell, a recent Harvard Ph.D. in human development, would be the ASPE staff member directly responsible for working with the Planning Unit on program planning. She had attempted to influence the Planning Unit program planning as early as July 1971, when she presented the Steering Committee with an example of the kind of program planning she thought the Planning Unit should engage in (Bissell, 1971). Her model was based on Secretary Richardson's 1971 "Research and Evaluation Guidance" memorandum, circulated throughout HEW, which required all research managers to analyze their research programs in cost/benefit terms: What is the problem the agency is trying to solve? What is the target population? What is already known about the problem? What are gaps in knowledge about the problem? How can those gaps be filled? What are alternative solutions to the problem? How appropriate is each solution in terms of feasibility? cost? potential impact? relation to other government programs? Silberman was not impressed with the model as a guide for Planning Unit behavior. He believed most of the interesting problems in education did not lend themselves to top-down, deductive analysis. So he had not systematically utilized the ASPE planning model while working on the Interim Report. With the assignment of Bissell to oversee program planning in the spring of 1972, the ASPE planning model would become more prominent.

After approximately nine months of work, the Planning Unit found itself buffeted by external criticism, bedeviled by advice-givers, somewhat estranged from Marland, and unsure of what to do next. No one had any idea when the NIE legislation might pass, yet the Planning Unit could not be allowed simply to stop work. A staff had been hired, a bureaucratic entity had been created. Planning must proceed.

The Spring of 1972

With the poor reception of the Interim Report, Silberman felt obliged to listen to some of the advice he had been getting from ASPE and the Steering Committee. So he agreed, according to the ASPE memo, that the Planning Unit would "develop a rigorous, comprehensive plan which identifies and analyzes program options for the Institute" (p. 2). One of the criticisms of the Interim Report was that it had been solely an internal effort; Silberman was urged to involve planners from policy research groups around the country. He organized the spring program planning into four teams of planners. One was directed by Amitai Etzioni of the Columbia University Center for Policy Analysis; another was directed by O. W. Markley of the Stanford Research Institute (SRI) Educational Policy Research Center. Beverly Kooi headed the third team, which was composed of Planning Unit and OE staff and consultants drawn from the OE-supported laboratories and R&D centers. Senta Raizen, on loan from NSF where she was special assistant to the associate director for education, headed the fourth team. She drew most of her consultants from the "wider community" of which the Unholy Trinity was fond.[12] On 1 February the team leaders received a copy of the suggested analytic framework and of Bissell's earlier planning model and were told to have their analysis—including statement of the problems, assessment of current knowledge and work, identification of critical knowledge gaps, and alternative program suggestions analyzed on all feasibility criteria—completed by 15 April.[13]

The four program planning analyses were completed and distributed by 20 April 1972. Their completion marked the end of Planning Unit new program planning and analysis. At a meeting held 2 May 1972, to review all four documents, attended by members of the Planning Unit and the Steering Committee, it became apparent that further planning would merely be running people around the same track again. Additionally, there were certain bureaucratic exigencies, such as a fast-approaching budget-submission deadline, that had to take priority.

The 2 May 1972 meeting is noteworthy not only because it marked the effective end of Planning Unit program planning, but also because it foreshadowed the kind of debate that would characterize much of NIE's first year. Attending the review meeting were many of the members of the federal community most interested in NIE, and meeting notes reveal the extent to which practically everyone present was operating from a different agenda (Silberman, 15 May 1972). A member of the HEW Comptroller's Office asked about legal commitments to ongoing OE programs. The OE deputy commissioner for development urged that the programs be transferred intact from OE. John Mays wanted to make sure they were not so intact that the first NIE director would be unable to split them up if he wanted to. Emerson Elliott, just arrived from OMB as Silberman's deputy, asked what the budget lines for NIE's first budget submission should look like. This question in effect asked the group to decide what NIE's first public statement of its programs and priorities should be. The Comptroller's Office representative suggested listing activities under "fairly broad goals rather than budget lines." Bissell and Mays suggested categorizing all the R&D initiatives that had been proposed in the program planning documents. Another ASPE representative believed those categories did not "add up to one" and proposed using Etzioni's categories of learner goals. Mays proposed the three categories used in the Levien and Raizen reports. A third ASPE representative seconded the suggestion. Kooi observed that the three categories were overlapping and would "allow placement of any program anywhere." An OMB budget officer questioned whether there was too much emphasis on the educationally disadvantaged. Raizen pointed out that this was a broad concept of providing equal access to those client groups who are not well served by the present system. At this point Silberman interrupted to ask people to comment specifically on the R&D programs proposed in the four documents.

Members of ASPE thought more work was necessary in establishing the logical connection between goals and analysis and suggested that the Raizen document be used as the model. Kooi pointed out the other documents also had strengths. Silberman questioned whether one would ever finish analysis of goals. His plaintive question was that of a tired planner—"How do you know when you're through?" At this point "many members of the group" agreed with Mays, who said the work was "pretty much done" for the time being but should become the basis of an ongoing program of analysis in NIE. Then Elliott, who had not spoken since asking about budget lines, said he would prepare a draft budget for review during the next few weeks. It was agreed that a summary of the four documents should be prepared; Bissell asked for more goal analysis; Mays cautioned not to get "locked into a single person's idea of what ought to be done in particular programs"; the Comptroller's Office representative reminded the group that a good budget justification would be necessary to convince Congress to meet the budget target of $125 million; and the meeting concluded (Silberman, 15 May 1972). This was not the first time, nor would it be the last, that reasonable people were unable to agree on a framework for NIE activities.

The Transition

Although Emerson Elliott had been officially invited to join the Planning Unit by Silberman, it had been at the urging of Steering Committee members concerned that the Planning Unit had no one skilled in the intricacies of federal management and budgeting (Kooi, 28 February 1974; Elliott, 28 November 1973). Elliott was probably one of the most skilled budget analysts in Washington. He had been a budget examiner for federal education programs in the Bureau of the Budget from 1960 to 1967; assistant director for education programs in the Bureau of the Budget Human Resources Programs Division from 1967 to 1970; and deputy chief of the Human Resources Programs Division from 1970 to 1972. He had been on the staff of the 1964 and 1967 White House Task Forces on Education and had principal responsibility for the special analysis of federal education programs included in the 1969, 1970, and 1971 presidential budgets.

Even though passage of the legislation was still close to two months away, Elliott's arrival signaled the beginning of the transition from a planning group to an operating agency. All the senior Planning Unit staff except Cody had either left the Planning Unit or shortly would announce plans to leave. Silberman announced that he had accepted a faculty appointment at the UCLA School of Education and would leave Washington at the end of the year. Kooi was preparing to return to California at the end of June. Raizen had decided to join Roger Levien at the Rand Corporation. The Planning Unit official in charge of dissemination was soon to be named president of a small college in Ohio.

Elliott became the center of all Planning Unit activity, and he was swamped with work. Both Levien and Silberman had been allowed the luxury of prefacing every proposal with a disclaimer: "For purposes of illustration . . ." or "NIE might choose among the following . . ." or "The first NIE director must decide . . ." But some decisions could not wait for the appointment of the director. Someone had to prepare the 1973 budget request and justification. Someone had to negotiate an OE personnel transfer plan with Marland. Someone had to attend to the evaluation of OE transfer programs. Someone had to close out the Pennsylvania State University planning contract and decide what to do with the dozen Planning Unit staff employed under that contract who wanted jobs with NIE. Someone had to find office space for the new agency. The days of analyzing the goals and problems of education and of designing elaborate organization structures were over, at least for a while. Pragmatic decisions and deadlines had begun to drive the system.

Conclusion

Twenty-six months after Levien had begun work on a preliminary plan for NIE, Congress passed its authorizing legislation. Did all the months of planning make any difference? Was the new agency any better off than it would have been if there had been no planning activities? We have suggested that it is possible to discern at least four models of the purpose of planning during this period. A brief assessment of each may help us answer these questions.

Levien's work embodied two of the models: planning as politics—gathering constituent support through a careful process of consultation—and planning as symbolism—convincing an audience through the style of analysis, as much as through its content, that the "plan" is worthy of support. In Levien's view, constituents were to be found inside, as well as outside, the government; thus he was careful to consult with and heed the advice of the Unholy Trinity. Insofar as Levien's plan convinced HEW and congressional staff that an NIE was an attractive idea, through its widespread consultation and rational, analytic style, his work was fruitful. Had there not been an impressive Preliminary Plan legitimating the idea of an NIE, the authorizing legislation might never have passed. (As we shall see in the next chapter, Levien's work substantially influenced the specific provisions in the authorizing legislation.)

Silberman's attitude toward planning as politics was more complicated than Levien's approach. Both Marland and Silberman believed that the Planning Unit should nurture interest in the idea of an NIE and in the idea of improving education R&D. In this regard, the Planning Unit Steering Committee could have become a mechanism for generating support for NIE inside the government review agencies. But because Silberman and the committee viewed each other with mixed emotions this potential was not fully realized. The committee's access to the Planning Unit reassured its members that irrevocable decisions about NIE were not being made by faceless bureaucrats in unnumbered offices. Committee members may have been dissatisfied with the quality of the Planning Unit work, yet at least they were kept informed of it. But Silberman's desire to involve people was counteracted by his desire to "protect the birth"—to prevent too many people from becoming too involved. Thus the Planning Unit did not emphasize public information and external constituency development activities. Nor did it attempt to assess or influence the likelihood of congressional support for the new agency. As a result of the conflicting desires to nurture interest and protect the birth, the Planning Unit behaved in a schizophrenic manner with respect to the political aspects of planning.

The Planning Unit's performance as a creator of symbols was also mixed. With the exception of Raizen and her consultants, the Planning Unit personnel did not look like the "good people" of which the Unholy Trinity was fond. Nor did Planning Unit documents and presentations have the crisp analytic assurance that characterized Levien's work. One of the reasons Levien's Preliminary Plan was so appealing was that nothing like it had ever been seen before. But once it had been created, the Planning Unit was expected to be even more analytic, more comprehensive, and more sophisticated. Its symbolic task was much more difficult than Levien's. Levien did not have to follow Levien.

The third model of the purpose of planning—planning as "laying out options"—was most strongly and consistently championed by ASPE. This is not a surprising preference. Laying out options—studying alternative courses of action—is exactly the sort of work ASPE staff are expected to perform in their own jobs. But the Planning Unit seemed incapable of meeting ASPE's expectations. Neither the Planning Unit personnel nor most of its consultants were trained or experienced in the analytic mode favored by ASPE. Further, many of those associated with the Planning Unit were not interested in presenting alternatives. They were committed to a particular point of view and course of action.

This commitment is characteristic of the fourth model—planning as early action, or "the baton theory of planning." In this view the Planning Unit would hand on its work to the first director of NIE who would pick it up and run with it. The Planning Unit firmly believed that the activities it was proposing and initiating were the most appropriate for the new agency and assumed that its plans could and would be implemented. However those who did not agree with the Planning Unit's specific proposals found it easy to object to them on the grounds that they had not emerged from the laying-out-options process.

In one sense the planning went on too long. Silberman arrived in Washington to find a completed, highly praised preliminary plan and expectations that the NIE legislation would be passed in late spring of 1971. When it became apparent that the legislation would be delayed until 1972, the status of the planning effort changed. The anti-OE contingent was unwilling to let planning proceed for a year inside NCERD, and Silberman was forced to separate himself from OE. But Silberman had no experience or authority of his own in the federal bureaucracy, owed his job to Marland, and was dependent on OE for administrative support. Because the months dragged on and there existed an identifiable entity called the NIE Planning Unit, the larger federal bureaucracy began making demands on it. The HEW Comptroller's Office and the Office of Management and Budget wanted NIE budgets and justifications for them in terms of programs and personnel. Neither Silberman nor Marland had authority to make fiscal decisions on behalf of NIE; no one would have that authority until Congress passed authorizing legislation. Yet officials in the executive branch insisted that unless those decisions were forthcoming, NIE would not be represented in the president's budget and therefore would receive no funds even if it were authorized. Silberman was caught in a bureaucratic crossfire. These bureaucratic pressures, plus its own growing commitment to a particular set of activities for NIE, led the Planning Unit to act in a certain way—proposing specific programs and a single organization structure. These actions resulted in a loss of Planning Unit legitimacy in the eyes of those who either did not believe in the baton theory of planning or did not happen to like the Planning Unit's particular suggestions.

None of the proposals from the planning efforts was ever formally adopted by NIE. Had Levien or Silberman been NIE's first director, the situation might have been different. But, as it turned out, the substantive impact of the planning years was negligible. In mid-1972, a small planning bureaucracy was phased out and a largely unrelated operating bureaucracy was born.

What then might planners of other new organizations conclude from the NIE planning experience? If the nascent organization can be characterized by ambiguous goals, unclear technology, and fluid participation, the four models of planning exhibited in the NIE case may be of some utility. But it is well to understand that they involve different activities and yield different results. Consider, for example, the degree of outside participation in the planning allowed by the various models. Planning as politics, by definition, guarantees substantial outside participation. Planning as symbolism will guarantee it only if the appearance of constituent support is important to the symbolic plan. Planning as laying out options may or may not require outside participation, depending on the method used. If the planning staff chooses to do its own analysis of alternatives, then no outsiders need be involved. On the other hand, the planning staff might choose to engage a variety of groups of outsiders, each to prepare the analysis of a separate alternative. Finally, planning as early action guarantees there will be little or no outside participation. If planners are engaged in making specific suggestions, the alternative interests and points of view inevitably accompanying outside participation will be viewed as a hindrance rather than as a help; therefore outside participation will be kept to a minimum.

Or consider the degree of specificity of the planning documents. Planning as politics will be accompanied by a low degree of specificity. To secure the support of a wide assortment of constituents it is necessary for the plan to appeal to all of them. The more general the plan, the easier this is to accomplish. Planning as symbolism will also be accompanied by low specificity. Because it is the style of proposals rather than their specific content that is important in a symbolic plan, one must make sure that the specific details do not overwhelm or obscure the style. Planning as laying out options, in theory, is usually characterized by high specificity. In practice it may be difficult to achieve the same level of specificity across options if they are at all complex. The final planning model, planning as early action, is of course characterized by high specificity.

Related to the specificity of planning is the issue of implementing plans. It seems reasonable to expect that the most specific plans, that is, ones generated under planning as laying out options or planning as early action, would be the easiest to implement. But there is a problem. In the NIE case there were two (three, counting Congress) major sets of planners, neither (none) of whom was the implementer. It is probably true that when planners are not implementers, specific plans are not likely to be carried out. How can this be? When an architect hands blueprints to a builder, the builder does not throw them away (usually). But when goals are ambiguous and the technology for achieving them is unclear, it is easier to have confidence in one's own plans than in someone else's. Generating a specific plan requires that the planner go through a very complicated learning process. There is a complex sifting of detail, weighing of alternatives, and application of personal judgment before the plan is fashioned. It is difficult to convey this process to someone who sees only the end product—the plan. In an organized anarchy, every new manager must go through his own learning process. In addition, most leaders of new organizations probably believe that plans can have an impact on the organization. Naturally they would prefer that impact to be of their own design rather than someone else's.

Another distinction may be useful. Most of the foregoing discussion has assumed that planning is concerned with Big Questions and Grand Proposals. But it may also be concerned with mundane issues and small suggestions. And, assuming there has been enough planning as politics and symbolism to insure that the new organization will come to exist, it is in this latter domain that planners who are not implementers may be of use to the first managers of the new organization. Attending to the minutiae of a new organization—the panoply of small procedures and details that make the organization work—may be the best service the planners can perform. Unfortunately, there is little glamor in it.

Three　　　　　　　　　Creating the Institute:
　　　　　　　　　　　　　　The Legislative Process

Introduction

On 23 June 1972, more than two years after he had proposed it to Congress, President Nixon signed the legislation that created the National Institute of Education. In this chapter we describe the major features of the new agency stipulated in the legislation and analyze the factors, both people and ideas, that led to them. We also examine the course by which the legislation moved through Congress—the process of hearings, debate, and vote. This chapter will attempt to answer three questions:

What were the major features of the NIE legislation?

How were they determined?

What degree of support did the NIE enjoy in Congress?

The Legislative Process Chronology

1970

March	Nixon proposes NIE
November	(Levien circulates draft of Preliminary Plan)
December	Moynihan leaves Domestic Council
	(Silverman hired by Marland)

1971

February	(Levien Preliminary Plan published)
	Brademas hearings begin on NIE
May	(NIE Planning Unit announced)
June	Brademas hearings end
August	Senate passes Education Amendments of 1971 including NIE title
November	House approves creation of NIE, 210 to 153
	Majority of House Appropriations Subcommittee vote against NIE

1972

March	House-Senate conference committee convenes on Education Amendments

May   Senate passes conference version of Education
               Amendments of 1972
June   House passes conference version of Education
               Amendments of 1972
               Nixon signs legislation creating NIE
August   NIE officially begins operations

The Legislation: Provisions and Expectations

The NIE legislation closely followed Roger Levien's suggested design. Levien had determined several important characteristics for the new agency that congressional hearings on the proposed NIE had reiterated. The organization must have high status within the federal government in order to attract first-rate personnel and bureaucratic authority. It must have prestigious advisory councils to help link practitioners and the research community and to provide stability and freedom from political influence for NIE's programs and policies. It must have an internal research office to help formulate policy and to help attract competent researchers. It must have a flexible personnel system to free the agency from Civil Service personnel constraints. And it must have the authority to retain funds unspent at the end of a fiscal year to facilitate multiyear program continuity. It is no accident that these features closely resembled those described by Vannevar Bush when he proposed the National Science Foundation twenty years earlier (see chap. 1). NSF and NIH analogies marked the path of NIE's legislation.

In its final form (see Appendix 3 for the complete text of the law), Public Law 92–318 provided the essential features articulated by Levien. It created an Education Division within HEW, to be headed by the assistant secretary of education, consisting of two coequal branches: the Office of Education and the National Institute of Education. In establishing NIE the legislation provided for a fifteen-member National Council on Educational Research and a director, to be appointed by the president. The director would receive a salary ranking equivalent to that of the commissioner of education (executive level V). It permitted the agency to spend up to 10% of its funds on internal research. In effect, it allowed the agency to disregard the Civil Service hiring laws: all professional and technical personnel could be given up to three-year appointments, and one-fifth of the professional and technical staff could be given permanent appointments without regard to Civil Service laws. It authorized a three-year expenditure of $550 million to carry out the functions of the institute and gave the agency the right to retain funds unspent at the end of any fiscal year.

Echoing Levien's words, the legislation declared that the NIE would "seek to improve education" through

A. Helping solve or alleviate the problems and achieve the objectives of American education.
B. Advancing the practice of education as an art, science, and profession.
C. Strengthening the scientific and technological foundations on which education rests.
D. Building a vigorous and effective educational research and development system.

The legislation and the accompanying conference report deviated in only a few respects from Levien's design. Levien had stipulated that the National Council on Educational Research (NCER) would be a high-level advisory committee. The House version of the legislation so provided. But the Senate version, and the resulting conference version, bestowed policy-making authority upon the NCER. This unusual provision apparently came about because one or two congressional staff members were determined to insure NIE's independence from Marland and the Office of Education. They believed that the only way to protect NIE completely was to stipulate that the NCER—not the secretary of HEW, not the assistant secretary for education, and not the Director of NIE—set policy for the agency (Wexler 1974). The final bill also explicitly charged the agency with improving career education. Levien had not advocated career education in the Preliminary Plan, but career education was Marland's favorite program. Including it explicitly in NIE's mandate may have been designed to soften Marland's displeasure over the role of the NCER. Or, because Marland had already begun research activities under the label "career education" within OE, unless those activities were specifically removed from Marland's jurisdiction, he would continue his own research program within OE. In addition to mentioning career education, the preamble to the legislation reflected some of the concerns of Moynihan and the White House group that made the original NIE proposal. The preamble declared it was the policy of the United States to provide to every person an equal opportunity to receive an education of high quality regardless of his race, color, religion, sex, national origin, or social class. And it declared that NIE was being created "in order to carry out [this] policy."

The Conference Report accompanying the law provided one significant departure from Levien's advice. Levien had argued that most dissemination activities, then housed in OE's National Center for Education Communication, and including the computerized ERIC system, should remain in OE. ·The Chairman of the House Select Subcommittee on Education, however, was convinced that, if the dissemination functions remained in OE, NIE would be unable even to utilize them, let alone to improve them. Thus he was adamant, and the Conference Report so stipulated, that the National Center for Education Communication be transferred to the institute. This was the only OE activity whose transfer to NIE was specifically mentioned in the Conference Report, but a set of OE research activities to be transferred had also been stipulated in the House Committee Report as a result of Marland's testimony. These included "basic and applied research, development and experimentation . . . researcher training, support of the Regional Educational Laboratories, and the Experimental Schools Program" (House Report 92–554, 1971, p. 66). Levien had argued that only the authority to spend the funds associated with these activities, not the activities themselves, be transferred to NIE. None of the committee reports or the legislation, however, made this distinction. Still, with these few exceptions, the legislation and its accompanying reports were substantially true to the conception of the institute articulated by Levien, a conception also articulated by many of the witnesses in the congressional hearings on the proposed institute.

The congressional hearings on NIE held before the passage of the legislation, particularly eight days of hearings held by the Select Subcommittee on Education of the House Committee on Education and Labor, not only affirmed the characteristics of the institute incorporated in the bill, but also articulated a set of expectations about the agency—how it would conduct its business, what kinds of results it could be expected to produce. Although these expectations were not codified in the legislation, they influenced its tone and provisions. And they established, "for the record," the expectations against which the new agency would be judged.

The fundamental assumption underlying the entire NIE proposal was that more knowledge was required in order to improve American education. As one witness observed,

> The principle behind [the NIE legislation] is almost ridiculously simple. It is that if a man will focus his skills, reason, and humaneness upon his problems, he can markedly improve his condition. [Bailey, p. 50][1]

Given this assumption, it followed naturally that "better" researchers must be attracted to education. Moynihan's view epitomized the expectations about personnel.

> The men we want are not career civil servants. Some may choose to spend their life with the Institute. A more typical pattern would be to spend 10 years or so. These are professional men. I think Congress would be wise to follow the President's proposal to let these people be picked on their merits, which is basically by assessment of their colleagues. With respect to some people we are talking about, there aren't three or four men in the country who are capable of judging. [Moynihan, p. 24]

In order to attract these people, it was necessary to have a "better," that is, more rational and scientific, agency. One witness cautioned,

> I think that for the NIE to make a contribution, it must be clearly recognized that this will be a controversial and risky enterprise and that the NIE must be set up in a way that will assure independence of judgment on the part of its officials. [Oettinger, p. 75]

Given that a "better" agency was created—and the features to be provided by the legislation were designed to do just that—the results that could be expected from this agency were grand indeed. Marland was almost poetic in his enthusiasm: "We will have in NIE a fountainhead of new and useful knowledge" (Marland, p. 120). Levien was less effusive, but no less optimistic. When asked by Congressman Mazzoli (D–Kentucky) for some grounds upon which to justify the expenditures of money on research and development to the people of Kentucky, Levien observed:

> There is disorder in schools. There is financial crisis. There are disadvantaged children entering the schools leaving with the same disadvantages. These are not problems that can be solved by money alone. We need knowledge to solve them. . . . What we are not talking about is research for research's sake, we are talking about improvement for improvement's sake. [Levien, pp. 216–17]

The time period within which these results could be expected was somewhat difficult to pin down. Moynihan himself championed both the long and the short view. He cautioned that it would take at least ten years to learn anything important. Yet later in the same testimony he seemed to undermine his own cautions about the length of time required to see results.

> The basic problem, as I say, is that it takes a long time for a child to grow up, so what you do today doesn't really appear to have consequences for 25 years or so. But it is entirely within the range of methodology technique today to begin seeing differences in rates of change very early on, and probably to make very accurate forecasts of where things will go. This is the kind of thing which, if you give men a little time and resources, they are likely to get you good answers. [Moynihan, p. 18]

Implicit in the discussions about the amount of time necessary for results was usually one of two assumptions about the work NIE should support. Either NIE should focus on basic research with the promise of long-term payoff (for example biophysical and neurological research into the mechanisms of human learning), or it should focus on applied research with the promise of short-term payoff (for example economic and legal research into the more equitable distribution of local education funds). Levien advocated a mixed strategy. This view was also championed by the chairman of the subcommittee, for political reasons. In his analysis, and he was not alone in this view, the short run strategy of addressing pressing problems through applied research would generate the congressional support (particularly in the appropriations committees) that NIE would need in order to pursue the long-run strategy of basic research.

Independent of all assumptions about the appropriate research strategy to pursue was the universally shared expectation that NIE would have a large budget. HEW Secretary Richardson assured Congress that, in addition to transferring $118 million in funds from OE, the administration would ask for $30–60 million in new funds for NIE's first year. Moreover, he predicted that NIE's budget would grow to between $320 and $420 million by fiscal year 1977 (Richardson, p. 115). Other witnesses pressed for even more generous appropriations early in NIE's life: $250 million in its first year (Bailey, p. 51); $400–500 million in new money, beyond funds transferred from OE, in its first three years (Howe, p. 145). Levien and Moynihan predicted a total NIE expenditure of $1.1 billion by fiscal year 1980 (Levien, p. 205; Moynihan, p. 19).

What would this money buy? Chapter 2 documented the wide range of program proposals generated during the planning process (see table 2.2). There appeared to be no boundary to the future responsibilities of NIE. According to Levien:

> Education in all settings, both within schools and outside of them, and all Americans, before, during, and after traditional school ages, would be within NIE's scope of interest. [Levien, p. 195]

In addition to articulating high expectations about the quality of personnel, research strategies, budget levels, and program proposals, the hearings before the passage of the NIE legislation also established the expectation that NIE was to be completely independent from OE. At one point during the hearings Marland stated his intention that NIE be "responsive" to OE. In reply, the chairman of the hearings indicated his agreement with a "very distinguished leader of American education" who had urged that "NIE must be able to spit in the eye of the Office of Education" (Brademas, p. 113). And he later reiterated:

> The autonomy and the independence of the NIE from either apparent or substantive captivity on the part of the Office of Education ... would be very important in terms of attitudes toward the NIE both in the educational community in the country and in Congress. [Brademas, p. 156]

The transition from OE to the new agency was to be thoughtful and orderly. During the hearings on the NIE proposal, held during the spring of 1971 when it was thought that the legislation would pass that summer, it was stipulated that the institute would spend the entire 1972 fiscal year hiring a staff and reviewing all OE activities slated for transfer. Marland assured

Congress he had arranged for the NIE Planning Unit, under Silberman's direction, to be responsible for initial formulation of NIE options and strategies during this transition period. Silberman himself, in the spring of 1971, described to the subcommittee the activities his Planing Unit would undertake on behalf of the new agency: identifying areas of important educational needs; documenting significant programs addressing those needs; assessing the effectiveness of current solutions; determining what development needed to be done; describing alternative R&D programs, including detailed cost and time projections; and setting forth alternative personnel policies and alternative program management policies (Silberman, p. 366). Chapter 2 examined the extent to which these promises turned out to be unrealistic. But, at the time they were made, they probably seemed both reasonable and reassuring.

To summarize thus far, when the NIE legislation was signed in June 1972, the institute could be described by two sets of characteristics: the specific structural features granted it by the legislation and a set of ambitious, but ambiguous, expectations about what it would do and how it would do it. In addition, it could also be described by a third set of characteristics, revealed through analysis of the legislative process—namely, the political strength and attractiveness of the agency.

The Political Insignificance of the NIE Proposal

Congress did pass NIE's authorizing legislation. President Nixon did sign it. In that sense, NIE had to happen. But anyone believing in the historical inevitability of NIE may be misguided. The course of the NIE proposal through the legislative process indicates that the creation of NIE—although it did happen—was a low probability event.

Almost one year passed between the president's initial NIE proposal in March 1970 and the beginning of hearings on NIE in February 1971. Legislation had been introduced in the 91st Congress, but it was not acted upon. Bills to create an NIE were reintroduced in January 1971. Commenting on the delay at the opening of the hearings, Moynihan recalled,

> The President's message on educational reform was sent to the Congress just a few weeks short of a year ago. For a while there it looked as if it had as well never been sent at all, considering the response or rather nonresponse it evoked. At the time, I was a member of the administration and more than once found myself thinking of the occasion on which the clergyman . . . met a friend of Fleet Street, [and said] "I am just on my way to St. Paul's to pray for you, . . . but with no very great expectation of success." [Moynihan, p. 7]

This eleven-month delay in considering the NIE proposal, one measure of the lack of congressional interest in NIE, is attributable to at least four factors: the

White House was not pushing the proposal; the executive branch had not given Congress any specifications for the agency; there was little public response to Nixon's proposal; and there was little inherent congressional interest in education R&D.

Certainly the NIE proposal did not benefit from strong White House lobbying efforts. Moynihan, father of the NIE proposal within the White House and a natural source for high-level lobbying on behalf of NIE, was neither visible nor voluble in public support of the proposal. Although he probably genuinely believed in the value of an NIE, he could not devote much time to it. Moynihan's credibility had been somewhat tarnished by the leaking of his January 1970 memorandum to President Nixon advocating "benign neglect" of "the issue of race" (*New York Times*, 1 March 1970, p. 1). News of this memorandum first appeared in the national press two days before Nixon sent his education message and NIE proposal to Congress. Thereafter Moynihan was kept busy defending his past policy advice, and his usefulness within the White House as a new program advocate was perhaps somewhat diminished. Rumors of his resignation were reported in the national press within four months, and by December 1970 Moynihan had left Washington to return to Harvard. With Moynihan's departure, John Ehrlichman, in theory, should have taken over the process of shepherding the NIE proposal through Congress. NIE was not a high-priority activity for Ehrlichman.

Not only was there no White House lobbying, there was no specific plan for NIE accompanying Nixon's proposal. Levien's report, the document that would provide the plan, was not circulated within the government until the end of 1970. Thus, until the beginning of 1971 there was no plan to provide a focus for congressional hearings and debate.

Further, there was no great outpouring of public support for the NIE proposal. In the national press, NIE was described as Nixon's ploy to avoid increasing education spending. The NIE proposal was described as "an indictment of most Federal efforts to help the schools." President Nixon was reported as calling for "a searching reexamination of the entire approach to learning before [providing] any massive increases in funds for education programs" (*New York Times*, 4 March 1970, p. 1). One columnist, commenting on the NIE proposal, asked, "Will education be largely the pause that relaxes the budget?" (Hechinger, 8 March 1970, p. IV:7). The education press was no more sanguine. One national education newsletter headlined its story on the Nixon speech that proposed NIE with, "Nixon's Reform Program Disappoints Educators." The story quoted the president of the National Education Association, who lambasted Nixon's "intention to fight education problems with words, not dollars" (*Education USA*, 9 March 1970, p. 1).

And, finally, education R&D had little support within Congress. John Brademas (D–Indiana), chairman of the House Select Subcommittee on

Education and the man who became the principal House sponsor of the NIE legislation, observed:

> My own perception is that educational research does not stand very well on Capitol Hill for several reasons, one of which is, we don't know what it is. Another is that, whatever it is, we don't think it makes much difference. And another, ... is that we have the apprehension that the fruits of investment in educational research are not really translated into the system. [Brademas, p. 158]

Nevertheless, Brademas and a small number of other congressmen were sufficiently impressed with Levien's work to support an NIE bill in the House in early 1971. Although sponsored by a bipartisan group of twenty-one congressmen, including Carl Perkins (D–Kentucky), chairman of the Education and Labor Committee, and Albert Quie (R–Minnesota), ranking Republican on the Education and Labor Committee, the legislation was in fact under the proprietorship of John Brademas. Brademas was a man on the way up in the House of Representatives. Although he did not yet command the kind of power and respect enjoyed by more venerable members of the House, he had been elected a deputy majority whip. A Phi Beta Kappa, magna cum laude graduate of Harvard in 1949 with a Ph.D. in social studies from Oxford University, Brademas was considered to be an expert on educational issues and a friend of education.[2] The eight days of hearings convened by his subcommittee provided the only intensive congressional consideration of the institute before its creation.

Few congressmen expressed interest in the hearings themselves. Only Chairman Brademas attended all of them. No other Democrat attended even half of the hearings, and a majority of the Democrats did not attend a single hearing. Two subcommittee Republicans, ranking subcommittee Republican Ogden Reid (R–New York) and Orval Hansen (R–Idaho), attended at least half the hearings. And Quie, though not a member of the subcommittee, attended half the hearings. If all subcommittee members (plus Quie) had attended all hearings, there would have been 144 "representative appearances." Attendance records indicate the NIE hearings had 35 "representative appearances"—a participation rate of 24%.

Even with a low participation rate by subcommittee members, a collection of impressive witnesses would have demonstrated that there would be powerful support for the new agency. The subcommittee heard testimony on behalf of NIE from twenty-two witnesses. An additional eighteen people submitted views for the record.[3] The majority of those testifying were present or past employees of the executive branch; an additional 20% had been Office of Education contract or grant recipients or consultants. The total group of witnesses also included three university professors, three representatives of private educational materials firms, and two representatives from state departments of education. One of these last two witnesses, the superintendent of public instruction for Illinois, testified *against* the creation of an NIE.[4] There was no representation from any major scholarly association or any national education organization. Indeed, not until after the NIE bills had passed both the House and Senate did the Big Six education associations (American Association of School Administrators, Council of Chief State School Officers, National Congress of Parent-Teacher Associations, National Education Association, National Association of State Boards of Education, and National School Boards Association) endorse the creation of NIE. According to the chief executive branch lobbyist for the creation of NIE, this endorsement was nothing more than lip service (Cross, March 1974). If interest in the NIE legislation can be measured by participation in the hearings, it seems to have been nonexistent among the education associations, scholarly associations, and general public; the NIE proposal was of interest to a small group, largely dominated by HEW officials.

The congressional insignificance of the NIE proposal was highlighted by the way its legislation was finally passed. While the Brademas subcommittee conducted its NIE hearings during the spring and early summer of 1971, an omnibus education bill was beginning to take form in both the House and the Senate. This massive piece of legislation included provisions for higher education student financial aid and institutional assistance, grants for community colleges, funds for occupational education and Indian education, funds for the support of innovation in higher education, and controversial antibusing amendments. It was decided that the NIE provisions should be included in this legislation rather than be offered in a separate bill. On the House side, Brademas and Quie believed this strategy would more likely insure NIE's passage. But on the Senate side the NIE provision was included in an attempt to placate the Nixon administration, which found many features of the very expensive bill objectionable (Wexler, March 1974; Cross, March 1974). The Senate passed its version of the omnibus bill on 6 August 1971, with little debate on NIE. However, NIE provisions in the comparable House bill barely escaped defeat.

During House debate on the omnibus bill on 4 November 1971, H. R. Gross (R–Iowa), an opponent of most spending measures, found a way to remove the NIE provisions from the House bill. He complained that NIE's proposed exemption from Civil Service hiring regulations invaded the jurisdiction of the House Post Office and Civil Service Committee and therefore would have to be approved by that committee before the House could vote on NIE. Gross's parliamentary objection struck the NIE provisions from the omnibus bill and forced Brademas to propose the creation of NIE, with the offending hiring provisions deleted, as a floor amendment. Seven representatives, including Perkins, Quie, and Brademas, rose to defend the amendment. But other members of the House urged its defeat. One representative argued that NIE would simply duplicate OE work at the cost of "additional waste of time and effort," utilizing the "same people who ran the old program." Edith Green reiterated her long-standing complaints about OE contracts and grants procedures, complained that the NIE provisions were too vague, and suggested that the money slated for NIE could be better spent on institutional grants to colleges. She counseled her colleagues in the House:

> If you want to save money, if you want to put money into the colleges and universities, if you want to improve education, and if you want to cut funds, this [NIE] is the place to cut them. [*Congressional Record*, 4 November 1971, p. H39275]

On a teller vote the NIE amendment passed by only two votes, 52 to 50. Congressman John Ashbrook (R–Ohio) demanded a recorded vote, and the House approved the creation of NIE by a vote of 210 to 153. Unnoticed at the time of the recorded vote on the NIE amendment was the fact that a majority of the House Appropriations Subcommittee on Labor and HEW—the subcommittee to which NIE would submit its budget requests—voted against the creation of NIE (*Congressional Record*, 4 November 1971, pp. H39272–H39277).

A lengthy conference followed House and Senate passage of the omnibus bill, with the student aid provisions and the antibusing amendments receiving most of the attention. NIE received little attention during this process, although one or two Senate staff members had suspected that the NIE provisions might be completely deleted by the conference committee (Wexler, March 1974; Smith, March 1974). The conference committee's final report on the bill was 228 pages long; NIE's share was 6 pages. The conference bill was passed by the Senate on 24 May, passed by the House on 8 June, and signed by the president on 23 June 1972.

Conclusion

And so the National Institute of Education was created. Some observations about the entire process of creation—the events, actors, and attitudes described in chapters 1–3—are appropriate in summarizing the process of creation for NIE.

First, the scientific model and the Unholy Trinity seemed to have triumphed. The structure created for the institute and the standards set for it were clearly predicated on a belief in the power of knowledge, which could be harnessed only by a rationally managed agency. Past education R&D efforts had been pronounced a failure; the cause of the failure lay in bureaucratic problems.[5] A bureaucratic solution—a new federal agency—would lead to success in education R&D.

Second, the process of creation generated an ambitious and ambiguous mandate for the new agency. It was easy to agree that the agency would attract "better" people to do "better" research. It was not easy to find consensus on an operational definition of "better."

Third, the creation of NIE was a convenient receptacle for a variety of problems and solutions only loosely coupled, at best, to each other and to the new institute.[6] Nixon needed an education initiative; Moynihan believed in research; the Unholy Trinity wanted to do something about OE. NIE was the result. Levien's work, applauded by Congress, was disregarded by the Planning Unit; Marland, disliked by the congressional proponents of NIE, made his own decisions about programs to be transferred from OE; the congressional proponents of NIE had little apparent connection with the users of education R&D; the congressional authorizing committees had no connection with the appropriations committees. NIE was the result.

Finally, the new agency was not very important. Its creation was a fairly low probability event. Attracting little support in Congress or among interest groups, it rode through Congress on a much larger bill. Viewed in a long-term perspective, it was simply the latest in a long series of attempts to reform OE's R&D efforts.

None of this is to say the institute was doomed to failure. We suspect that almost all new agencies exhibit these first three characteristics—offering a bureaucratic solution to substantive problems, possessing ambitious and ambiguous goals, and providing a convenient receptacle for a collection of diverse interests and issues. They may differ only on the last characteristic— the amount of support provided to the new agency by its environment. The process of creation, however, endows a new agency with an air of significance. For the people who come to staff it, its creation takes on an air of heroic and historic inevitability. The fact of its existence is proof that powerful people believe in its importance. It may turn out, however, that one of the most important responsibilities of the first managers is to disbelieve the rhetoric of creation. The creation of NIE did not solve the hard problems of education R&D. The goals and technology were still unclear; the participants and environment were still unstable. In the next chapter, we explore the effects of NIE's environment upon the new agency.

Four

Who Cares? Research and the Appropriations Process

Introduction

Any agency operating inside a larger bureaucracy is inevitably shaped by the desires, constraints, and demands of its bureaucratic environment. When the agency is new, it is particularly vulnerable to these influences. The chief personnel in the new agency are usually selected by people in the larger bureaucracy. The new agency may be the recipient of programs or responsibilities transferred from other agencies. Further, it may find itself constrained to act in ways inimical to its own best interests because of the need to follow policy set by the larger bureaucracy.

In its infancy, NIE was directly shaped by HEW, OE, and the White House. In this introduction, we briefly document the initial impact of these three organizations upon the new NIE before turning, in the body of the chapter, to how NIE attempted to influence its environment.

In July 1972, HEW Secretary Richardson named Emerson Elliott the NIE project manager, and in August he named him acting director of NIE. These appointments simply confirmed officially what had occurred unofficially during the last months of the Planning Unit—Elliott had taken charge. By September 1972, HEW Secretary Richardson had chosen the person he wanted to see as first director of NIE—Thomas K. Glennan, Jr., then assistant director for planning, research, and evaluation at OEO.[1] Richardson sent his recommendation to the White House; President Nixon sent it to the Senate, where it was confirmed on 18 October 1972; and Glennan was sworn in by Richardson as NIE's first director on 1 November 1972.[2]

Richardson was also influential in naming members to the National Council on Educational Research (NCER). In the standard procedure for creating advisory councils, the secretary's office sends a list of its nominees to the White House; the White House combines that list with lists from other sources—in the NIE case, from the Domestic Council, for example; adds any of its own preferences; then sends the list directly to the Senate. As a result, the list sent to the White House is often the last the secretary's office knows of the matter until the nominations, sometimes a surprise to the secretary, are announced. But this procedure was somewhat altered in the case of NIE. Believing the NCER to be the most important education council he would nominate during his tenure at HEW, Richardson both took a personal interest in the selection of candidates to be recommended to the White House and won from the White House the right to review the final presidential list before it was sent to the Senate for confirmation (Mastrangelo, March 1974). As a result of Richardson's interest, which led to negotiations between HEW and the White House over four or five out of the fifteen names submitted by Richardson, the final list was not agreed upon until December 1972 (Mastrangelo, March 1974). By then Nixon had decided to move Richardson from HEW to the Department of Defense. Richardson was in the midst of the transition, and the White House staff was relaxing after Nixon's reelection. Also during this period, Moynihan, one of Richardson's choices for the NCER, accepted the post of ambassador to the UN, and HEW had to find someone to replace him. Further, the omnibus bill that created NIE and its NCER also created a number of advisory councils in education, all of which had to be filled with presidential appointees. The combination of congestion in the White House offices handling advisory councils, a relaxing White House staff, and the absence of Secretary Richardson meant there was little pressure to announce the NCER nominees immediately; and, in fact, Nixon did not announce them until March 1973.[3]

Named as chairman of the NCER was Patrick Haggerty, chairman of the board of Texas Instruments, Inc. Other prominent nominees were James Coleman, a sociologist then at Johns Hopkins University, and William Baker, president of Bell Laboratories. The complete council was composed of five university presidents or chancellors, three businessmen, two university professors, one state school superintendent, one state administrator of aid to nonpublic schools, one local school superintendent, one school principal, and a graduate student.

Even though it took close to a year to give NIE its council, it took no time at all to give it $110 million worth of R&D programs. During the 1971 hearings on the proposed NIE, Marland had told Brademas that he intended to transfer most of OE's R&D activities to NIE. On 1 August 1972, he gave NIE responsibility for the R&D centers, the laboratories, ERIC, and the other dissemination programs from the National Center for Education Communications, Career Education research, and a host of other smaller projects. NIE thus became an instant $110-million operating agency. As a result it lost its transition year that had been promised during the 1971 hearings—the year for hiring a staff, evaluating OE programs as candidates for transfer to NIE, and planning its own new programs.

One of the principal ways NIE found itself constrained as a result of being a part of HEW was in its attempts to develop good relationships on Capitol Hill. The Office of the Secretary of HEW has traditionally had difficulty reining in the congressional relations of its constituent offices and bureaus. A number of these bureaus had developed direct channels of communication with influential congressmen and were thereby able to lobby quietly and effectively against HEW legislation they found displeasing. In an effort to remedy this subversive behavior, the HEW assistant secretary for legislation announced, in 1972, that all agency contacts with members of Congress must go through his office. This policy was intended to tame politically powerful bureaus; applying it to NIE was incongruous at best, debilitating at worst. The HEW Office of Legislation could devote little attention to creating a foundation of good congressional relations for the fledgling agency. NIE, a $100-million-a-year agency employing 300 to 400 people, got lost in the crowd of HEW agencies employing 100,000 people and spending close to $100 billion a year.

The HEW comptroller and the OMB also shaped NIE's world. NIE's authorizing legislation gave it the authority to retain any funds unspent at the end of the fiscal year. This important provision was to assure that funds could be spent wisely with no last-minute year-end rush. But the HEW comptroller and OMB opposed NIE's exemption from the fiscal-year requirement because it caused bookkeeping headaches and allowed the agency too much autonomy. NIE's request for fiscal-year exemptions, with no strong backing from HEW and OMB, was turned down by the appropriations committees.

NIE also felt the impact of White House policies created for purposes not directly related to the new agency. Nixon was determined to hold down education spending and, in fact, was vetoing education revenue bills as early as 1969. After the 1972 presidential election, the policy on education spending grew even more stringent. NIE thus found itself in the uncomfortable position of being perceived as a Nixon initiative by the education lobbies who were not fond of Nixon. Even more embarrassing was the fact that, because Nixon did not propose cuts in NIE's budget, NIE seemed to be profiting from the cuts made in other education programs.

These, then, were some of the major ways NIE's environment shaped its early existence. Now let us turn to how NIE attempted to influence its environment, principally to its attempts to win more money from Congress. Previous chapters have detailed the widely accepted expectations that NIE's budget would grow substantially and rapidly. There was, indeed, to be a quick and significant change in the NIE budget—but not in the expected direction.

In this chapter we first briefly present the history of NIE's budget negotiations with Congress for three annual budgets and one request for supplemental funds. This history is based primarily on the public record—NIE's congressional budget justifications, statements by members of Congress in hearings and on the floor of the House and Senate, and appropriations committee justifications as recorded in committee reports. We then amplify and extend the public record by inquiring into possible reasons for NIE's misfortunes in the budget process, suggesting there are four major categories of reasons: accidental, bureaucratic, political, and programmatic. We then attempt to set the NIE story in a larger context by speculating about the conditions under which Congress is likely to support research and assessing the degree to which NIE met those conditions.

Who Cares? Research and the Appropriations Process Chronology

1972

June	Nixon signs NIE legislation
July	Elliott named NIE project manager
August	$110 million worth of programs transferred from OE
	Elliott named NIE acting director
September	Glennan becomes Secretary Richardson's choice for director
October	$110 million granted for NIE fiscal year 1973
November	Glennan sworn in as NIE director
December	Richardson and White House agree on NCER nominees

1973

January	NCEC complains that, without a council, NIE is operating illegally
February	Brademas holds oversight hearing on NIE
	NCEC files suit against NIE
March	Glennan requests $162 million from House for fiscal year 1974
	Nixon announces NCER nominees
June	NCER confirmed by the Senate
	House Appropriations Committee recommends $142.7 million
July	$34 million worth of programs transferred from OE and OEO
	NIE appoints director of external relations
	Glennan requests $162 million from Senate for fiscal year 1974
October	Senate Appropriations Committee recommends $75 million
November	Conference Committee recommends $75 million
December	HEW advises NIE to ask for a supplemental request (NIE declares five priority areas)

1974

February	Glennan requests $25 million in supplemental funds from House
March	Glennan requests $25 million in supplemental funds from Senate

April $0 recommended by House Appropriations Committee
                      for supplemental funds
                 Glennan requests $130 million from House for fiscal
                      year 1975
May $0 recommended by Senate Appropriations Committee
                      for supplemental funds
                 $0 recommended by Conference Committee for
                      supplemental funds
June   Glennan requests $134.5 million from Senate for fiscal
                      year 1975
                 $100 million recommended by House Appropriations
                      Committee
                 $80 million voted by full House for fiscal year 1975
                 NIE director for external relations resigns
August   Senate Appropriations Committee recommends $65
                      million for fiscal year 1975
                 Glennan resigns
September   Haggerty, NCER chairman, resigns
                 Senate Appropriations Committee recommends $0 for
                      fiscal year 1975
November   Conference Committee recommends $70 million for fiscal
                      year 1975

NIE Budget History

NIE did not begin operations until after the 1973 fiscal year had already begun and so could not follow the standard government schedule and procedures for obtaining its fiscal year 1973 funds.[4] In July 1972, Emerson Elliott, then project manager for NIE, hastily prepared a request for a supplemental appropriation to fund NIE's first year of operation. Elliott based the budget on the fact that NIE was receiving $110 million worth of programs transferred from OE and on the belief it could spend $30 million on new programs, thus totaling $140 million in expenditures by 30 June 1973. The OMB, which reviews all budget requests before they go to Congress, reduced that estimate to $110 million on the grounds that NIE would not be sufficiently organized to spend any money on new programs in its first year of operations. Elliott presented the request for $110 million to the appropriate House and Senate Appropriations Subcommittees, where it was routinely approved and later approved by Congress as a whole.[5] (See table 4.1 for a chronology of all the NIE budget requests discussed in this chapter.)

For fiscal year 1974, NIE decided[6] to ask for an increase of close to 50% over its fiscal year 1973 budget allocation in order to provide substantial funds for beginning new programs and to support a second set of transferred

Table 4.1   NIE Budget Chronology

Fiscal Year 1973 Budget	
9 Oct. 1972	$110 million requested from Senate Appropriations Subcommittee
10 Oct. 1972	$110 million requested from House Appropriations Subcommittee
13 Oct. 1972	$110 million recommended by Conference Committee
Fiscal Year 1974 Budget	
9 Mar. 1973	$162 million requested from House Appropriations Subcommittee
21 June 1973	$142 million recommended by House Appropriations Committee
23 July 1973	$162 million requested from Senate Appropriations Subcommittee
Sept. 1973	$50 million recommended by Senate Appropriations Subcommittee
2 Oct. 1973	$75 million recommended by Senate Appropriations Committee
8 Nov. 1973	$75 million recommended by Conference Committee
Fiscal Year 1974	
Supplemental Request	
27 Feb. 1974	$25 million requested from House Appropriations Subcommittee
7 Mar. 1974	$25 million requested from Senate Appropriations Subcommittee
4 Apr. 1974	$0 recommended by House Appropriations Committee
18 May 1974	$0 recommended by Senate Appropriations Committee
29 May 1974	$0 recommended by Conference Committee
Fiscal Year 1975 Budget	
23 Apr. 1974	$130 million requested from House Appropriations Subcommittee
6 June 1974	$134.5 million requested from Senate Appropriations Subcommittee
24 June 1974	$100 million recommended by House Appropriations Committee
28 June 1974	$80 million voted by full House
Aug. 1974	$65 million recommended by Senate Appropriations Subcommittee
11 Sept. 1974	$0 recommended by Senate Appropriations Committee
21 Nov. 1974	$70 million recommended by Conference Committee

programs—these transferred from OE and OEO on 1 July 1973. And so the fiscal year 1974 budget request was set at $162.2 million. NIE's director, Glennan, presented this request to the House Appropriations Subcommittee in March 1973. In June the full House Appropriations Committee recommended a modest cut, about 12%, in NIE's request, recommending that NIE be allocated $142.7 million for fiscal year 1974. The committee intended that NIE's fiscal year 1974 budget not provide funding for new programs; their recommended increase over the fiscal year 1973 budget was to be spent on the newly transferred programs (House Report 93–305, 21 June 1973, p. 64).

In justifying their allocation, the House committee indicated they believed NIE was not yet ready to launch new programs. They observed that NIE's policymaking council had not been nominated until after Glennan had presented his 1974 budget request and thus had had no opportunity to review it. They further noted that NIE had been slow in organizing its fiscal year 1973 expenditures. The institute had not received its fiscal year 1973 budget allocation until 31 October 1972. By 31 May 1973—one month before the end of the fiscal year—NIE had obligated only slightly more than half of its fiscal year 1973 allocation. Thus, the committee believed, the new agency would probably not be in a position to spend new funds effectively (House Report 93–305, 21 June 1973, p. 64).

In July 1973 Glennan took his $162.2 million request to the Senate Appropriations Subcommittee, where he presented the same budget justification, statement for the record, and verbal overview of the budget request that he had used before the House subcommittee. After making his request, Glennan was briefly questioned by Senator Warren Magnuson (D–Washington), chairman of the subcommittee. Magnuson's questioning was approximately one-fourth as long as had been that of the House subcommittee, and, according to the representative of the HEW comptroller attending the hearings, the hearings had gone fairly well (Forbush, quoted by Glennan, 5 October 1973, p. 5).

Subsequently, to the incredulous dismay of NIE, the subcommittee recommended that NIE's fiscal year 1974 appropriation be set at $50 million. The full Senate Appropriations Committee raised the recommendation to $75 million and reported it to the full Senate on 2 October 1973. The committee justified its deep cuts on the grounds that NIE had not established a clear sense of direction and was unable to specify its long- and short-range goals.

> To date … NIE has done little to assert its role of leadership. The committee is discouraged by what appears to be a total lack of understanding of purpose on the part of the agency. Persistent questioning by the Committee as to NIE's long and short range goals prompted little more than vague, often obscure, references to educational exploration. The Committee is certainly mindful of the fact that research efforts of any kind cannot be related to a timetable; however, research must be undertaken with a purpose in mind. … The Committee feels strongly that in order to succeed, NIE must first determine its proper role within the educational system. In the future, the Committee would expect to receive a more cohesive, better defined plan of operations. [Senate Report 93–114, 2 October 1973]

NIE and HEW immediately attempted to appeal the cut. HEW prevailed upon Senator Jacob Javits (R–New York), customarily a friend of HEW, to defend NIE's cause on the Senate floor. Javits read into the *Congressional Record* a letter from HEW Secretary Caspar Weinberger, who had replaced Elliot Richardson, asserting that the cut would all but put NIE out of business (*Congressional Record*, 4 October 1973, p. S18635). Javits also urged the House-Senate Appropriations Conference Committee to review the NIE evidence in order to provide a basis for restoring some of the cut funds.

Magnuson reacted angrily to Javits's intervention:

> Here is their own [NIE's] justification. They have spent $142 million. If any of them can tell me what they have been doing or what the program is instead of just sitting around thinking about it and hiring people, we might learn something. They have 462 people. They have not given us one scintilla of evidence. Here is their own justification. . . . We could not find out anything that had been done by this group. . . . I never saw anything like this outfit. [*Congressional Record*, 4 October 1973, p. S18634]

Senator Norris Cotton (R–New Hampshire), ranking Republican on the Senate Appropriations Subcommittee, supported Magnuson:

> I think perhaps this was a case where someone poorly presented the case on this particular appropriation.
>
> I feel that we tried in this bill to put the money right straight where it would go to the education of the children and where it would take care of the needs of the children and not for planning and evaluating. If there is any cut [in the HEW appropriations bill], it has to be there [in NIE's budget]. [*Congressional Record*, 4 October 1973, p. S18634]

Senators J. Glenn Beall (R–Maryland) and Milton Young (R–North Dakota) also attempted to defend an increase for NIE, pointing out that NIE was only one year old and that education research had been chronically underfunded and was worthy of increased support. Senator Edward Brooke (R–Massachusetts), a Senate Appropriations Subcommittee member, tried to reassure Javits, Beall, and Young:

> I assure the distinguished Senator from Maryland that the committee felt that with the $75 million that was ultimately agreed to, there would be some give in conference [with the House] and there was a possibility that in conference we might end up with $125 million [for NIE]. [*Congressional Record*, 4 October 1973, p. S18636]

Magnuson then closed the debate over the NIE budget by inserting in the *Congressional Record* all the NIE testimony and documents received by his subcommittee, concluding dourly with, "When Senators read this, they will wonder why we did not [cut] it even farther" (*Congressional Record*, 4 October 1973, p. S18644).

When the House-Senate conference committee resolved differences in the appropriations measures passed by the two houses, the final NIE appropriation for fiscal year 1974 was marked at $75 million (House Report 93–626, 8 November 1973, p. 13). Given the usual proclivity of conference committees to split the difference between two figures, a practice that in this case would have given NIE $109 million, the final decision represented a distinct slap in the face for NIE.

NIE estimated that $76.1 million was required in fiscal year 1974 to meet commitments for work the institute was already sponsoring.[7] Thus, the $75 million appropriated by Congress would be entirely consumed by "old" projects, leaving no money for "new" ones. But Glennan and the institute staff believed it was essential for NIE to begin supporting its own new work. The HEW Office of the Deputy Assistant Secretary for Budget, offering assurances that the Appropriations Committee would be receptive to such a request, advised NIE to ask for a supplemental appropriation for fiscal year 1974 that would allow it to begin some new programs (Elliott, 11 March 1974). Acting on the basis of this advice, NIE deferred $16.25 million in current fiscal year 1974 obligations to transferred programs in order to free this amount for new programs. NIE intended to use funds from the supplemental appropriation to honor the deferred obligations. Instead of asking for a supplemental appropriation request of $16.25 million however, NIE decided also to seek an additional $8.75 million for new programs. Thus NIE's total supplemental request was $25 million. This request was incorporated with other HEW supplemental requests in a total package of $177 million (House Report 93–977, 4 April 1974, pp. 68–9).

Glennan presented NIE's request for a $25 million fiscal year 1974 supplemental appropriation to the House Appropriations Subcommittee on 27 February 1974. There he discovered that the institute's strategy had backfired. The House subcommittee, previously cordial to NIE, had turned distinctly hostile. The ranking Democrat on the subcommittee, Congressman William H. Natcher (D–Kentucky), bridled at the fact that NIE had deliberately created the need for a supplemental appropriation by spending money appropriated for existing projects on new ones (House Appropriations Subcommittee, 27 February 1974, p. 256). Other representatives also resented NIE's seeking a supplemental appropriation to restore congressional cuts made only a few months earlier when supplemental appropriations are theoretically to be used only for unforeseen emergencies. Congressman Robert Michel (R–Illinois), the senior Republican on the subcommittee, was offended by NIE's seeming disregard for programs transferred to the agency, coupled with their eagerness to begin new programs:

> I am curious about the ... statement that NIE would have nothing but rhetoric to show if it did not begin work in new areas. Taken literally, that statement implies that you [NIE] are spending $60 million on the transferred programs for nothing. Is that what they meant? But on the other hand, if they did not mean that, the statement carried the implication that the NIE must pursue new work in order to justify its existence, doesn't it? I don't like the impression that leaves with me, that the important thing is to keep busy, to show some movement, some new activity, and never mind how much of it pans out in the long run. [House Appropriations Subcommittee, 27 February 1974, pp. 318–19]

The reception at the Senate subcommittee hearing was no less icy. Magnuson observed that NIE would be returning in about sixty days to request a fiscal year 1975 appropriation and told Glennan, "You can wait until then [for more money]" (Senate Appropriations Subcommittee, 7 March 1974, p. 294). Both committees refused to grant NIE any supplemental funds (House Report 93–1070, 29 May 1974).

In April 1974, less than two months after his defense of the supplemental request, Glennan was back before the House Appropriations Subcommittee to present his request for NIE's fiscal year 1975 budget. NIE was asking for $130 million and the mood was amicable. Congressman Daniel Flood (D–Pennsylvania), chairman of the subcommittee, complimented Glennan on his answers and gave him opportunities to insert in the record materials supporting his case. Congressman Obey (D–Wisconsin) assured Glennan that his questions were not "any attempt to hatchet your operations" (House Appropriations Subcommittee, 23 April 1974, p. 832).

On 24 June 1974, the full House Appropriations Committee recommended that NIE be granted a fiscal year 1975 appropriation of $100 million. The committee declared that all of the $30 million cut must be borne out of the agency's research and development activities; none could come from dissemination activities. The $100 million figure was a disappointment to NIE. The cost of projects to which the agency was already committed, increased by the $16.25-million deferral, had grown to $91 million. Once again NIE was faced with the prospect of having little money to begin new programs. However, within a few days the NIE appropriation would be debated on the House floor and even the $100 million figure would come to appear generous.

The $33-billion Labor–HEW appropriations bill for fiscal year 1975, containing the $100 million recommendation for NIE, was debated on the House floor on 28 June 1974. There was a brief attempt to restore the $30 million cut from NIE's request when Congressman John Dellenback (R– Oregon) proposed a package of four amendments providing increases in various HEW programs, including NIE. In the face of objections, however, all four amendments were withdrawn (Congressional Record, 28 June 1974, p. H5974). Congresswoman Edith Green (D–Oregon) then spoke briefly on the "wisdom" of withdrawing the NIE amendment because education R&D needed no more support. She reminded her colleagues of past failures in the management of education R&D in OE, then sat down. Two representatives then paid tribute to Green, who would be retiring at the end of 1974, indicating that her departure would strip the House of one of its sharpest overseers of executive branch spending. Then a bizarre event occurred, demonstrating the ease with which an insignificant agency may be harassed by congressional caprice. Representative John Ashbrook (R–Ohio) moved that the NIE appropriation be slashed to $10 million, as a tribute to Green. His complete "justification" for the cut was nonsensical:

Mr. Chairman, because my amendment is short, I need not take more than 30 seconds. There is a line from "1776" which says, "Is anyone listening? Does anyone care?"

Mr. Chairman, I would like to offer this amendment as a tribute to the gentlewoman from Oregon, Edith Green. We can cut $90 million out of [the NIE allocation] and let them squawk over at the Institute. I think it would be great for them. [*Congressional Record*, 28 June 1974, p. H5978]

Ashbrook demanded a record vote and the House floor filled as members were summoned. The Ashbrook amendment was easily defeated, 331 to 34, with each member of the Appropriations Subcommittee, including Green, voting to reject it. But now there was a larger audience on the floor, and Green herself moved that NIE's appropriations be cut to $80 million. She recapitulated her attacks of the past six years on OE contracts and grants management and argued that NIE was guilty of the same sins: "I suggest to the Members that the NIE is not one single bit different from the Office of Education except in name" (*Congressional Record*, 28 June 1974, p. H5979). Green concluded her attack with a withering indictment of the "nonsense" of education R&D.

This is the kind of stuff we are financing and that the taxpayers in the Members' districts are paying for and that my taxpayers are paying for, when our schools and our classrooms do not have enough money for basic essentials, but we can pay out millions and millions [for research] and say, oh, yes, there is an unlimited amount the Federal Treasury can give out in research, some of it for esoteric research but some of it just plain nonsense and we ought to stop it. [*Congressional Record*, 28 June 1974, p. H5979]

At the end of her remarks the congresswoman was afforded a standing ovation by her colleagues, an unusual event in the House. Flood, her own subcommittee chairman, rose immediately and sought to repair the damage to NIE's cause:

What we were applauding, and so did I, what we were standing for and so did I, was respect for the gentlewoman of course, but not for the argument, because it has nothing to do with the case at all, nothing at all to do with the amendment at all. ... Now fun is fun, but may I suggest that the [Appropriations] committee cut the NIE $30 million. ...

This [the Green amendment] is a proposal to do the opposite of what the Congress originally intended in creating the NIE. [NIE] was espoused by the administration and proposed in the budget. But it was cut back by your committee by $30 million. It is my hope that this National Institute of Education will do the things needed to benefit the things that you insist back home that you want done at every parent-teacher meeting you have attended—every one of you. That is what NIE is supposed to be all about. You asked for it. [*Congressional Record*, 28 June 1974, p. H5980]

Representative Quie joined Flood in asking the House to defeat the Green amendment. Representative Gross, who had moved to delete the original NIE provisions from the 1972 omnibus bill, responded to Quie by criticizing NIE for spending $8,000 to send forty-three employees to the Chicago convention of the American Educational Research Association and blasted "Thank God It's Friday" parties that he alleged had been held at NIE offices. The senior Republican on the Appropriations Subcommittee, Congressman Michel, made one last plea for his colleagues to support the committee's judgment and defeat the Green amendment.

A congressional staff member recorded at the time:

> People shouted, "vote, vote!" from the floor, and when Flood, Quie, and Michel tried to stem the tide, they were laughed at, and met with shouts of "cut more." It was a zoo ... and the voice vote was overwhelming for Green's cut. [Personal letter to the authors, 30 June 1974]

And so it was that NIE emerged from the House with $80 million.

Three weeks earlier, on 6 June 1974, Glennan had testified before the Senate Appropriations Subcommittee. Except for a brief appearance by Senator Mike Mansfield (D–Montana), only Senator Cotton was present to hear him. Cotton's questions were not hostile; nor were Glennan's answers heroic. The entire two hour and five minute session was low-key. A congressional staff member, present at the hearings, described them this way:

> [Glennan] continues to try earnestly to explain things. . . . As for substance, it was a very disjointed session, Cotton knowing literally nothing about the Institute. . . . Cotton was not particularly hostile, just uninformed and hence not very helpful in getting the Institute to show itself to advantage. [Personal letter to the authors, 30 June 1974]

The Senate subcommittee later recommended $65 million for NIE, an amount just one-half of its request, but $15 million more than it had recommended the previous year. When the subcommittee's recommendation had gone to the full committee the previous year, it had been increased by $25 million. But in 1974 that practice was not repeated. On 11 September 1974, the full Senate Appropriations Committee slashed NIE's fiscal year 1975 budget request to zero. As it had done the previous year, it complained that NIE had shown "little progress" in reaching its goals.

A few days later the Labor–HEW appropriations bill was presented to the full Senate. Javits once again rose to defend the institute. He reminded the Senate that NIE was new and asked that the institute be supported until the Senate Education Subcommittee had the opportunity to review NIE in 1975 (*Congressional Record*, 16 September 1974, p. S11691). Magnuson conceded that eliminating NIE funding was a "drastic step," but argued that "considering the tight budget situation other tried and proven programs are facing, the committee believes the [NIE] money could be better used elsewhere in the bill" (*Congressional Record*, 16 September 1974, p. S16668).

After a Thanksgiving recess, the conference committee agreed upon a $70 million fiscal year 1975 budget for the agency—a sum $60 million below NIE's original request and $20 million less than the agency's commitments to ongoing projects (House Report 93–1489, 21 November 1974, p. 15).

On 28 August 1974, after the Senate subcommittee had recommended a fiscal year 1975 allocation of $65 million for NIE but before the full Senate committee cut that to zero or the conference committee recommended $70 million, Thomas Glennan, NIE's first director, resigned. His letter of resignation cited "personal reasons" for his decision (Glennan, 28 August 1974), but he and others hoped his departure might improve NIE's budget problems (Glennan, July 1975). Shortly thereafter, Patrick Haggerty, first chairman of the NCER, also resigned for "personal reasons." Neither departure had a positive effect on the size of NIE's fiscal year 1975 budget.

Thus, by the end of 1974 the institute had been thoroughly battered in the congressional appropriations process; was without the funds to launch new initiatives; and was working without the leadership of a permanent director or NCER chairman. The visions of budget growth created by Moynihan, Levien, Richardson, and the other believers in NIE less than four years earlier had vanished in the cold light of the appropriations process.

Everyone with an interest in NIE had an explanation for its budget troubles. Some of the explanations were fairly trivial; others were comprehensive; all had at least some basis in fact. We indicated above that these explanations can be grouped in four categories: accidental, bureaucratic, political, and programmatic. Because this is an examination of NIE's failure to win more funds from Congress, in some sense every explanation is a political explanation.[8] But simply saying that NIE was politically naive or maladroit, although correct, obscures as much as it illuminates. In examining various classes of explanation, we try to move beyond that observation in order to discover how a new agency might avoid the problems that plagued NIE.

Explanations for NIE's Appropriations Problems

Accidents and Mistakes

In any drama with as many actors as the NIE budget history—all the NIE staff and officials, HEW legislative staff and officials, White House staff, congressional staff, committee members—someone is bound to miss a cue or flub a line. The NIE history probably contained no more accidents or mistakes than the history of any other agency, but because NIE's budget went down, not up, they were all duly noted as having contributed to NIE's problems. The four major actors charged with accidents or mistakes are the White House, Congress, HEW, and NIE.

White House delay in the appointment of the NCER, a delay that does not appear to have been intentional (Mastrangelo, March 1974), has been blamed for NIE's congressional problems. It meant that Glennan was unable to present a legitimate request to the appropriations committees for the 1974 fiscal year. He had to begin his first congressional testimony by pointing out that the budget requests he was making were tentative and subject to the approval of the council. This led Congressman Flood to open his first questioning of Glennan with, "Does not that mere fact [that the council had not yet been appointed] render all of this testimony of yours here this morning somewhat fruitless?" (House Appropriations Subcommittee Hearings, 9 March 1973, p. 144). After NIE's first budget cut, Congressman Brademas suggested that White House negligence had contributed to NIE's problems:

Nobody has put the blame where it really belongs—on the White House, which delayed appointing the Council. That's what put Glennan between the rock and the hard place. [New York Times, 22 October 1973, p. 64]

This view probably overemphasizes the significance of the delayed council appointments. The absence of a council did not hinder NIE from pruning the transferred programs or from asking Congress for a substantial budget increase. Second, while the House questioned Glennan about the absence of the NCER and later justified its cut of the NIE fiscal year 1974 request by the lack of a council, it was the Senate that administered the larger cut to NIE's budget, and the Senate committee did not mention the NCER absence in either its hearings or its justification of the large cut. Finally, the institute's fortunes in the appropriations process have hardly grown since the council began its meetings.

Some mistakes or unintended actions also were made by members of Congress. During the determination of the fiscal year 1974 budget, congressional signals may have crossed more than once. In the Senate Appropriations Subcommittee closed session, the proposal to cut the NIE budget to $50 million apparently originated with Senator Cotton. Cotton, whose job it was to support administration programs and propose cuts in nonadministration programs, must have misunderstood his assignment on the NIE appropriation. But once Cotton had made his proposal, pro–NIE Senators, such as Ted Stevens (R–Alaska), were hard pressed to build a case for more funds. In the full Senate Appropriations Committee markup session, Senator Birch Bayh (D–Indiana) was prepared to ask for $142 million for NIE. But as a result of a misunderstanding between Bayh's staff and Stevens's staff, Stevens spoke first and, thinking he was doing NIE a favor, proposed an increase to $75 million (Glennan, 31 July 1975, reporting congressional staff conversations; Glennan, 5 October 1973, p. 1).

When Magnuson reacted angrily to Javits's defense of NIE's fiscal year 1974 budget request on the floor of the Senate, he made several mistakes in his characterization of NIE, mistakes unflattering to NIE.

> The Senator from New Hampshire (Mr. Cotton) and I would ask, "Isn't this on top of the real research evaluation? These millions for those people?" . . . They have spent $142 million. . . . They have 462 people. . . . We said, "You had better go back and shape up a little bit and then come back and tell us." They never showed up. They knew that we felt that way about it. I told them some weeks ago. They never came around. [*Congressional Record*, 4 October 1973, p. S18634]

Each of these statements is incorrect. Senator Cotton did not ask any questions at the NIE hearings. He did not even attend the NIE hearings (Senate Appropriations Subcommittee Hearings, 23 July 1973, pp. 4169–4217). There is no indication in the record of the hearings that Magnuson asked any question about research evaluation. NIE had not spent $142 million in fiscal year 1973; it had spent $106.5 million out of a $110 million appropriation, a fact Magnuson had had some difficulty grasping during the NIE hearings.[9] NIE did not employ 462 people; it had asked for funds to support 462 people in its fiscal year 1974 budget. At the time of the Senate hearings, NIE employed approximately 325. Nowhere in the record of the hearings is there any indication that Magnuson asked Glennan to "shape up" and "come back" with better testimony. Further, Glennan said he never received such a request at any time after the hearings, nor did the HEW budget office (Glennan, 5 October 1973, p. 5; Miller, deputy assistant secretary of HEW for budget, quoted by Glennan, 5 October 1973, p. 5). Magnuson no doubt believed he had good reasons for his antipathy toward Glennan and the NIE, but the record indicates that his statements made on the Senate floor, quoted above, were simply incorrect.

Another congressional figure who contributed to NIE's misfortunes in—by her own admission—an unpremeditated way, was Congresswoman Green. When she introduced her amendment on the floor of the House to reduce NIE's fiscal year 1975 appropriation to $80 million, she admitted she had not intended to suggest such a cut. "I did not intend to offer an amendment, but if there is one thing it seems to me that this House ought to look at it is the $18 billion in research, contracts, and grants in the Department of Health, Education, and Welfare" (*Congressional Record*, 28 June 1974, p. H5977). Her spur-of-the-moment amendment cost NIE $20 million in the House appropriations bill.

Although it may be the case that mistakes, misinterpretations, or spur-of-the-moment actions on the part of members of Congress may have contributed to NIE's short-term problems, their significance was probably not large. Cotton's forgetfulness may have cost NIE $50 million in the subcommittee, but that could have been restored in the conference committee. Magnuson may have made inaccurate statements about NIE, but his misperceptions were probably more symptoms of his implacable dislike than causes of it. Green's amendment was totally consistent with her past behavior with respect to education R&D and NIE. Further, in spite of her amendment, the House had still voted to give NIE $80 million more than had the Senate.

The major mistake made by HEW was in counseling NIE to request a supplemental appropriation in fiscal year 1974. That mistake is discussed below in the section on bureaucratic problems.

NIE staff and people acting on behalf of NIE committed a number of gaffes that did nothing to contribute to budget expansion. One NIE staff member precipitated an incident that became grist for Capitol Hill rumor mills and later was even published in a *New York Times* analysis of NIE's difficulties (*New York Times*, 22 October 1973, p. 64). In late March 1973, before any of NIE's budget troubles had begun, the associate counsel to Senator Claiborne Pell's (D–Rhode Island) education subcommittee—the subcommittee that had sponsored NIE's authorizing legislation in the Senate—called the NIE staff assistant temporarily in charge of NIE's congressional liaison. The associate counsel had called to complain. He had been influential in establishing the policymaking role for the NCER in NIE's legislation and he was angry that NIE was conducting business without its NCER (Smith, March 1974). After an exchange of somewhat heated words, the NIE staff assistant reportedly challenged the associate counsel with, "Who cares?" and hung up on him. The incident spurred a letter of protest to Glennan from Pell (Pell, 30 March 1973), and elicited a personal apology from Glennan to Pell and, later, to the associate counsel (Glennan, 7 December 1973). Although both parties later discounted the significance of the incident (Smith, March 1974; Emery, March 1974), it was certainly not something a fledgling agency needed on its record. Further, it was later cited by Pell as one of the reasons he was unwilling to join Javits in supporting NIE on the floor of the Senate (Glennan, reporting congressional staff conversation, 5 October 1973, p. 4).

Pell had another reason to be annoyed with NIE. A group of senior NIE personnel, including Glennan, had visited Rhode Island early in 1973 at the invitation of the Rhode Island state superintendent of schools. Glennan viewed the visit as an opportunity to learn about work under way at the state level. The Rhode Island State Department of Education viewed the visit as encouragement to submit funding proposals to NIE. As a result of the visit, seventeen applications were submitted to NIE's basic research grants program. Subsequently, the Rhode Island state superintendent of schools was informed in a mimeographed form letter that all seventeen applications had been rejected (as had been 2,920 other applications). Pell and his staff were furious over such cavalier treatment (Smith, March 1974; Wexler, March 1974; Glennan, July 1975).

During the period when NIE's request for supplemental funds was before the House Appropriations Subcommittee, NIE managed to offend Congressman Obey, usually counted as supportive of NIE, without doing a thing. Apparently Obey had been advised by his best friend, a teacher in Wisconsin, to vote for the NIE supplemental request. Obey found this blatant pressure highly offensive and was "openly insulted" (Elliott, reporting congressional staff conversation, 11 March 1974, p. 21). NIE had no knowledge of how this pressure was generated, but Obey apparently blamed NIE (Elliott, 11 March 1974).

The above by no means exhausts the list of congressional mistakes or instances in which the institute and its friends were alleged to have offended outsiders. It is probable that these incidents do not form a major part of the explanation for NIE's budget difficulties. They do demonstrate two points of interest, however. They provide a reminder that, in a complicated situation, there is a high likelihood someone will be offended. And the popularity of these stories among NIE supporters demonstrates the natural tendency of those intimately involved with an organization to attribute "failure" to "personalities" rather than to bureaucratic, political, and programmatic factors.

Bureaucratic Problems

NIE was bureaucratically tied to HEW and OE. Both sets of ties caused it problems. Because NIE was established as a part of HEW—unlike, for example, NSF, which is independent of all cabinet departments—it was the recipient of advice, support, requirements, and constraints from the department. In the case of the supplemental budget request, it appears that NIE received very bad advice indeed from HEW.

The HEW deputy assistant secretary for budget told Glennan and Elliott that he and his staff had talked with members of the appropriations committees during the conference on the fiscal year 1974 appropriations bill. They had been assured that during supplemental hearings, without the pressure of the full appropriations bill deadlines, the committees would have more time to listen to the institute's case (Elliott, 11 March 1974, p. 14). The deputy assistant secretary for budget even reminded members of the House Appropriations Subcommittee of this understanding during the hearings on the NIE supplemental request:

> We felt at the time the conference occurred that there was not enough opportunity at that point to make our case, and we talked to a number of people and they said, "Look, there is an awful lot of business before the Congress. Please leave us alone. We will be willing to listen to you when there is some time to catch our breath and we come back in January."

> You are right, you can't regard this [NIE's request for supplemental funds] as an emergency item but we had some indication the Congress would be receptive to a supplemental if we held off so the item could be discussed deliberatively in the next [i.e., the supplemental] session. [Miller, House Appropriations Subcommittee, 27 February 1974, p. 302]

But the representatives flared at the suggestion they had agreed to a rehearing. Congressman Obey thought NIE had been given "plenty of opportunity" to make its case at the regular hearings (House Appropriations Subcommittee, 27 February 1974, p. 302). Congressman Kenneth Robinson (R–Virginia) explicitly rejected the HEW statement.

> And I do not agree with what [the HEW deputy assistant secretary for budget] says that there was any commitment on the part of this committee to the effect that this matter was going to be reviewed before the end of this fiscal year, certainly not on the part of this member. [House Appropriations Subcommittee, 27 February 1974, p. 306]

After the hearings the HEW comptroller asked his assistant, the deputy assistant secretary for budget, which members of Congress had agreed to NIE's returning with a supplemental request. It turned out that only one staff member for the Senate Appropriations Subcommittee had been approached directly; HEW had not discussed the issue with a single committee member (Elliott, 11 March 1974, pp. 13–15). HEW did not force NIE to ask for supplemental funds, but it did provide misleading advice and encouragement. Further, at least in part because HEW policy required that all NIE contacts with Capitol Hill go through the HEW office, NIE had not developed its own network of congressional friends who might have given warning of the danger of asking for a supplemental appropriation.

Even though NIE suffered some disadvantages from its association with HEW, by far the larger share of its congressional problems in the bureaucratic category came from its association with OE. There were three major ways NIE's association with OE led to problems. There was congressional confusion over the missions of the two agencies. OE's reputation for poor management rubbed off on NIE. And the transfer of more than $100 million worth of OE R&D programs denied NIE the opportunity to plead "newness" as a reason for lack of accomplishments.

Some members of Congress were unable to understand the difference between NIE and OE because the creation of NIE did not end research and development activities within OE. The omnibus bill that created NIE also included the provision that OE would continue its research in vocational education and education for the handicapped. In fact, in fiscal year 1974 OE was spending approximately $40 million for these activities. In an apparent duplication, NIE had its own career education program and also sought funds for research on learning disabilities. In addition to its research funds, OE spent $931 million in fiscal year 1974 for a broad array of discretionary programs, some labeled "demonstration," "planning," or "dissemination." Many of these activities also sounded similar to proposed NIE activities. Congresswoman Green could not see the difference between NIE's bilingual program and OE's bilingual program (House Appropriations Subcommittee, 27 February 1974, p. 285). Congressman Michel wanted to know how NIE's reading program related to OE's Right to Read program (House Appropriations Subcommittee, 23 April 1974, p. 827). Congressman Flood pointed out four major areas of possible overlap in the work of the two agencies (House Appropriations Subcommittee, 23 April 1974, p. 810). The distinctions between NIE work and OE work were in fact not clear. It was not surprising, therefore, that members of Congress assumed that NIE and OE were asking for duplicative funds.

NIE's association with OE was most troublesome to Congresswoman Green, who seemed unable or unwilling to believe that NIE was separate from OE. One-quarter of her remarks and questions during Glennan's appearance for the fiscal year 1974 budget request were specifically about OE activities that had not even been transferred to NIE.[10] Another 20% were about OE programs that had been transferred, but the queries were not about the substance of the transferred programs.[11] She wanted to know, for example, the annual salaries of the directors of the regional laboratories and R&D centers (House Appropriations Subcommittee, 9 March 1973, p. 198). During Glennan's defense of the NIE request for supplemental funds, more than 45% of Green's comments and questions were again about OE activities.[12] As far as Green was concerned, NIE was guilty by association.

> I have been lied to—and I use those words very advisedly—I have been lied to so many times by the people in the Office of Education, and as we have looked at contracts and grants, that, as far as I am concerned, there isn't any credibility among some of the higher-ups in that Office [of Education] or in the Department [of HEW]. . . . We see collusion, corruption, shoddy work inefficiency, waste throughout the whole operation. It gives me grave doubts about NIE. I am just not persuaded that NIE is going to be any different. [House Appropriations Subcommittee, 9 March 1973, pp. 188–90]

Congress wanted to know about the programs transferred to NIE from OE. The appropriations subcommittees had heard various OE commissioners of education and directors of research asking for money for some of these programs every year for the previous eight years. Glennan had not asked for these programs—indeed he had not even been hired until after they were transferred—but he had to explain to Congress what he was going to do with them. Glennan emphasized early in his first testimony before both the House and Senate subcommittees that NIE was reviewing every transferred project, usually with the assistance of outside experts, in order to determine whether to continue or withdraw funding support. But at least some members of Congress were not interested in reviews; they wanted results. Congressman Shriver would not accept Glennan's plea that Congress be patient:

> You caution us . . . not to expect too much from your efforts in the first few years. According to your [budget] justifications, all but $25 million of your $162 million budget request is for programs which have been going for years. I think it's time to expect results. [House Appropriations Subcommittee, 9 March 1973, pp. 177–78]

NIE was caught in a dilemma. If it terminated all the transfer programs it would be telling the subcommittees that years of government funding had been wasted. If it continued them it would have to produce results from them immediately. These results would have to satisfy some of the same committee members who had been unhappy with these programs for years.

By the time Glennan testified for NIE's fiscal year 1974 supplemental request, he could report that NIE had completed an "arduous" review of all projects transferred to NIE (105 from OE and 13 from OEO). Of the 68 projects at laboratories and R&D centers, NIE had phased out 11; declared 5 ineligible for funding; continued 23 for only one year; and continued 26 for two or three years. In all, 29 projects were either not funded or phased out for an annual savings of $30 million, and the 89 remaining projects were reduced by a total of $14 million (Senate Appropriations Subcommittee, 7 March 1974, p. 313; House Appropriations Subcommittee, 27 February 1974, p. 295). But the continued congressional reductions in NIE's appropriations indicated that NIE had not produced the necessary results.

Political Problems

NIE was troubled by a host of political problems—some of its own making, some as a result of particular programs transferred from OE or OEO that were of interest to powerful people in NIE's environment, and at least one as a result of presidential social policy over which NIE had absolutely no control.

The institute's congressional experience might have been different had NIE not been part of a Republican administration that was warring with a Democratic congress. Some members of Congress were incensed at the Nixon administration's attempts to reduce funding for social programs they considered essential. The administration's fiscal year 1974 budget request, which contained the $162 million request for NIE, proposed $3 billion in cuts for health and education programs. Magnuson, in introducing the Senate version of the fiscal year 1974 Labor–HEW appropriations bill on the Senate floor, railed against these reductions:

> Practically every program designed to assist people to better help themselves is reduced or terminated under the proposed [Nixon] budget. . . . In a time of inflation, this request can only be interpreted as an administration recommendation that Congress cooperate in taking a step backward in programs relating to better health and education of our citizens—a step backward into a time when many of the aged, the poor and the infirm were relegated to the scrap heaps of our society. [*Congressional Record*, 4 October 1973, p. S18617]

Viewed in the context of a budget that recommended, for example, the termination of all federal support for public school libraries, 50% cuts in health manpower programs, phasing out of community mental health centers, and only a 3% increase over the previous year's cancer research budget, the administration's request for a 50% increase in NIE's funds was particularly galling.[13] Congressman Obey singled out the disparity between the NIE-requested increase and the decreases recommended for other programs as one of the reasons for the cut in NIE's fiscal year 1974 budget.

> One of the reasons . . . the committee acted as it did was simply because at a time when there was an increase being requested in this program area [NIE], you were having cutbacks requested in some other areas which applied much more directly to local levels in the eyes of people at the local level. [House Appropriations Subcommittee, 23 April 1974, p. 833]

The situation was no different in the fiscal year 1975 budget. The Nixon administration was still proposing cuts in popular programs. As Magnuson described it, "As has been the case for several years, the architects of the [fiscal year 1975] budget estimates somehow lost sight of many of the real needs" (*Congressional Record*, 16 September 1974, p. S16667). At the same time, the administration was asking for a 70% increase in NIE's budget. It may very well have been the case that, had spending for social programs in general been on the rise, NIE would have received budget increases almost automatically. But NIE's requested increases were very noticeable and very vulnerable in the Nixon budgets.

It is possible that NIE might have fared better had its first director been more of a politician. Glennan was a researcher, and his forays into the political arena, particularly his first budget testimonies, were not very successful. His answers to congressional questions were discursive rather than crisp. His explanations were abstract, practically devoid of examples or anecdotes. And he did not always have ready answers for specific questions.[14]

One of the more damaging exchanges occurred in Glennan's first appearance before the Senate Appropriations Subcommittee, when Magnuson asked Glennan what NIE was doing in the field of desegregation. Glennan replied that local districts might need information on teacher-training and the problems that might occur in integrated classrooms:

Senator Magnuson: Do they come and ask you for the advice?

Mr. Glennan: Nobody comes and asks us for advice. That is, as far as I know.

M: Nobody asked you for any advice on it.

G: No sir.

M: They don't ask you for advice and if they don't ask you, I don't know why you should be involved with it.

G: We would be producing knowledge that would be available to people who ask.

M: You said nobody asked for it.

G: To my knowledge, no one specifically.

M: What do you do with the knowledge?

G: The knowledge is made available.

M: But nobody asked you for it. [Senate Appropriations Subcommittee, 23 July 1974, pp. 4188–89]

Magnuson's assessment of the quality of Glennan's testimony was low indeed. In justifying the Appropriations Committee's cut of NIE's fiscal year 1974 budget from $162 million to $75 million on the floor of the Senate, Magnuson attacked Glennan and his testimony:

We based our conclusions, first, on what we were told [by NIE]. . . . Maybe the fellow they sent up [Glennan] did not do the right thing. But he was probably the most miserable witness I have ever seen in my career in Congress, when he sought to justify $162 million. . . . He did not know what they were doing. He had no idea what they are going to do. [*Congressional Record*, 4 October 1973, p. S18634]

Glennan's testimony improved noticeably in his appearances for the supplemental request and the fiscal year 1975 budget. His answers were shorter and were illustrated with examples of products and projects supported by NIE. More familiar with his data, he was able to provide accurate numerical support for his answers.[15] Twice, when Congresswoman Green began complaining about OE programs, Glennan reminded her firmly that NIE was not OE (House Appropriations Subcommittee, 27 February 1974, pp. 285–86). To counter his initial exchange with Magnuson, he was able to provide long lists of people who had indeed asked NIE for advice. Had the quality of Glennan's initial testimony been the main reason for NIE's first budget cut, as Magnuson implied on the floor of the Senate, one would not have expected to see NIE's budgets continue to fall as Glennan's testimony improved. Further, it was after Glennan's resignation that the Senate committee cut NIE's budget to zero.

While Glennan's lack of political finesse probably contributed to NIE's difficulties, there were certainly other political problems. One of the most serious of these seemed to be that NIE could not demonstrate convincing constituent support. Had NIE begun its existence with a very small budget, Congress might have been less concerned about its apparent lack of constituent support. But NIE was asking for more than $100 million each year and could demonstrate little public demand for or support of these requests.

An agency usually derives political support from those groups who are the direct beneficiaries of its existence. For nonregulatory agencies this means support comes from the recipients of its contracts and grants.[16] In this case, the two groups most likely to support NIE were the Council on Educational Development and Research (CEDaR), the organization composed of the regional education laboratories and the R&D centers, and the American

Education Research Association (AERA), an association of approximately 11,000 scholars and researchers. The CEDaR organizations receive 90% of their funding from federal sources (House Appropriations Subcommittee, 27 February 1974, p. 292). Although there is no comparable estimate for AERA members, Glennan estimated the institute's requested fiscal year 1974 budget would support approximately 5000 researchers (Senate Appropriations Subcommittee, 23 July 1973, pp. 4184, 4186). While neither of these is a particularly powerful political force, their enthusiastic support for the agency might have been helpful. But CEDaR had cause to be restrained in its enthusiasm, and AERA was simply not organized to provide political support.

The tension in the NIE–CEDaR relationship grew from the fact that NIE had implemented an OE decision to discontinue the policy of institutional support to the laboratories and R&D centers. Thus, these organizations were no longer able to rely on continued financial support simply as a consequence of having been created by federal dollars. Instead, they had to finance themselves out of the "sale" of their programs to NIE or other buyers. In this process they were in competition with other laboratories and R&D centers and other private and governmental research organizations. In addition to terminating institutional support, NIE also gave some of the laboratory and R&D center programs low marks in its evaluation of programs transferred from OE. As a result of these two actions on the part of NIE, the CEDaR organizations lost close to $9 million in funds even before NIE's first budget cut.[17] A Brademas aide described CEDaR's "support" of NIE on Capitol Hill in discouraging terms.

> The people from the labs and centers come by and start off by saying, "We support NIE." Then they immediately start talking about their complaints against NIE. With friends like that, the Institute doesn't need enemies. [Duncan, March 1974]

The AERA did not oppose NIE, but its support was far from impressive. Traditionally governed by educational psychologists uninterested in political lobbying, the association was not organized to defend its interests on Capitol Hill (Dershimer, July 1974). Indeed, when the executive officer of AERA testified on behalf of the creation of NIE in early 1971 he could present only his personal views, because the AERA, up to that time, had "no provision for formulating public statements in the name of the Association" (Senate Committee on Labor and Public Welfare, 27 April 1971, p. 1194). AERA was silent when NIE's fiscal year 1974 budget request was cut in half. Its first public support of NIE did not occur until after NIE had sustained the House cut to $80 million in its fiscal year 1975 budget. In July 1974, Professor Robert Thorndike, a psychologist from Teachers College, Columbia University and president of AERA, submitted a statement of support for NIE to Magnuson's subcommittee (Senate Appropriations Subcommittee, 18 July 1974, pp. 6378–80). Thorndike did not appear before the subcommittee to testify on NIE's behalf, however.

The major education lobbies in Washington, such as the education administrators' groups and the teachers' unions, had little to gain from NIE. Their primary concern is the total multibillion-dollar budget spent by the Education Division of HEW each year. NIE's budget represents only about 1% of that total. But instead of ignoring NIE or supporting it with 1% of their resources, the major lobbies complained that NIE was not paying enough attention to them.[18] After NIE's first budget cut, Brademas castigated the lobbies, "who, not seeing some immediate benefit to their own interests, responded like some county highway commissioners, complaining that there was not enough pork in the barrel for them" (19 November 1973, p. 3).

The Senate subcommittee's recommendation that NIE's budget be cut to zero did provoke a unified reaction from education groups. In a 17 September 1974 statement fifteen national education associations urged that NIE be granted the $80 million approved by the House.[19] The associations declared, "It would be unthinkable for the Federal Government to renege on $90 million of committed and morally obligated research grants and contracts" (American Council on Education, 17 September 1974, p. 1). In the wake of Glennan's resignation two weeks earlier, HEW and the NCER were requesting the advice of the major lobbies on who should replace Glennan. The associations found this consultation to be "a genuine recognition of the necessity to guarantee that the Institute will, in the years ahead, concentrate its resources on the immediate, real-life-practical problems facing American education" (American Council on Education, 17 September 1974, pp. 1–2).

Also damaging to NIE's cause were complaints about NIE from individual educators to members of Congress. Congresswoman Green reported that the state superintendent of schools in her state complained that NIE was "plowing the same ground over and over" (House Appropriations Subcommittee, 27 February 1974, p. 306). Senator Magnuson read into the record of the fiscal year 1974 NIE hearings an angry letter from the president of Eastern Washington State College, who charged that OE's research program had been preferable to NIE's. In July 1973 Magnuson also received a letter from the Washington state superintendent of schools, complaining that "much of NIE activities will turn out to be inappropriate to the cause of elementary and secondary education" (Brouillet, 13 July 1973, quoted in Senate Appropriations Subcommittee, 6 June 1974, p. 2915).

Thus NIE found itself in the position of having at best only lukewarm support from the education research organizations, complaints from the national teacher organizations, and no support from the local educators. Senator Stevens, one member of the Appropriations Subcommittee generally friendly to NIE, pointed out the liability of having no local support.

The impact that I had from the discussion we had in the [fiscal year 1974 House-Senate] conference—and it was a heated discussion—was that there is really no support being reflected back to Members of the House and Senate from their own . . . consumers [of education R&D] in the districts of their States, and that they think they could do more with their money if it were just made available to them. . . . The complaint we heard, and I think we heard it vociferously, was that local school officials of all types believe that [NIE] was going to be another group of people who were going to tell them how to teach and what to teach, and what is wrong with the way they are teaching. . . . [members of Congress] are not hearing from home that [NIE projects] are effective, or that they have any desire for their continuance. As a matter of fact, just the opposite, just to the contrary. [Senate Appropriations Subcommittee, 7 March 1974, pp. 284–86]

After the first budget cut, NIE was caught in a vicious circle. Without new money for new programs, the institute found it difficult to win favor from the education constituencies. And without constituent support, it seemed impossible for the institute to win new money from Congress.

Furthermore, its management of the programs transferred from OE and OEO won NIE few political friends. The irritation of CEDaR, caused by reduction in funding of the laboratories and R&D centers, and the irritation of the teachers unions, caused by support of the education voucher experiment, were two of the political consequences of the transferred programs. NIE's early management of a third transferred program, the Mountain Plains Education and Economic Development Program, managed to annoy Senator Mike Mansfield (D–Montana) and the governors of six states.

Mountain Plains, one of the Career Education projects transferred from OE, was a $4–5 million residential program in a former Strategic Air Command base at Glasgow, Montana. This program had been initiated by OE in response to considerable political pressure from people who did not want the former air base unoccupied (*Education USA*, 9 October 1972, p. 35). When it was transferred to NIE, its credibility as an R&D program was questioned by its evaluators (Raizen, et al. 1973, p. 47). Instead of simply continuing Mountain Plains as a political service project as OE had apparently done, the NIE managers attempted to improve its R&D potential. While waiting for requested revisions in the project's activities, NIE temporarily withheld funds from the project (Senate Appropriations Subcommittee, 23 July 1973, p. 4201). This action caused the governors of the six states served by the project to "urge" that Mountain Plains be supported in a letter to Glennan with a copy to Magnuson. In the fiscal year 1974 appropriations hearings Magnuson read this letter into the record and questioned Glennan about the project (Senate Appropriations Subcommittee, 23 July 1973, pp. 4199–4203). In the fiscal year 1974 supplemental hearings Magnuson again asked Glennan about Mountain Plains (Senate Appropriations Subcommittee, 7 March 1974, pp. 305–6). In the fiscal year 1975 hearings, Senator Mansfield, not a member of the Labor–HEW Appropriations Subcommittee but a member of the full Appropriations Committee, appeared to question Glennan about Mountain Plains (Senate Appropriations Subcommittee, 6 June 1974, pp. 2875–85). He reminded Glennan that "this Committee maintains a high level of interest in the progress being made in the Mountain Plains project" (p. 2875) and closed his questioning with, "I would like to see a more personal interest taken in the project itself" (p. 2885). In the Senate committee reports accompanying both the fiscal year 1974 and 1975 appropriations bills, Mountain Plains was extolled (Senate Report 93–414, 2 October 1973, p. 80; Senate Report 93–1146, 11 September 1974, p. 84).

To marshal its defenses against the onslaught of political problems, NIE had only a small, weak external affairs unit. This unit, composed of two offices—the Office of Public Information that handled mass media and written communication, and the Office of External Relations which handled constituent group and legislative relations—was not even fully staffed until after NIE had received its first budget cut. The first director of external relations, George Gustafson, a former school administrator and executive secretary of the California Commission on Teacher Licensing and Preparation, had no prior experience working on Capitol Hill.[20] His first day on the job was the day Glennan first testified before Magnuson and announced that "nobody asked NIE for advice" (Gustafson, March 1974). The Office of External Relations had its work cut out for it.

But it was difficult to mount a creditable effort. The office was small and inexperienced, consisting of Gustafson and two staff aides—none of whom had significant contacts on Capitol Hill. There were no other NIE staff members who could supply such contacts, nor were there staff with close ties to the major education groups. Further, the office was not close to top-level decision-making or policymaking within the institute. It rarely had the opportunity to review and modify budget justifications before 'they were presented to Congress (Nicosia, October 1974). Nor was it consulted frequently by the NCER. In August 1973 the NCER asked how NIE would involve external constituents in the development of plans and programs. Gustafson prepared a memorandum in response, but in the following seven months it never reached the NCER because, he was informed, their agenda was always too full (Gustafson, March 1974). Because much of the institute's budget and energy was devoted to projects inherited from OE and OEO, the office felt it had nothing new "to sell" on Capitol Hill. In addition, it was difficult to explain NIE's mission in clear and compelling terms. Finally, there was persistent criticism of Gustafson, charging that he was not doing his job adequately and that key congressional staff members had not even met him (Duncan, March 1974; Smith, March 1974; Wexler, March 1974). In the summer of 1974, Glennan appointed a person to supervise both the Office of

External Relations and the Office of Public Information; Gustafson resigned shortly thereafter.

Even had NIE not had any accidental, bureaucratic, or political problems, it still would have had difficulties. NIE was unable to convince Congress that the programs it wanted to support were intrinsically worth supporting.

Programmatic Problems

All of NIE's budget requests were criticized by members of Congress because the substance of those requests—the projects and programs NIE wanted to support with its funds—seemed unsatisfying. Members complained about vague language in the budget justifications, difficulty in understanding the NIE mission, and a lack of tangible products resulting from NIE work.

One of the reasons the fiscal year 1974 request was somewhat vague was that the NCER, not then appointed, had not been able to approve it. As a result, the entire justification and Glennan's testimony were peppered with the phrase "subject to NCER approval." But that was not the only vagueness in the requests. The language describing NIE's projects proved a substantial stumbling block, which remained even after the NCER had been approved. Senator Cotton was unable to grasp the intended topic of a proposed "Conference to Define Concepts of Divesting (*sic*) and Pluralism and How They Relate to Equality in Educational Opportunity" or the import of a "Study of Infants' Ability to Control Their World in Home and Non-Home Situations" (Senate Appropriations Subcommittee, 6 June 1974, pp. 2898–2901). Congressman Obey reacted to the language used by NIE in more caustic terms. NIE wanted to spend $150,000 to design a survey to "query teachers, principals, school board members, and others about problems in the schools. The survey will provide a base for a research and development program to be undertaken to meet the express needs of educational practitioners." Obey's response was, "language like that drives me nuts" (House Appropriations Subcommittee, 27 February 1974, p. 304).

What some members of Congress perceived as vague language, or "mushy education jargon that doesn't tell us a damn thing," as Obey characterized it (*Wall Street Journal*, 28 June 1974, p. 36), was symptomatic of a more serious problem. NIE was unable to persuade Congress that it knew what it was doing. It could not make a convincing case that the money requested from Congress would be spent on coherent, compelling programs. Congressman Michel (R–Illinois) could not understand what NIE was proposing to do about improving basic skills:

> If per chance you and I were around here 10 years from now would we still be asking this question and still trying to find out ways of teaching?. . . I am looking down the road someplace hoping what I am doing here is the right thing and voting the right sums of money. Are we doing more than just funding jobs down in your shop? Are we going to get some good? What is your goal? [House Appropriations Subcommittee, 23 April 1974, p. 827]

After NIE's fiscal year 1974 budget cut, the institute attempted to provide a clear picture of its plans by announcing that its funds would be allocated among five priority areas. The priorities were:

1. The provision of essential skills to all citizens
2. The improvement of the productivity of resources in the education system
3. Understanding and improving the relationship of education and work
4. The development of problem-solving capability in education systems at the State and Local level
5. Increasing diversity, pluralism and opportunity in American education[21] [House Appropriations Subcommittee, 27 February 1974, p. 273]

The Five Priorities appear to have achieved little success in giving the appropriations committees a better sense of NIE's purpose, however. Both the "productivity" and "problem-solving" priorities provoked congressional demands for further definition and explanation (House Appropriations Subcommittee, 27 February 1974, pp. 319–20; Senate Appropriations Subcommittee, 7 March 1974, pp. 287–89; House Appropriations Subcommittee, 4 April 1974, p. 842). Members of the subcommittee could not understand, for example, why federal funding was necessary to identify local problems or why NIE should be given money to help solve them.

In spite of having declared priorities, NIE was still asking for funds for a wide range of small, seemingly unrelated projects, prompting Congressman Obey to ask, "Do you think that your people have accomplished an adequate degree of focussing to be really productive in the research that you are conducting?" (House Appropriations Subcommittee, 23 April 1975, p. 833). The twelve projects NIE intended to support with its fiscal year 1974 supplemental appropriation ranged from "field testing curriculum units to inform children about work careers" to "beginning a program of research to identify the causes of mental and emotional handicaps and their effects on learning" (House Appropriations Subcommittee, 27 February 1974, pp. 249–55). Asking for funds for twelve separate sets of activities obscured any sense of fundamental priorities. Further, almost all the items would receive relatively small amounts of money, thereby offering little hope that any one of them would have a major impact. In addition, many of the items represented a continuation or expansion of transferred activities, thereby further clouding any sense of NIE priorities. Magnuson captured the situation bluntly with, "I just do not understand what you people are doing down there with all of that money—and neither do the members of this committee, this subcommittee; and neither do the members of the House Appropriations Committee" (Senate Appropriations Subcommittee, 7 March 1974, p. 294).

The most serious of NIE's programmatic difficulties were not of its own making; they are inherent in the fundamental character of education and education R&D. Education is not endowed with the mystique of professional expertise that has served medicine and some of the natural sciences so well. Everyone who has been to school knows about education. As a consequence, there is little deference paid to the "experts" in education R&D. It is easy to ridicule their "scientific" efforts. Moreover, questions about education are rarely objective. Individual values and moral judgments are rarely absent from decisions about education or, by extension, from decisions about what to support in education R&D. Finally, while education is important, in the eyes of Congress it is no more important than a number of other social services. And because education R&D is not likely to solve many of the serious problems in education, at least not in the short run, it is difficult to argue that money spent on education R&D—even if it is "only" $100 million—would not be better spent on medical research or on programs that will affect children directly.

NIE encountered congressional ridicule of at least two of its research activities. Congressman Obey would not accept that a needs-assessment survey, the kind of exploratory work that precedes many scientific or technology development programs, was a reasonable activity for NIE to support. His judgment was, "If I tried to defend supporting $150,000 for that kind of project to my own education administrators [in Wisconsin], they would laugh me out of the room" (House Appropriations Subcommittee, 27 February 1974, p. 304). Senator Magnuson was no more impressed by a $334,000 project to study the effects on a national population of introducing standardized achievement tests. NIE defended the project on the grounds that, "for the first time in educational history an experimental study of the much argued effects of tests of ability and attainment on various social institutions and public can be undertaken ... planned social change will benefit educational and governmental agencies in developed and underdeveloped nations" (Senate Appropriations Subcommittee, 7 March 1974, pp. 297–98). Magnuson could not believe it.

Senator Magnuson: Of what? Say that again.

Mr. Glennan: The introduction of standardized tests in Ireland.

M: In Ireland?

G: Yes; let me try to explain why that is an important issue. There has been a great deal—as you undoubtedly have heard—of criticism about the use of standardized tests within classrooms. They are used to track kids when they should not be used to track kids; kids who find—

M: What are we doing in Ireland?

G: Ireland was the only English-speaking country remaining without a test program. It provided an opportunity to try to understand, in an experimental sense, how people will use those tests.

M: Why do you not write Dublin and get the book—the review of it—and get one of these paper shufflers [NIE staff] down there to read it?

G: This would not have been done without the resources to permit the analysis which we share with other organizations.

M: You mean you cannot read about it?

G: No. It is set up as an experiment.

M: They have got reports on it. I am sure they have.

G: No they do not. We are helping to produce them.

M: They have their own reports.

G: They have not introduced them as yet.

M: You could get the reports.

G: Let me provide a description, for the record, of that particular project because I believe it is—

M: Put it in the record. [Senate Appropriations Subcommittee, 7 March 1974, p. 297]

Magnuson's disbelief and Obey's ridicule are not the products of ignorant congressmen who have never heard of research and development. These men listen to testimony about and appropriate hundreds of millions of dollars for medical research every year. Many of them have served on other appropriations subcommittees, where they hear testimony about R&D in, for example, the Department of Defense or the Department of Agriculture. But when the topic is education rather than medicine, their minds work differently.

The political nature of education and education R&D was exemplified by the controversy over the funding of the education voucher experiment. Under the banner of "this program will destroy public education," the teachers' unions fought against a small experiment in parent choice in education.[22] Questions of individual values were also exemplified by an exchange between Glennan and Congressman Silvio Conte (R–Massachusetts) over the question of support for bilingual education. The exchange began innocuously enough when Conte asked Glennan to explain the theory behind bilingual education. After Glennan briefly explained two or three different theories, it turned out that Conte was not interested in the theory at all. What really troubled him was the idea that money should be spent on research in bilingual education when his parents and many other immigrants had come to this country without knowing a word of English and had become successful without the help of special programs.

What troubles me is that I had immigrant parents myself, and know how they and all the others, groped with the English language. We all made it. We made it well. How long are we going to spend the taxpayers' money on this kind of program? You have got to convince me.

We have great doctors and lawyers and engineers and Members of Congress and the Cabinet who had immigrant parents who couldn't speak a word of English when they came here. They made it. They went to college and became great leaders of the United States. . . .

When my father and mother landed on Ellis Island they were 12 and 13 years old. Everything they had was on their backs. My mother worked in a mill and ran 15 looms when she was 12 years old. They had no wealth; they had nothing. And they made it and they made sure we made it. How long are we going to need bilingual education? Is it just another gimmick to spend a little more money and set up another program? Is it really essential? I want to know. [House Appropriations Subcommittee, 27 February 1974, pp. 293–94]

Every project and program in education R&D is subject to this same kind of questioning. If a program does not seem important based on his own experience, or square with his own sense of values, the member of Congress feels free to oppose it. Scientific data cannot change a person's experience or values. It is difficult to argue against this kind of opposition. But if individual members of Congress do not place a high value on education research, this does not mean they are hardhearted. One of the complaints about NIE's programs was that they did not seem to be helping people. Congresswoman Green complained that NIE's fiscal year 1974 budget did not seem to be concerned with "the lives of kids" (House Appropriations Subcommittee, 9 March 1974, p. 203). Magnuson complained that NIE's programs "don't get at the basic needs here" (Senate Appropriations Subcommittee, 23 July 1974, p. 4192). Obey complained that NIE's programs seemed superfluous when "we have pressing problems on the local level in just trying to pay teachers, to build schools, and to provide some of the other items that are very crucial" (House Appropriations Subcommittee, 27 February 1974, pp. 301–5). And Stevens complained that NIE was not helping the education community "at the grassroots level" (Senate Appropriations Subcommittee, 17 March 1974, pp. 285–86).

In an era of budget stringency, each million dollars added to the education research budget may well mean the deletion of a million dollars from the medical research budget. Many of the advocates who appear before appropriations subcommittees represent causes only the most callous could bear to cut. Dozens of groups appeared before the House Subcommittee for Labor–HEW Appropriations, in support of funding requests for fiscal year 1975: their numbers included the American Cancer Society; the American Heart Association; the Arthritis Foundation; the National Kidney Foundation. There is a simple and compelling calculus that does not place education research high on the list of worthy concerns in comparison with the causes represented by these kinds of groups. A top Appropriations Subcommittee aide of Magnuson stated the case baldly, simplistically, but not inaccurately: "After all, not very many people die for a lack of educational research" (Dirks, March 1974).

Congressional Support of R&D

That NIE did not fare well in the appropriations process is clear. That a complicated set of factors probably contributed to its misfortunes should also be clear from the explanations above. Perhaps a more general look at the congressional support of R&D will set NIE's troubles in a broader context.

Without attempting a sophisticated or exhaustive analysis of congressional motivation or intent in funding R&D, it seems apparent that there are three broad, elementary strategies for persuading Congress to support R&D. The first is to bury R&D in a service agency. The Department of Transportation can win funds for R&D year after year—$370 million in fiscal year 1974 alone—because it is spending most of its money seeing to it that highways are built in every representative's state (Office of Management and Budget 1975, p. 255). Similarly, OE could support its small research office, albeit with criticism, because most of its funds were going directly to school districts and state departments of education in every representative's state.

The second strategy for winning funds from Congress is to have a compelling mission. The Department of Defense has funded enormous amounts of R&D under its mission of national defense—$8.4 billion in 1974 alone (OMB 1975, p. 255). Of course, if the mission is ever completely accomplished, the agency must find another one or run the risk of losing its congressional favor. NASA has fallen on hard times in recent years, having been unsuccessful in finding a new mission that would be as appealing to Congress as was going to the moon. From 1967 to 1973 the NASA R&D budget steadily declined—from $4.4 billion in 1967 to $3 billion in 1973 (OMB 1975, p. 254) For at least a part of its existence, the National Science Foundation also had a compelling mission—to upgrade the nation's scientific resources in comparison with those of the Soviet Union. It too has suffered periods of congressional disenchantment, the first one in the early fifties and the second one in the seventies, when its mission did not seem worthy of increased support. Indeed it is more than slightly ironic that NSF, one of the prime exemplars for NIE, in the mid-1970s has had its own problems with Congress (*Congressional Record*, 9 April 1975).

The third straightforward way to win R&D money from Congress is to help people. Every year in their budget justifications the National Institutes of Health can report how many lives were saved or rehabilitated the previous year as a result of their research. Of course some agencies are able to combine strategies. In the 1970s, the National Cancer Institute used both the second and third strategies. It is carrying out the national mission to cure cancer and, even before it finds the definitive cure, it is helping people live longer through the discovery of new drugs and treatments.

How does NIE fit within this context of three strategies? As history turned out, it is possible to argue that NIE was marred by serious flaws in both its conception and its creation that would make none of the strategies appropriate. In the thoughts of the Moynihan White House group, Levien, the Planning Unit, and many of those who testified at the Brademas hearings, NIE was endowed with a particular set of expectations. It was to be stable, scientific, and comprehensive. It was to have high status and visibility. And it was to have a large budget. In its creation, NIE was endowed with a director who shared the expectations of the conception, $110 million worth of programs, and utter political insignificance. As a result of this combination NIE was in trouble.

The act of creating NIE denied it the opportunity to use the first strategy. Education R&D was no longer buried within the multibillion-dollar Office of Education budget; it could not slip by unnoticed in a much larger budget. Did NIE have a compelling mission? The evidence seems to be that it did not. The legislation creating NIE declared that its mission was to "seek to improve education" through education R&D. Congressman Brademas may have found that compelling, but no members of the appropriations committees seemed to do so.

The only strategy open to NIE was to demonstrate that it helped people. But that was very hard. At least part of the justification for the creation of NIE was that past efforts in education R&D had *not* resulted in many products or findings that helped people. Improving the productivity of education R&D, particularly given that the technology was fairly weak, would take time. Until that occurred it would be difficult to demonstrate tangible, satisfying results from education R&D. To be sure, in its second and third budget requests NIE did attempt to emphasize how the work it was supporting, principally the transferred programs, helped people. It also found itself in the position of trying to win favor from the powerful education lobbies so that they, in effect, would testify that NIE was helping people. But it was not very successful in these endeavors.

If none of the three strategies was feasible, does this mean NIE was doomed to failure? There is, in fact, another way to gain temporary congressional support for R&D, a short-term strategy that NIE in fact thought it would be able to employ. If an R&D agency is new, Congress may be willing to invest funds against the prospect of future returns. This buys the agency enough time either to find the compelling mission or to begin to generate evidence that it is helping people. But Congress was not willing to invest in the case of NIE. In retrospect the reasons are threefold, and obvious. NIE was asking for more money than any member of Congress could be reasonably asked to commit on the basis of no more than vague promises. Had NIE asked for $3 million rather than $162 million, Congress might have been willing to make the investment. Second, NIE was not only asking for a lot of money, it was also asking for large increments in its budget.[23] The new-agency strategy probably works best with small budgets and modest increments. And third, although NIE was a new agency in the sense that it had to hire people and get organized, it was not at all a new agency in the programmatic sense. When members of Congress looked at NIE's budget, they did not believe they were investing in the prospect of future returns. They believed they were investing in OE transfer programs.

If there is a tragedy in the NIE story it may be that the first director and his close advisers actually believed in the expectations for NIE that were established during its conception. They believed in them and tried to make them come true. One of the principles underlying NIE's creation was that the way to improve education was to make it more scientific. And Glennan agreed. "I believe that an emphasis on comprehensive thinking through of problems and vigorous attention to research design will provide us with the foundations for a truly productive system" (House Appropriations Subcommittee, 9 March 1973, p. 178). But the appropriations committees scoffed at scientific studies.

A second principle was that good research cannot be produced on demand. NIE's authorization stipulated no year funding at least partly in recognition of this fact. Glennan concurred. "[We must] avoid the temptation to beat the clock, to succumb to demands to produce immediate flashy results. ... questions can not be formulated and answered over night or even in a few years" (House Appropriations Subcommittee, 9 March 1973, pp. 141; 178). But the appropriations committees operate on an annual calendar, refused NIE's funding-year exemption requests, and wanted to see results.

A third principle was that education R&D had been chronically under-funded and needed more support. NIE's authorization therefore provided $550 million for its first three years of operation. Glennan agreed. He asked for a 50% increase in his first year's budget, asked for supplemental funds, and asked for a 70% increase in his second year's budget. But the appropriations committees were not persuaded and gave NIE less than half its authorization.

NIE was conceived and created by thinkers: Moynihan, Brademas, Levien, Silberman, Richardson, the Unholy Trinity, Glennan. The process was a cerebral one, not a political one. It was conducted, by and large, by a small group of analysts—believers in the efficacy of research and creators of ambitious expectations for the new agency. The first director shared these beliefs and expectations and attempted to realize them. But, by the end of twenty-seven months of operation, NIE was a faltering agency, crippled in the appropriations process. Thinkers can create an agency, but they cannot fund it—cannot guarantee its survival.

Part Two   Bureaucratic
                          Development

Part 2 of this book is concerned with the bureaucratic development of NIE. Any new agency undertakes a very heavy load of bureaucratic activities. People have to be hired; procedures have to be invented; policies have to be established; money has to be spent in a way that can be made accountable; paper has to be processed; office space and furniture have to be obtained.

Each of the next four chapters emphasizes a particular aspect of bureaucratic elaboration: the recruiting and hiring of personnel; the design and management of programs; the creation and implementation of organization structures; and the making, not making, and unmaking of decisions. We discuss each separately, but of course all are interrelated. Additionally, all are influenced by five characteristics common to most new bureaucracies. It may be helpful to keep them in mind while reading part 2.

Conflict between Rationality and Ambiguity

Most new organizations can be characterized by a high desire for rationality. A new organization—a fresh beginning—affords the opportunity to impose an order based on analysis rather than on exigencies. Indeed, one reason offered for establishing new organizations is that existing ones can no longer be influenced by analysis or rational judgment; they have become captured by politics or bureaucratic ennui. The rhetoric surrounding the creation of NIE established the strong expectation that the new agency would act in a rational fashion. In addition, the agency's leadership seemed commited to an analytical approach to programs, procedures, and policies.

At the same time that a new organization is operating under expectations of rationality, it must cope with an extraordinarily high degree of ambiguity. Without the benefit of organizational memory or precedent, the agency must discover what it wants to do and how to do it. Even if an agency's mission is relatively straightforward and clear, the process of moving from the idea to the action requires confronting uncertainties and unknowns. Part 1 has documented the extent to which reasonable people differed over what NIE's major goals should be. The agency's mission had never been stated in precise, operational terms. As a result, the desire for clear criteria against which to evaluate competing claims for attention or resources was never fulfilled, thus frustrating every attempt at rational behavior.

No New Organization Is Completely New

Every new organization is influenced by its legacy. At the least, the legacy includes the promises and compromises necessary to establish the organization in the first place and the attitudes and experience brought by employees from other organizations. Part 1 has described NIE's legacy of belief in a scientific model and in the "failure" of OE; the products of a two-year planning period; and the collection of ambitious and ambiguous congressional promises. NIE's legacy also included large numbers of people and programs from OE and OEO. Transforming these into the "new" NIE staff and program was not an easy task.

Discovery of Who and What Are Important

One of the time-consuming activities in most new organizations is discovering who is important and which activities are rewarded. In a well-defined organization, the process is fairly straightforward. With each new senior person hired, patterns of relative importance and influence emerge and are stabilized. In the case of NIE, the patterns never stabilized: NIE was characterized by a shifting set of influential people and ideas over its first two and a half years. As a result, the discovery process never ceased.

Cycling of Issues

In the development of a new organization there is inevitably too much to do. Complex issues, which take time to resolve, often cycle through several iterations. When personnel are in short supply, this cycling is often accompanied by a concommitant cycling of personnel who manage the issues. Each new manager feels some necessity to redefine the problem, thereby further impeding resolution. NIE was characterized by a rapid cycling of issues and managers through center stage for its first two years of existence. Under the pressure of externally imposed deadlines, an issue received close attention for a short period, only to recede into the background once the deadline had passed. After several rounds of such cycling, it became difficult to generate any enthusiasm for yet another attempt to resolve any particular issue.

Delicate Relationship with Environment

Early in their existence, most new organizations expect a fairly unobtrusive environment. Often called "the honeymoon period," a time when few external demands are placed on the organization, this period allows an organization to pursue the process of getting organized in an undisturbed manner. Until systems or procedures for dealing with external demands are developed, responding to such demands is time-consuming and energy-diverting. If the early intrusions are many or severe, they leave little time for the organization to stabilize, to institutionalize its responses, or to begin to initiate its own contacts with its environment. NIE was confronted by so many external demands that it was unable to develop any reasonable degree of control over them during its first two and a half years of existence.

None of these five characteristics need adversely affect bureaucratic development. We suspect every successful bureaucracy has encountered and coped with every one of them, to a greater or lesser extent. Yet if an agency early falls on hard times, these features may interact in such a way that the agency's difficulties are exacerbated. This was the case with NIE. Once resources were constrained by the first budget cut, the tensions between rationality and uncertainty were compounded. It became more difficult to overcome the OE legacy, because there were few funds for new programs. Because the agency seemed to have a "problem," competing "solutions" and their peddlers vied constantly to establish their importance. And the environment—the larger federal bureaucracy, Congress, and constituents—became more demanding.

Five   Personnel

Introduction

A new agency's personnel influence its development in three major ways. Most obviously, they contribute their skills to solving problems and building structures. They also bring with them a way of looking at the world that influences their definition of problems and their design of solutions. And they bring with them beliefs about what the organization should do for them—their own career expectations. The process of recruiting and hiring also affects the new agency's development in three ways. It creates demands on the time of agency leadership, who must manage a recruiting process in addition to all their other duties. It becomes a convenient arena for ideological debates over who and what are important to the new agency. And its style and outcomes provide symbolic indicators to those looking for early signs of agency "success" or "failure."

In this chapter we examine the various processes used in recruiting and hiring NIE personnel. We suggest several models of hiring and growth and examine the extent to which NIE fulfilled the requirements of each of the models. We also speculate on the consequences of different hiring models for the agency. The questions we attempt to answer in this chapter are:

Who worked for the new agency?

How were they hired?

What impact did both the people who were hired and the hiring processes have on the new agency?

Personnel Chronology
1972

June	Nixon signs NIE legislation
July	Elliott named NIE project manager
	OE personnel lottery is held
August	Elliott named acting director
	Eighty-four people are transferred from OE
	($110 million worth of programs are transferred from OE)
	Coleman turns down position of NIE director
October	Glennan nominated as director
	Planning Unit staff hired by NIE
	Eight-step recruiting process is outlined

November   Glennan sworn in as first director
                Elliott and Martin are hired
                Mays concentrates on recruiting "good people"

1973
Spring   Recruiting becomes responsibility of young management
                    assistant
March   (Nixon announces NCER nominees)
June   NIE staff size is 375
                Twenty-three "key positions" unfilled
October   (Senate Appropriations Committee recommends $75
                    million for fiscal year 1974)
                Wise named associate director for Office of Research
December   (Five Priorities announced)

1974
April   Raizen named associate director for Office of
                    Dissemination
                (House denies supplemental request)
May   (Executive Committee formed)
                Executive recruitment moved into the Office of
                    Administration
                (Supplemental budget request denied)
June   NIE staff size is 426
August   Glennan resigns
November   (Conference Committee recommends $70 million for
                    fiscal year 1975)

Hiring in Bulk: The Transfer of OE Personnel

One powerful theme recurring throughout the NIE planning period was that NIE must not be another OE. It was imperative that NIE attract "better people" than OE had done. OE personnel were perceived to be uninterested in the substance of research—to be paper pushers, and not even competent paper pushers at that.[1] Nevertheless, on 1 August 1972, NIE announced it had just hired eighty-four people from the Office of Education.[2] It is difficult to answer the question, "How did it happen?" There were eight major actors: Congress, the American Federation of Government Employees (AFL–CIO), the Civil Service Commission, the NIE Planning Unit, the Unholy Trinity, Sidney Marland, John Ottina, and Emerson Elliott. Most were only loosely related to one another. No one actor was in charge of the entire process.

Congress stipulated in the NIE legislation that the budget authority associated with certain OE programs, for example the Cooperative Research Program, would be transferred to NIE. This meant that the personnel positions or "slots" associated with these budget authorities would also transfer to NIE.[3] But those slots were not empty; at the time of the budget transfer most of them were occupied by OE employees. The American Federation of Government Employees began insisting in 1971 that every OE employee whose program transferred to NIE must be transferred with it. Union threats of lawsuits against both OE and NIE if this policy were not carried out led OE to ask for a review of the applicable Civil Service statutes. It was the opinion of the Civil Service Commission that if OE programs were transferred intact to NIE, the OE personnel working in those programs must be offered positions commensurate with their current positions, but they did not have to be positions in NIE. Comparable OE position would suffice.

The Unholy Trinity did not launch a strong protest against NIE's receiving the OE budget authority, because the budget transfer was viewed as a sure way to provide funds for NIE. At the time the legislation was written, it was believed that OE programs would be transferred, evaluated, and—presumably—drastically reduced on the basis of the evaluations. These actions would thereby provide substantial amounts of "new" money for the agency. At the time, the possible attendant transfer of personnel did not seem a pressing issue. ASPE assumed that all OE personnel could remain in OE. Furthermore, the orderly transition year envisioned by Levien and Moynihan and promised by Marland would allow for an open search for the best candidates to fill NIE positions. Any OE people judged best in open competition would come to NIE.

As we described in chapter 2, the Planning Unit had proposed allowing each interested OE employee to "try out" for a position in NIE by writing papers for the Planning Unit. On the basis of an evaluation of the papers, the Planning Unit would write a job description for each slot that would specifically include or exclude the current occupant of the slot (NIE Planning Unit, January 1972, p. 128). When this proposal was criticized by ASPE, who wanted no personnel transferred, and turned down by Marland, who did not want all the "rejects" to remain in OE, the Planning Unit effectively ceased work on the question of personnel transfer (Silberman, 28 February 1974). This meant no one was working on this question until the NIE legislation passed.

Sidney Marland, then commissioner of education, was determined to avoid any congressional criticism of his role in the early days of NIE. And so he vowed that on 1 July 1972—the day stipulated by Congress for NIE to receive program responsibility—all positions in OE associated with those programs would be abolished, and the personnel occupying them would be reassigned (Marland, 22 March 1974). Marland's interpretation of congressional intent created and imposed a very early deadline for the transfer. Marland asked John Ottina, his deputy commissioner for planning, evaluation, and management, to develop a personnel transfer plan. The main objectives of the plan were "to offer each individual a position that is compatible with his skills and interests, is at least equal to his current salary and GS classification, which will lead to the more effective accomplishment of NIE and OE objectives, and is legal" (OE, n.d., p. 1). Ottina's office recognized only two possible options for dealing with the problem: either "offer NIE positions to all OE personnel whose positions are affected" or "make decisions on an individual basis, offering some NIE positions and some OE positions" (OE, n.d., p. 1). The third option, offer OE positions to all OE personnel whose positions were affected, was not mentioned.

During this period Emerson Elliott was overwhelmed with responsibilities. He had neither time nor resources to study or alter the plan Ottina developed. Furthermore, Elliott had no power base of his own from which to launch an alternative plan even if he had wanted to; technically, Marland was his supervisor during this period.

Ottina's plan created the OE personnel lottery.[4] On 5 July 1972 meetings were held with the 147 OE staff members occupying slots to be transferred to NIE, informing them of openings in NIE and OE, assuring them that each person would receive a job offer from one of the two agencies, and asking them to complete preference sheets indicating in which agency they would prefer to work. The preference sheets were sent, with each person's employment history and official personnel folder, to representatives of NIE (Emerson Elliott) and OE (four deputy commissioners). On July 22 these five individuals met in the commissioner's conference room to divide up the people.

In the initial round, each of the five selecting units—NIE plus the four OE bureaus—named its first five choices of individuals. NIE was allowed to name first because it had the largest number of vacancies to fill. After this initial round, in which the twenty-five "most desirable" people were chosen, the order of selection was based on the number of vacancies in each unit. For every four people NIE selected, the deputy commissioner for school systems selected one; for every five people NIE selected, the deputy commissioner for higher education selected one, and so on (OE, 12 July 1972, p. 2). Elliott had prepared a list of the people he wanted to bid for, based on recommendations from Silberman and the heads of transferring programs and on a brief reading of personnel folders. The list included the thirty-four members of the two programs transferred intact plus enough other individuals to reach his quota of eighty-four people.[5] But as the lottery proceeded, many of the people on Elliott's list were chosen by other units. He recalled, "By the time we got to the middle of the voting, I was very hard pressed each time my turn came up to find five people that I wanted . . . and you could not pass" (25 March 1974, p. 25).

The selection continued until everyone was placed, with NIE receiving eighty-four people including the last ten to be chosen. Only one day before the lottery Ottina had discovered NIE was entitled to four more slots than he had realized. Instead of revising the selection formula to reflect the additional

NIE slots or allowing NIE to choose four more people in the initial round, he decided that each of the four OE units would "give up" its final selection to NIE. Elliott later remarked, "I didn't think about it at the time. And nobody else did, either. It was a perfectly honest mistake" (25 March 1974, p. 26).

Thus through a combination of events and actors—congressional stipulation, union threat, bureaucratic regulation, Planning Unit and Unholy Trinity inattention, Marland's self-imposed deadline, Ottina's interest in fairness, Elliott's crowded schedule, and a last-minute juggling of the lottery—NIE acquired its first personnel.

In addition to the OE transfers, NIE soon hired the entire Planning Unit staff. Silberman had assured Elliott that no promises of long-term employment had been given any member of the Planning Unit; each would have to compete for an NIE job on the same basis as other applicants. But the Planning Unit staff insisted they had been promised jobs, and by 15 October 1972 Elliott had agreed to hire them all (Silberman, 28 February 1974; Elliott, 25 March 1974). This added fifteen more people to the personnel roster. Thus before the agency was four months old or had a director, it had bulk-hired seventy-four professionals and twenty-five secretaries and clerks. In those early days, no one was overly concerned; the agency would grow quickly and would have no trouble absorbing those people.

The Director

The process of choosing an appropriate first director for NIE had begun long before Congress had authorized the new agency. Before externally imposed deadlines changed the nature of the process, thinking about the selection of the first NIE director had an almost religious quality. This person would be chosen to lead education R&D out of the Office of Education and into its own place in the sun. A 1971 memorandum from ASPE to the counselor to HEW described the kind of person who could fill such a position. He (*sic*) should be:

(1) *A humanist* . . . who never loses sight of the gravity and immediacy of the human problems whose solutions our research seeks.

(2) *An eminent scientist* . . . who can elicit the support of [education] researchers and of practitioners, as well as direct the attention of other intellectuals currently outside the education research area to the solution of education's important problems. . . . The best person . . . would be an eminent man of science, not himself an educational researcher, but knowledgeable, and acknowledged to be so, in the profession.

(3) *A capable administrator and representative* . . . [with] experience in administering large scale research projects or similar undertakings . . . [and] able to articulate [NIE's] mission and its value to the remainder of the government and the general public.

(4) *Politically neutral or independent.* . . . It is hard to see how the Institute can retain the bipartisan support which has thus far characterized its legislative history unless its Director is clearly non-political. [ASPE, 1971, pp. 1–3]

Beginning in early 1971, staff in ASPE, OST, the Planning Unit, and the OE commissioner's office drew up lists of candidates who might meet these criteria. During the spring of 1972 several candidates, including Professor Lawrence Cremin of Columbia University Teachers College, turned down informal offers, citing other professional commitments or a distaste for working in Washington (Elliott, 25 March 1974). By July 1972 James Coleman, then professor of sociology at Johns Hopkins University, was the leading candidate. Secretary Richardson formally offered him the directorship at the beginning of August 1972. Coleman was deeply intrigued by the offer; he envisioned it as an opportunity to implement an idea he strongly advocated—to replicate within an organization the national population age distribution. Had he become NIE's first director, he would have wanted infants, schoolchildren, working adults, and senior citizens all on the NIE payroll. But Coleman decided he was "a man of ideas, not a man of action," and so he turned down the NIE offer at the end of August (Coleman, May 1975). In mid-August, Elliott had gone on vacation thinking that when he returned his new boss would be James Coleman. Instead, on a rainy day in a telephone booth in Ogunquit, Maine, Elliott learned that Coleman had turned down the offer and that Thomas K. Glennan, Jr., would be nominated as first director of NIE (Elliott, 28 November 1973).

With Coleman's rejection of the directorship, the pressure intensified to find someone quickly; early expectations about qualities necessary in a director were modified. A new criterion was added to the top of the list—immediate availability. Glennan's name had been on several of the lists of candidates as a result of his senior position at OEO and his work on various White House task forces. But Glennan, then assistant director of OEO for planning, research, and evaluation, was only mildly interested when Marland approached him about NIE. However, Secretary Richardson intervened and, in a long personal interview, explained his hopes for NIE and persuaded Glennan to take the job, assuring him he would have the complete support of the secretary[6] (Upp, 27 March 1974). Glennan's nomination was confirmed by the Senate on 18 October 1972, and he was sworn in by Richardson on 1 November.

Tom Glennan had graduated from Swarthmore in 1957, majoring in electrical engineering. He earned a master's degree in industrial management from MIT and a Ph.D. in economics from Stanford University in 1967, writing his dissertation on "New Product Development: Some Observations Based on the Development of Military Aircraft." He worked for the Rand Corporation as a research economist for eight years, coming to Washington in

1969, at the age of thirty-four, as director of research and evaluation in OEO. While at OEO he had developed a reputation for supporting interesting social policy programs—for example, performance contracting and education vouchers—and for competent management in the sticky area of social research. He had also become a member of the informal club of OE critics.[7]

Glennan, a large, usually slightly rumpled man with an engaging grin and informal style, seemed well suited for the new agency. He spent much of his day bursting in and out of offices, complimenting someone on a good piece of work, asking someone else for an opinion on a new memorandum. He liked nothing better than a rousing intellectual debate on a social policy issue and encouraged talented young members of the institute to participate extensively in important decisions. His management style resembled that of the leader of a good university seminar in which strength of intellect is more important than seniority and the free exchange of reasoned criticism is highly valued.

Although his policy research credentials were good, Glennan had little political or educational research experience. At OEO he had been a relatively protected staff member; the OEO director managed most of the external political relationships. Furthermore, he had never had to develop the skills of an office politician. His staff at OEO had been small, fewer than a hundred at its largest, and almost all had been hand-picked by Glennan. He had never had to live with someone else's personnel selections or delegate authority to people he had not hired or did not know. Nor was he well known within the education community. (To some OE critics this might have been considered an asset.) While at Rand, he had published papers on topics familiar or of interest to only a few members of the education community.[8] After coming to OEO, if he were known at all, it was as an advocate of performance contracting and the education voucher experiment—two programs viewed with great disfavor by the teachers organizations. Within the informal club of Washington staff concerned with education, Glennan was respected as a sharp analyst. He had no particular ideological preferences, no personal interest in any specific age-group or educational problem, but was willing and able to apply his analytic skills to whatever seemed important.

Second-level Leadership

Glennan immediately named Emerson Elliott his deputy director. He also named Bernard Martin, whom Elliott was using as a consultant, as associate director for the Office of Planning and Management. Martin, thirty-five at the time of his appointment, belonged to the informal OE-critics club. He had been an education budget officer in OMB, did staff work for the White House group that had recommended the creation of NIE, and had been a member of the Planning Unit steering committee. Glennan, Elliott, and Martin formed the senior leadership triangle for much of NIE's first year. Although all were relatively young, each had extensive staff experience in federal agencies. They brought well-sharpened analytic tools to their jobs, although none had ever managed an agency before. If these three could be said to have a constituency, it was to be found in that group to which they all belonged—bright, competent staff members primarily in such offices as OST, OMB, and ASPE—an intelligent but not, by and large, bureaucratically or politically experienced group.

Glennan could not fill the entire senior staff with analysts, however. As a result of the bulk hiring, Glennan inherited six men who—as a result of their civil service classification—comprised a portion of the senior leadership cadre. Three of the six remained at NIE for only a year or less.[9] The departure of these three men symbolized NIE's early, perhaps unintentional, rejection of the educationists—educational psychologists, school practitioners, and the Office of Education. Of the three remaining members of the senior personnel inheritance, one saw his program abolished at the end of the first year. The other two won at least chary respect from the leadership trio and, although they never became members of the inner circle, continued to operate their programs for at least two years.[10]

Shortly after hiring Martin, Glennan named Ernest Russell associate director for the Office of Administration. Glennan had known Russell at OEO, where he had held a similar position. At about this same time Glennan also hired two senior advisers. He named Richard Werksman, who had been assistant general counsel in OEO, his legal adviser, and named John Mays from OST his science adviser. These were fairly easy hiring decisions. Both were "good people"; that is, they had excellent education credentials and records with the "right" government agencies.[11] Both were available, because President Nixon was about to abolish OEO and OST was near extinction. And neither was important in any formal programmatic sense—neither had permanent responsibility for running any of the institute's programs. Two more advisers—one for human rights and one for external affairs—were also hired by the end of the first year.

During NIE's second year, two out of three associate directors for programmatic areas were hired. In October 1973, Glennan appointed Arthur Wise, associate director for the Office of Research. Wise, thirty-one at the time of his appointment, came to NIE from the University of Chicago, where he was associate professor in the economics of education and associate dean of the School of Education. In March 1974, Glennan named Senta Raizen, who had briefly worked with the NIE Planning Unit and then joined the Rand Corporation, associate director for dissemination. Raizen had just completed a Rand design for the evaluation of the Head Start program. When she came to NIE, she brought with her experience in the design of policy evaluation for large-scale social intervention programs as well as her nine years' experience in managing curriculum development programs for NSF.

The Younger Managers and the Inner Circle

Because Wise and Raizen were not appointed until NIE's second year (and indeed an associate director for programs was never appointed), the managers of individual programs such as career education and education vouchers reported directly to Glennan throughout NIE's first year. Some of these managers were very important figures during the institute's first year, not only because they ran the agency's programs, but also because they participated vigorously in debates over agencywide issues.

Table 5.1   The Younger Managers: July 1973

Age	Sex	Race	Education			Government Experience	
			Highest Degree	Institution	Field	Number of Years	Agency
33	M	W	M.A.	Berkeley	Political Science	2	OEO
30	M	W	Ph.D.	Ohio State	Political Science	1	OEO
33	M	W	Ph.D.	U. Michigan	Psychology	2	OE
34	F	W	Ed.D.	Harvard	Education Development	1	ASPE
42	M	W	Ph.D.	U. Wisconsin	Psychology	6	OEO
34	M	W	B.A.	Brown	Literature	0	–
36	M	W	Ed.D.	Harvard	Statistics	0	–
28	F	W	–	–	–	3	OEO

As a group these people were very young; they were also well educated (see table 5.1 for characteristics of this group). One of the younger managers had been a Planning Unit consultant; another had worked for ASPE. Four came from OEO, one came from OE, and one came from Harvard University.

Although they lacked substantial government experience, Glennan believed they were competent. And they were certainly confident and enthusiastic. Some of the members of this group came to constitute an inner circle around Glennan.[12] They were willing, even eager, to take on special assignments for him and were often to be found in his office after six in the evening debating the most recent agencywide issue. They were his advisers, assistants, and friends. In the words of one of the members of the inner circle, "[We are] immodest, young, foolishly willing to deal with a broad range of issues beyond our competence, curious, quick studies." In the words of another, who left the inner circle after the first budget cut, "[It's] a children's crusade."

Analogous to Glennan's inner circle was a small group of management specialists that revolved around Elliott. In their late twenties or early thirties, trained in business management or economics, these young men were given responsibility over a wide range of areas. One developed the plan for the first formal organization structure. One was in charge of congressional relations for the first year. Two, at separate times, were responsible for senior personnel recruitment. One ran the Office of Administration until its associate director was hired. One ran the research grants program. Although they were perceived as bright and talented by some members of the senior staff, at least two of them developed reputations as arrogant upstarts. Given to remarks such as "[the OE-transfer personnel are the] eighty or ninety most nonenthu-siastic, nondynamic, noncreative people you can imagine," they did not move through the institute in a diplomatic fashion. It was one of this group who hung up on Senator Claiborne Pell's staff assistant. Because these men had easy access to Elliott, many people assumed their attitudes and actions reflected, or were at least condoned by, the senior leadership of the agency.

Recruiting

During NIE's first two years, the process for recruiting senior personnel cycled through a number of phases. It began in a highly rational style, in the early fall of 1972, with a memorandum from Martin's office describing an eight-step process for recruiting:

1. Agreement on positions to be filled
2. Further definition of job requirements and characteris-tics to be pursued
3. Suggestions by all NIE interested staff of prospective candidates
4. Further identification of candidates
5. Paper review of interested candidates by a NIE staff panel
6. Interviewing of top several candidates by appropriate NIE staff people
7. Preparation of a written summary presenting staff reac-tions and reference checks with recommendations of top two or three candidates to the Director
8. Interviews and selection by Director. [Task Force on Planning and Management, n.d., pp. 6–7]

Had there been early agreement on an organization structure, this deductive strategy might have been both efficient and effective; however it was not until May 1973 that the first official organization structure was decided upon. Recruiting could not wait for an organization structure.

In the late fall of 1972, in the absence of "agreement on positions to be filled," recruiting efforts centered on the "great minds." As a result of the conferences organized by Mays and the Planning Unit during the previous eighteen months, NIE had a list of approximately ninety prime recruiting targets, the majority of them university-based academicians. During the late fall of 1972, NIE leadership assumed that attracting notables to NIE was a good strategy, no matter what the final organization structure would look like. The rhetoric of the planning period had advocated attracting high-status researchers; to the extent that NIH staffing was a model for NIE, it suggested the same strategy. Finally, the senior staff member who devoted the most time to thinking about recruiting during this period was John Mays, whose prior experience at NSF and OST emphasized attracting the "best minds" to contribute their knowledge to solving government problems.

One consequence of the great-minds strategy was that NIE began to hear rejections from the people who were most attractive to the institute. Although a number of reasons having nothing to do with NIE can explain such rejections, they were interpreted by NIE leadership as a signal that the agency was not yet rational and scientific enough to be attractive to the great minds.[13] Mays, with at least the tacit support of Glennan, Elliott, and Martin, continued to press for a tighter, more compelling rationale for the agency's structure and activities.

During the spring of 1973 Mays, who was then directing the $10-million basic research grants competition, had little time to devote to senior personnel recruitment. Glennan asked one of the young management assistants, who had come to NIE from OMB, to take on this responsibility during that period. Although the assistant willingly accepted the task, he was not well prepared for it. He had no professional reputation or stature within the scholarly or education R&D community that he could use to promote personal contacts. And he received little guidance from Elliott and Glennan in terms of projected organization or program structure. Glennan and Elliott attended to the recruiting process only sporadically. They would vigorously pursue an attractive candidate for a period but when, for whatever reason, that candidate decided not to accept an offer, Glennan and Elliott would turn their attention to any of the other demands competing for their time.

At the end of the first year there were twenty-three senior positions, described as "key positions," still unfilled. By this time, the nature of the 375 people already hired was beginning to constrain further choices.[14] Younger program managers who were already well on the way to establishing their programs and reputations within the institute had won for themselves the implicit right of approval of any person who would be their superior. In some cases the institute had to hire leaders for programs whose staff size had already reached capacity as a result of OE transfers or the early hiring of junior people. These conditions persisted until the time of the budget cut, then a new set of constraints—based on political considerations—was added to the system.

Several factors external to the recruitment process itself contributed to its lack of success. Time constraints, ambiguity of purpose, and the budget cuts were the principal factors. Glennan and Elliott had so many competing demands for their time that they devoted personal attention to recruitment only sporadically. Uncertainty about the agency's agenda—the kinds of research and development it should be supporting—made it difficult to settle on an organization structure. Uncertainty about the organization structure made it difficult to project specific openings. It also made it difficult to describe to desirable candidates what their responsibilities would be and where they would be located in the agency's structure and hierarchy.[15]

Uncertainty about purpose and structure led to changes over time in the descriptions of desirable characterictics or job responsibilities for persons filling senior positions. The position description for the associate director for the Office of Programs was rewritten four times from the fall of 1972 to the spring of 1974 (see table 5.2). The first description was created by Martin's staff during the rational period in the fall of 1972. It emphasized management and conceptualizing abilities. In June 1973 the management assistant created the second description, which emphasized sensitivity to internal politics. In this description the "supervisory skills" characteristic from the fall of 1972 had become, "experience in supervising independent research managers." This change signaled the realization that the "independent research managers" were already a feature of the organization; therefore whoever stepped in above them must be able to cope with them. In February 1974—after the first budget cut—John Mays prepared a job description emphasizing sensitivity to external political problems. In April 1974 Martin's assistant, who had replaced the previous management assistant as the day-to-day director of the recruiting efforts, prepared yet another "list of possible criteria" for the position. By this time, the process of accumulating more and more criteria for the role of associate director led to a set that no one person could fill.[16]

In spite of the incompatibility of several of the criteria listed in any of the position descriptions, all had their advocates inside the agency. In any meeting held to evaluate a candidate for the position of associate director for the Office of Programs, each participant would champion his or her favorite criterion. Mays, for example, could be counted upon to evaluate carefully the candidate's scholarly reputation; the human rights adviser was unhappy with anyone not sensitive to minority concerns; one of the assistant directors always pressed for someone with extensive school experience, and so on. In the absence of a higher authority (for example, a completely specified program of research) against which these competing opinions could be measured, no candidate could be judged "better" than any other. The director did not arbitrarily impose a decision, and so no decision was made.

Events or factors external to the recruiting process affected its course dramatically. Several factors inherent in the process itself—principally its day to day leadership, the changing nature of sources for names, and its

Table 5.2   Job Descriptions for the Position of
                                                  Associate Director for the Office
                                                  of Programs: Fall 1972 to Spring 1974

Fall 1972
    Management experience
    Conceptualization skills
    Supervisory skills, preferably with experience in supervising fairly large numbers of people
    Knowledge of research and education

June 1973
    Experience in managing large-scale research or similar programs
    Experience in supervising independent research managers
    Capacity to delegate responsibilities
    Demonstrated flexibility
    Familiarity with education issues
    Demonstrated analytical and conceptual skill
    Experience in evaluating social programs

February 1974
    External relations
        1. Public presentation of the program
        2. Relations with school people and others in education
        3. Relations with the R&D community (including social and behavioral and other science
            departments as well as research oriented schools of education)
    Conceptualization, planning, and evaluation of
        1. The individual programs
        2. The overall Office of Programs' effort
    Resource allocation among individual programs
    Program management
        1. Management of the individual programs
        2. Coordination of the operation of the several programs, e.g.,
            a. pursuing opportunities for useful interaction
            b. common procedures for development, data-gathering, etc., where appropriate
        3. Establishment and maintenance of internal operating procedures

---

April 1974
    Substantive knowledge of the major federal policy issues facing education and
        educational R&D
    Management experience under following conditions
        1. Large-scale development
        2. Broad span of control
        3. Aggressive immediate staff
    Strong scholarly reputation
    Strong reputation to educational practitioner and research communities
    Bureaucratic/political experience in government
    Effective public spokesman
    Credibility with minority and disadvantaged communities

                                        Sources: Task Force on Planning and
                                        Management, n.d.; Goldman, 17 May 1974.

cumbersome procedures—also impeded its progress. We have noted that the major day-to-day responsibility for recruiting during NIE's first year rested with one of the young management assistants. During the second year the responsibility continued to rest with a staff assistant, but three different assistants held the job during the year, thereby adding lack of continuity to the original problematic situation. Each time the responsibility changed hands, the process slowed down. The process was sensitive not only to who was directing it, but also to who was recommending candidates. Early in the process many of the nominees were scholars, recommended by academicians who had attended Planning Unit conferences. As the process continued, more of the recommendations came from NIE staff—only five outside sources of names were acknowledged for the first six months of 1974—and from a small number of NIE staff at that. In addition to Glennan and Elliott and two of the staff assistants, only eight members of the NIE staff made formal recommendations during the first half of 1974 (Goldman, 17 May 1974).

In spite of specific procedures that were to be completed before introducing a name at a senior staff meeting, those who attended those meetings could—and did—short-circuit the process. For example, at a meeting in April 1974, six individuals were "identified as potential candidates who should be contacted." For each of these individuals background information, collection of resumes, and preliminary reference checks had been completed. After agreement had been reached on these six candidates, Mays reintroduced a name he had submitted two months earlier, one in which there had been no interest at the time. Martin's staff man then proposed a candidate who had never before appeared on any list. These two names were also added to the contact list (Goldman 17 May 1974, pp. 18–19). This kind of short-circuiting indicated tacit recognition by senior staff that the formal procedures were slow, unwieldy, and unlikely to produce results.[17] At the end of May 1974, executive recruitment was moved into the Personnel Division in the Office of Administration. This move was formal recognition of the same point.

Staff Growth and Personnel Characteristics

NIE approximately tripled in size during its first year, from 84 people on 1 August 1972 to 375 people on 30 June 1973. During its second year, growth slowed. Nevertheless the staff size did increase 14% to a total of 426 employees by 30 June 1974. The majority of NIE's professional staff came to NIE from one of three different employers: OE, OEO, or a college or university.[18] The largest proportion were from OE (25%); 17% were from OEO; and 15% were from colleges or universities. Although their similarities are probably greater than their differences, even after the agency was two years old the groups were perceived by those inside the agency to be distinct. The OE group was the oldest of the three, with an average age of forty-two.

The university group was the youngest, with an average age of thirty-four. And the OEO average age was thirty-eight. As a group, the university people tended to work late at the office more than the other groups. (Thus these people tended to be found at the informal gatherings Glennan held in his office after 6 P.M. "for whoever was around.")[19] When asked to characterize the kind of person they believed it was most important for NIE to hire, the majority of the OE people believed it was most important to hire school practitioners and experienced civil servants; the majority of the OEO people believed it was most important to hire managers; the majority of the university people believed it was most important for NIE to hire scholars. The distribution of these three groups was not uniform across major offices (see table 5.3). The density of OE personnel was lowest in the Office of the Director and highest in the Office of Dissemination. The density of OEO personnel was lowest in the Office of Dissemination and highest in the Office of Administration (second highest in the Office of Programs). The density of university personnel was highest in the Office of Research.

Table 5.3   Distribution of NIE Professional
                                        Personnel by Office and Career
                                        Background: June 1974

Immediate Prior Employer	NIE Organization Unit					
	Director	Administration	Programs	Research	Dissemination	Total
OE	3	11	15	19	12	60
OEO	8	17	11	14	1	51
University	5	1	8	24	4	42
Other federal	8	17	4	6	4	39
State and local education agencies	2	2	5	4	2	15
Other	14	5	14	9	–	42
Total	40	53	57	76	23	249[a]

[a]This represents 86% of the professional staff. Data taken from questionnaire administered June 1974 ($N = 288$).

Models of Hiring and Growth

Despite the limited success of the formal executive recruiting process we have described above, the agency was obviously hiring people. As we have noted, by the end of its second year NIE employed more than four hundred

people. Several different models of hiring and growth are useful in understanding how they were hired.

One standard hiring model is that of cell division, a top-down model in
which the three or four most senior people are hired immediately; they, or
their deputies, in turn create subdivisions and hire all the junior people.[20] Of
the early senior leadership trio—Glennan, Elliott, and Martin—Martin is the
only one who hired a personal staff of more than three or four people. This
model was of only limited usefulness to NIE for several reasons. As a result of
the bulk hiring, a large number of junior people were in place before senior
people were hired. Second, as a result of the transferred programs, NIE had to
conduct business like an ongoing agency from its first day of operation; there
was no start-up time available to look for senior people who could establish
their own divisions de novo. Third, Glennan had not yet firmly settled on an
organization structure, and so it was not possible to offer a senior person the
opportunity to create a specific division within that structure.

When a cell-division model is not applicable, hiring and growth may
proceed by imitation. NIE's Office of Administration was the fastest-growing
unit during the early days. Everyone knew what an Office of Administration
should look like; therefore the lack of a master plan for the entire agency did
not impede the hiring of eighty people for that office in six months. But an
imitation model was also of only limited utility. Constantly reiterated during
the NIE planning period was the theme that NIE was to be unique. It was to
embrace certain features of other agencies, to be sure, but no single agency
provided a template for the entire organization.

Another possible model, for an organization that cannot use cell-division or
imitation, is the paint-by-numbers model. If the leader of the organization
has a clear picture of what the organization should look like—what its major
activities should be, how it should be structured, what kinds of people should
fill its positions—then all job applicants can be evaluated against that picture.
(In effect, that was the model employed in the senior personnel recruiting
system.) But the NIE picture was so unclear that position descriptions kept
changing, based on an ever increasing set of criteria that was impossible to
fulfill.

None of the three most common models of hiring and personnel growth
was very appropriate for NIE. In each case the combination of an ambiguous
mission and expectations for rational, comprehensive analysis confounded a
pure strategy. Three additional models are potentially useful for an agency
with an ambiguous mission—a political model, an entrepreneurial model, and
a "good people" model.

In a political model the director would say, "I may not know what I want to
do, but no matter what it is I will need political support to do it, so I will hire
people who are politically astute and who have ties to constituencies I must
serve."[21] Several factors militated against the employment of a political

model, the most powerful being the expectations and norms of rationality and comprehensive analysis. OE had been excoriated for politicizing educational R&D; NIE could not embark upon that course. Additionally, even if Glennan had wanted to pursue a political strategy, it was not clear to NIE's leadership during its first year of existence just who the NIE constituents were. Finally, with respect to staffing the Office of External Relations, it was difficult to find a person with Washington political experience eager to work for such a small agency.

In a second model appropriate to an agency with an ambiguous mission—the entrepreneurial model—the director would say, "I may not know what I want, but I will hire people who have specific plans. One or more of these people is bound to produce something successful. When those successes occur, I will have discovered what I want."[22] Again, the norms of rational comprehensive analysis blocked this approach for NIE. A patchwork quilt of good, but unrelated projects would have been an unacceptable comedown from the comprehensive designs of the Levien Preliminary Plan and the promises made during the congressional hearings.

In the third model—the "good people" model—the director would say, "I may not know what I want, but I will hire 'good people' who will be flexible enough to fit any strategy, and together we will build a good agency." Had this model been implemented, we would expect to see a small group of individuals closely surrounding Glennan and participating in a very broad range of policy decisions. In fact, the younger managers and the "inner circle" described above do fit this characterization.

Thus it seems that a reasonable explanation of how NIE's staff grew to more than four hundred people in two years would invoke several hiring models, each of which applies to a different portion of the institute. Cell-division describes the growth of Martin's staff; imitation, the growth of the Office of Administration. A paint-by-numbers model describes the senior personnel recruitment process. A "good people" model describes the growth of the younger manager and "inner circle" contingent. (And, of course, hiring in bulk describes the acquisition of the Planning Unit and OE transfer personnel.)

Conclusion

NIE experienced disappointments in its personnel search. The fact that the early expectations for a rational, deductive recruiting process were unrealized was only one indication that NIE would not be as perfect as its creators had hoped. The fact that some of the "best minds" in the country turned down job offers was another such indication. The bulk hiring of the OE and NIE Planning Unit personnel constrained the new agency in several ways. The presence of the OE transfer personnel was a symbolic indication that NIE was little different from OE. More practically, the presence of these ninety-nine people meant that recruiting for most senior managerial positions could not rely on the standard new organization enticement of giving new managers the opportunity to build their own staffs.

The persistence of identifiable differences among the three major groups of personnel—those from OE, OEO, and universities—impeded the development of an agencywide spirit of cohesiveness. Further, it led to somewhat erratic internal communications patterns. And it engendered some ill-will by fostering the belief that some kinds of people were favored by top management over other kinds of people.

The existence of an inner circle undoubtedly affected the agency. It led to a denigration of the notions of formal status, authority, and power. One member of the senior staff observed, "There's a perception that power is personalized, if you're friends with the director you don't have to abide by the bureaucratic rules" (Martin, June, 1974a). Because membership in the inner circle was somewhat fluid, reaching consensus in that forum on any major issue was difficult. Within the inner circle the criteria for closure—What is an "acceptable" solution?—and indeed, the issues themselves—What is an "acceptable" problem?—changed over time. Thus, although the inner circle may have served Glennan well in providing a forum for deliberations, it probably impeded the making and implementing of major decisions (chapter 8 discusses the role of the inner circle in three major decision situations).

NIE leadership believed that superior staff would create a superior agency. Of course everyone would prefer to work with more competent and congenial people rather than less competent and congenial ones. And on balance NIE probably hired more than its share of the former. But to expect that paragons of political, managerial, and intellectual genius existed, let alone would choose to work for NIE, was bound to lead to disappointment. It also led, as we shall see in chapter 9, to an undervaluing of some of the people who had been hired by the agency.

Six   Programs

The core of any R&D agency is the R&D programs it supports; the significance and quality of the agency's programs are often thought to be an important determinant of external evaluations and continued appropriations. NIE had difficulties in establishing its own R&D identity. In its first two and a half years NIE had to manage more than $100 million in programs transferred from other agencies, principally OE. In addition to their problematic political legacy which we discussed in chapter 4, these programs also presented NIE with a vastly complicated bureaucratic and managerial inheritance. The fate of these programs within NIE illustrates the wide range of strategies that may be employed by a new agency in managing its inheritance. Furthermore, the interactions among these programs and such other factors as the hiring of personnel and the creating of organization structures illustrate some of the consequences associated with the strategy of creating a "new" agency out of "old" components.

In this chapter we first examine the programs transferred to NIE and then describe NIE's "new" programs. The level of analysis is fairly general. We do not detail the internal management, structure, or content of the program units—that would require a separate book. Rather we attempt to convey some sense of the range and scope of the activities composing NIE's R&D program.

We attempt to answer four questions:

What strategies were used in managing the programs transferred from other agencies?

What was the impact of NIE's new program during its first year of operations?

How did NIE's inheritance influence the development of the Institute's own programs?

What might have been plausible alternative strategies for dealing with NIE's programmatic structure?

Programs Chronology

1972

June	Nixon signs NIE legislation
August	$110 million worth of programs transferred from OE to NIE

1973

January	NIE announces new Field Initiated Studies program
June	NIE funds 6.5% of the Field Initiated Studies proposals
July	$34 million worth of programs transferred from OE and OEO
October	(Senate Appropriations Committee recommends $75 million for fiscal year 1974)
December	Five Priorities announced

1974

April	(House denies supplemental request)
August	(Glennan resigns)
November	NIE reorganized, abolishing field initiated research and revising five priority areas
	(Conference Committee recommends $70 million for fiscal year 1975)

The Inherited Programs

On 1 August 1972, NIE inherited $110 million worth of programs from the Office of Education. A year later it inherited an additional $34 million worth of programs from OE and OEO (see table 6.1 for major inherited programs). The fate of these programs within NIE was shaped by a complicated interaction among personalities, bureaucratic momentum, politics, and the initial expectations for rationality and comprehensiveness.

The Regional Education Laboratories and R&D Centers program, whose creation within OE was described in chapter 1, was the largest inherited program. It comprised $35.9 million worth of contracts with twenty-three institutions. At the time of transfer, the majority of the funds were devoted to development work such as teacher training and curriculum development (more than $17.4 million for curriculum development alone). In addition, almost every institution had at least a small basic research unit.

In the early months of NIE's existence, managing the laboratories and R&D centers program was hampered by two factors. The first was a lack of useful documentation about the content of the work under way at the various institutions.[1] The second was an NIE management decision that assigned responsibility for the program to two different managers at the same time. Glennan and Elliott gave one of the younger managers, Marc Tucker, responsibility for the laboratories and centers evaluation and "transition," that is, the process of negotiating new, often lower, funding levels on the basis of that evaluation. And Wilmer Cody, from the Planning Unit, was directing the "Applied Studies Task Force," which monitored the transferred projects on a day-to-day basis. This dual management impeded effective internal communications about the program. (It also confused and frustrated the

Table 6.1   NIE Programs Inherited from
                                            Other Agencies

		Amount (in millions)	
Date	Donor Agency	FY 1972	FY 1973
1972			
Regional Education Laboratories and R&D Centers	OE	$35.3	$35.9
Career Education	OE	16.7	11.5
Experimental Schools	OE	15.0	30.0
Dissemination (ERIC and other projects)	OE	7.6	15.8
Education for the Handicapped	OE	5.2	2.6
D.C. Schools Project	OE	2.2	2.2
Researcher training	OE	3.3	2.6
Unsolicited research	OE	7.7	—
1973			
Education Voucher Experiment	OEO		$20.0
Teacher Competence Study	OEO		6.5
Education Technology Program	OE		7.5

Sources: "NIE 1973 Budget Request,"
6 October 1972; "NIE FY 1972 Allocation
of Funds by Major Organizational Unit,"
10 July 1973. All figures are approximate.

laboratories and centers personnel in the field.) And it reduced the likelihood that a strong internal champion for laboratories and centers would emerge. As long as Tucker was on the scene, Cody was effectively prevented from building personnel and financial support for his contracts. Because NIE leadership did not see the laboratories and centers program as a coherent and cohesive entity, it would become fairly easy to split up that program during NIE's first reorganization.[2]

Career Education, a $11.5 million transfer, fared quite differently from the laboratories and centers program. Conceived in 1971 by Marland, Career Education began as an effort to infuse the entire K–12 curriculum with "awareness" about various careers. By the time it was transferred to NIE, it had grown into an elaborate four-component project. The school-based component or model continued the original notion of a large-scale curriculum project. The employer-based model, moving career education into the workplace, gave eleventh and twelfth grade students the opportunity to learn job skills and academic lessons on job sites in the community. The third component, the home-based model, had funded developmental work on a

daytime television program for unemployed adults. And the fourth component, the Mountain Plains residential-based model, moved low-income
families from a six-state region to a former Air Force base in Glasgow,
Montana, for intensive job training and schooling.

Corrine Rieder, another of the younger managers, took over this program
in the fall of 1972 and acted as the internal advocate which the laboratories
and centers program lacked. She commissioned independent reviews of all
career education projects. Then on the basis of those reviews, she cut back
most of the inherited projects by about 50% and refocused many of them on
the problems of adolescents and mid-career adults. After these cuts and
redirections, Rieder and her staff emphasized to NIE top management that
Career Education possessed an institutional and intellectual foundation they
were committed to protect and expand (Datta, June 1974). Glennan and
Elliott judged Rieder to be a first-rate analyst; her program prospered.

Experimental Schools, transferring with $30 million worth of contracts,
changed very little during NIE's first year.[3] Begun as an OE experiment in
1970 to test the hypothesis that comprehensive school reform was more likely
to lead to educational improvement than was a piecemeal and incremental
approach, the Experimental Schools program funded large-scale, multiyear
projects in a small number of school districts. Because of the multiyear
funding provision for this program, most of its expenditures, with the
exception of awards to any new sites, were predictable and difficult to reduce.
Additionally, the program director, Robert Binswanger, was supremely
assertive and self-assured. When the Planning Unit had attempted to gather
information on transferring programs in 1971, Binswanger refused to provide
it. And Silberman had no way to compel him to do so. Thus in the fall of 1972
his program was practically a complete mystery to Glennan and Elliott. When
NIE moved into its own first offices in October 1972, about two blocks away
from the OE building, Binswanger chose to keep his offices and staff in the
OE building. It was months before Experimental Schools was even under the
same roof with the rest of NIE.

Also transferred was the $15-million dissemination program that included
as its largest component ERIC, the network of eighteen clearinghouses for
computerized storage and retrieval of education documents. The program
also included an educational change-agent program based loosely on the
model of the agricultural extension agent, an information service for
educational publishers, and the beginning stages of a consumer-information
project. After the transfer, the director of the dissemination group, Lee
Burchinal, found himself and his group shut off from the top management.
Glennan and Elliott took the view that dissemination was an issue to be
studied. They believed that Burchinal's program, which was based on the
assumption that dissemination was primarily an issue of information transfer,
needed reassessment, and that Burchinal needed to be redirected. Unwilling

to see his program studied to death, Burchinal left NIE, and his group did little more than mark time for its first year at NIE (Burchinal, 23 June 1974).

In addition to these four very large programs, NIE received a number of smaller miscellaneous projects. Two consumed agency time and political capital far out of proportion to the size of their budgets. The first, the D. C. Schools Project, was a $2-million contract to upgrade eighteen elementary and secondary schools in the Anacostia district of Washington, D. C., through introducing open classroom techniques, individualized instruction, team teaching, and school-community advisory boards. This project had received some attention in the late spring of 1972 when OE announced it was terminating its funding. A sit-in by Anacostia parents and community representatives in Commissioner Marland's office brought newspaper stories, embarrassment, and continued funding. When the project was transferred to NIE, the agency felt some compunction to transform this into an R&D program, not an easy task for a school district with only a small research office, nor a welcome one for a community-school coalition that wanted action, not research. Complicated and delicate negotiations were necessary to bolster the R&D component of this program. The second project was the OE day-care center. Perhaps because the original contract to design the day-care center was with one of the educational laboratories, or perhaps because OE had no personnel to manage it, NIE inherited the responsibility for funding and monitoring a day-care center in the basement of the OE building for the children of forty OE employees. This was even more difficult to justify than the D. C. schools project. NIE funds were buying care for the children of OE employees at an annual cost of almost $4,000 per child (Tomlinson, 9 August 1974). Additionally, there was very little research going on. Although in theory the day-care center might have been an attractive laboratory where NIE-funded researchers could study early childhood learning, in practice it was simply an expensive day-care center.

Despite their varied subject matter, most of the programs transferred in July 1972 had several characteristics in common that shaped NIE's first year. They were all complicated; they required hours of attention from new NIE managers to understand their purposes and procedures. They were demanding; many of them required contract renegotiations or extensions before December 1972. Even the smallest of them had built-in constituent support—someone who would complain loudly if funds were withdrawn. (At least two of the programs, Career Education and the laboratories and centers, were represented directly on Capitol Hill by their own lobbying groups.) And some of the programs were politically controversial. The D. C. Schools Projects and the Mountain Plains Career Education Project both had congressmen interested in their well-being. Finally, many of the transferred programs—begun as service projects, as grants-in-aid to deserving sites, or as hurry-up efforts to put something "in the field"—simply were not research and development programs. A different director might have chosen to ignore those programs completely, allowing them to die a quiet, bureaucratic death when their contracts expired. But Glennan felt obliged to recover the government's prior investment and to turn them into creditable programs.

At the beginning of its second year—1 July 1973—NIE inherited three more programs: the OEO Education Voucher Experiment, the OEO Teacher Competence Study, and the OE Education Technology Program. The Voucher Project, originally funded by Glennan's staff at OEO in 1970–71, was supposed to give parents the opportunity to select the school their child would attend, then to pay for his education with a voucher worth the per pupil cost of educating the child. Conceived as an experiment in accountability and alternative delivery systems for education, the program was first implemented in the Alum Rock District in San Jose, California.[4] The move from OEO to NIE had little immediate effect on the Voucher Project. Glennan was familiar with the project, respected and liked its manager, and was happy to see it continue within NIE. After the budget cuts began, however, the Voucher Project came to be defined as a political liability. The program was not comparatively large—the Alum Rock budget was less than $2 million in 1972, one-third the size of the Career Education school-based model, for example. But it was almost the only piece of social engineering the agency was funding. Because it was well publicized, it was very visible to the powerful national teachers' organizations, who found it objectionable.[5]

Unlike the Voucher Project, the Education Technology program and the Teacher Competence Study aroused few strong sentiments. One major component of the Technology program was a regional educational television program run by the State University of Nebraska, offering courses for college credit to students unable to reach the university. A second component, the Education Satellite project, paid for the development of curriculum materials and the use of a NASA communications satellite to beam educational programs into remote parts of the Rocky Mountain states and Alaska. The Teacher Competence Study was intended to document the behaviors of successful teachers. With the transfer of these three programs, NIE was monitoring more than $144 million of programs designed and initiated by other agencies (House Appropriations Hearings, 9 March 1973, p. 205).

The New Programs

During its first year of operation, NIE launched only one new program, Field Initiated Studies—a $10 million basic research support program.[6] It funded research proposals from established research investigators in the areas of learning and instruction; human development; objectives, measurement and evaluation; social thought and processes; and organization and administration. It also funded "younger scholars" through a small grants project, providing up to $10,000 for up to eighteen months of work for each project.

And it funded research in disciplines usually not attracted to the problems of education; for 1973 these disciplines were anthropology, political science, economics, and legal research. OE had also funded a basic research program; however, the NIE program was designed to provide a more stringent technical review of all proposals and attract scholars who never would have applied for OE funds.

The Field Initiated Studies task force was overwhelmed by the number of proposals received in response to their grants announcement in January 1973. By the close of the competition, 3,126 proposals filled the NIE offices. Every researcher was required to submit twenty copies of his/her proposal; estimating conservatively twenty-five pages per proposal, NIE had to manage more than 1.5 million pieces of paper. The total amount of money requested by the researchers was more than $250 million; NIE had less than 4% of that sum to award.

Every proposal was read by NIE staff and screened on the basis of "technical quality and relevance to education." The top 25% of the proposals were then sent to panels of outside reviewers, drawn primarily from prestigious universities.[7] After the outside review process was completed, NIE funded 6.5% of all the proposals it had received (table 6.2 indicates how funds were allocated among those submitting proposals).

The Field Initiated Studies program achieved some of its goals, but its positive contribution to the new agency was small. It allowed NIE to fund research in some disciplines usually underrepresented in educational research. Not surprisingly, however, the largest number of proposals received and funded were from people identifying their discipline as education or psychology. The program used a number of respected academicians with national reputations on its review panels. However, some researchers complained that their proposals never reached the review panels because they were screened out by NIE staff unqualified to judge the technical merits of a proposal (Lipman-Blumen, June 1974; Lake, 1973). It demonstrated that NIE cared about basic research, and this in itself was important to counteract the image created by OE that development and field experiments were the only activities worth funding. The program must have offended at least a few people; undoubtedly not all of the 2,920 people whose proposals were turned down had viewed this as a long shot. (We reported in chapter 4 the dismayed reaction of the Rhode Island State Department of Education and the resulting anger in Senator Pell's staff.) It did not give Glennan any politically attractive projects with which to enliven his congressional testimony. It drained staff energies at a time when there was no energy to spare. On balance, if the Field Initiated Studies program helped the new agency more than it hindered it, its positive impact was marginal. Of course, at the time it was begun no one envisioned any budget cuts. It was an appropriate program for an agency committed to upgrading education R&D. For an agency attempting to win short-run political support however—which NIE became

Table 6.2

Descriptive Statistics by Type of
Institution for 1973 Field Initiated
Studies Program

Organizations	Proposals Submitted	% of Total	Proposals Funded			$ Amount Funded	% of Total $
			N	%[a]	% of Total		
Colleges and universities	2,072	66.28	161	7.8	78.16	9,280,315	81.65
State education agencies	67	2.14	2	3.0	.97	56,242	.49
Local education agencies	176	5.63	4	2.3	1.94	150,003	1.32
Elem-sec schools	18	.57	1	5.6	.48	12,000	.11
Non-profit	255	8.15	20	7.8	9.70	1,302,328	11.46
Profit	106	3.39	1	0.9	.48	59,895	.53
Professional associations	22	.70	0	0	0	0	0
Ed. labs and R&D centers	89	2.84	1	1.1	.48	9,911	.09
Individual	195	6.23	5	2.6	2.42	43,930	.39
Other	126	4.03	11	8.7	5.33	452,002	3.98
Total	3,126	~100.00	206	6.6	~100.00	11,366,626[b]	~100.00

Source: Adapted from S. G. Brainard, 25 June 1973, Memorandum to John Mays concerning an evaluation of Office Research Grants programs.
[a]Percentage funded of number submitted.
[b]Includes $1.1 million of Career Education funds.

after the budget cuts began—the Field Initiated Studies program was not helpful.

Although NIE initiated only one new program during its first year—Field Initiated Studies—senior staff devoted a considerable amount of attention to thinking about how to create and organize an appropriate R&D agenda. During NIE's first year this process (which was called the "Paradigm Search" and is described in chap. 8) yielded no acceptable framework. In NIE's second year, spurred by friends and critics alike who wanted an explanation of the NIE program, NIE announced its five priority areas. These were derived from work NIE was then sponsoring, that is, the inherited programs, and from topics many of the planning documents had identified as important. They were to be areas "on which to focus public attention and the Institute's energies" (NCER minutes, 5 November 1973).

The five priority areas were Essential Skills, Local Problem Solving, Productivity, Education and Work, and Diversity and Pluralism. Essential Skills would support R&D on reading and writing, focusing particularly on the development of those skills in the nine- to twelve-year-old child. Local Problem Solving would fund projects generated within local school districts such as teacher centers and in-service training programs. Productivity would support the technology programs and work in education finance. Education and Work was a new name for the Career Education program. Diversity and Pluralism would support R&D on individual, social, and cultural learning differences. (See Appendix 3 for descriptions of these programs as they were presented to Congress in April 1974.)

Glennan budgeted 70% of the agency's funds to these five areas;[8] he announced a new organization structure consonant with them; and in all ways he behaved like a person who had made a major decision, knew it was not perfect, but intended to make it stick. He had no illusions that the five areas encompassed all of education—for example, he pointed out to the NCER that postsecondary education and early childhood learning would each receive little attention. Nor did he believe that these were areas in which all the problems would ever be "solved." But they were areas in which the agency had invested energy and money. Four out of the five would be managed by people in whom Glennan had confidence. (The fifth priority, Diversity and Pluralism, had no manager at that time.) And they represented the realization that the search for a grand, rational synthesis must give way to pragmatic attempts to accomplish something. As one senior staff member observed:

> We have long passed the day we can afford the luxury of abstract debate over which five topics, or if it should be three or seven, or for that matter even one. What is critical for staff morale, agency momentum and responsiveness to our critics, we have chosen five areas that are appropriately encompassing, relevant and difficult to give the Institute the lift-off it has been awaiting. [Binswanger, quoted in Martin, 13 November 1973]

After the second budget cut and Glennan's resignation in the fall of 1974, the Five Priorities were slightly revised. Local Problem Solving and Experimental Schools were united in a task force called "Organization and Management for Change." Diversity and Pluralism was combined with activities from the Office of Human Rights and some basic research projects into a task force called "Education Equity." Essential Skills became one unit in the "Basic Skills" task force. Education and Work and Productivity remained unchanged, while Dissemination received new prominence. Furthermore, Field Initiated Studies—NIE's one new program from 1973—was abolished.

Conclusion

By the time NIE was two and a half years old, in the late fall of 1974, the general outline of its R&D agenda was fairly well established.[9] Three attributes of individual programs seem to be associated with their importance in the R&D agenda. They are bureaucratic momentum, characteristics of the program managers, and external political support. During the first year and a half of NIE's existence, bureaucratic momentum and personal characteristics of program managers determined the relative security and status of programs. After the budget cuts began, political attractiveness became an important characteristic.

When the first $110 million worth of programs were transferred from OE to NIE, they were accompanied by thirty-six cardboard cartons of contracts and grants (Duby, June 1974). Simply learning about the contents of the cartons took time. The larger programs such as the laboratories and R&D centers were particularly difficult to fathom. And meanwhile the projects themselves were not in limbo. Money was being spent; reports were being written; work was being performed. As a result, in many cases it would cost just as much, if not more, to attempt to close out some of the contracts and grants as it would to allow them to run to completion (Elliott, 11 June 1974).

Clearly, programs managed by certain individuals fared better than those managed by others. On balance the more prominent programs were managed by individuals who had not come from OE. And they were managed by individuals whom the NIE leadership believed had a fondness and aptitude for systematic analysis. (The fate of the Education Voucher project, however, illustrates that a program manager's personal qualifications are not enough to support a program that seems to be a political liability.)

Of course the third program characteristic—which became important only after the budget cuts began—is the ability to attract or generate useful external political support. For example, even though the laboratories and R&D centers program was dissolved, its contracts came to benefit from lobbying on their behalf by CEDaR. ERIC and the other dissemination programs attracted the support of state departments of education. Field Initiated Studies, which had no political support, was abolished.

Another View

To anyone caught up in the daily activities of an organization, much of what occurs takes on an air of inevitability; people come to believe that what happened had to happen. Often even more detached observers of organizations convey this sense of inevitability in their descriptions, thereby reinforcing belief in the inevitability of a particular course of events. As we suggest in the Introduction, however, our view of history is much more probabilistic. Here we explore some alternative histories for the NIE programs.

It was not inevitable that NIE inherit the transfer programs. In his preliminary plan for NIE, Levien stipulated that there should be a one-year transition period after NIE's creation during which OE would continue to operate its programs (Levien 1971, pp. 153–54). This year would allow for an orderly, legitimate evaluation of any candidates for transfer and would permit OE to close out all noncontinuing contracts. Congressional staff were sufficiently impressed with Levien's work to insert sections of it into the legislation practically verbatim. They could just as easily have mandated a one-year transition period. Perhaps one reason there was no such provision in the final NIE bill was eagerness to see the institute in operation and out of the hands of Marland and the OE. Nevertheless, it seems more than slightly naive or careless to assume that allowing Marland to determine which programs would transfer, with no representation from the first director of NIE, would result in a situation advantageous to NIE.

It is a common, though not inevitable, congressional procedure to create a "new" program or agency from "old" money. Brademas had been warned in his 1971 hearings against doing this for NIE. It was not inevitable that specific OE programs be named in the NIE legislation. Had Levien or any of the informal club of OE critics been in charge of the planning effort during 1971, they might well have lobbied against including specific mention of any OE programs in the authorizing legislation (Levien, 21 March 1974). Because some programs were mentioned specifically, Marland could cite the legislation as his justification for a complete transfer on 1 August so as "not to offend Congress" (Marland, 22 March 1974). And one of the reasons Silberman cited for not questioning the advisability of transferring programs during the Planning Unit period is that "they were mentioned in the legislation" (28 February 1974).

Even though programs were transferred, it was not inevitable that they be nurtured. An early, decisive announcement that no transferred program would be funded again would have eased the burden on strained staff resources. Of course this would have produced outraged complaints from jilted contractors, but weathering those complaints initially might have put the institute in a better long-run position than did badgering those contractors for months but finally giving them their money anyway. Alternatively, a few of the transferred programs were essentially ignored during NIE's first year. A policy of benign neglect toward all the transferred programs might have fared well. (Of course, hiring aggressive program managers for those programs would foil such a strategy.) Particularly, had the first director indulged in entrepreneurial promotion of one or two of his own special interests, ignoring the transferred programs might have been feasible.

Even though the programs were transferred and supported, it was not inevitable that they be justified in the NIE R&D program plan. During his appearances before the appropriations subcommittees, Glennan was heavily abused whenever he attempted to justify those programs. He might have said, "Gentlemen, I did not ask for those programs. I am monitoring them to make sure government funds are properly accounted for, but attempting to convert them into a creditable R&D program would be no more efficient or effective than trying to convert an aircraft carrier into a rocket ship." Of course this statement would have required an immediate display of blueprints for the NIE rocket ship—the plans for building its own R&D program. Glennan might have been ridiculed for such an unorthodox stance, but on the other hand he might have won some respect for his position.

Finally, even though the programs were transferred, supported, and justified in the NIE R&D program plan, they do not have to be blamed for NIE's lack of success. It is quite possible the agency would have been no more successful without them than it was with them. A depressed economy, a decline in enthusiasm for R&D of every variety, the absence of a strong theoretical foundation for education R&D, the political irrelevance of NIE, all might have meant that not even an agency with nothing but new money could have flourished. On the other hand, NIE might well have prospered, even with the transferred programs, had any of these conditions not prevailed, or had Senator Magnuson been out of town on the day of NIE's first budget hearings.

Introduction

The formal structure of an organization—the patterned interrelationships of authority, communication, and coordination—shapes the organization in a number of ways. Structural coordination and control can be powerful means to achieving organization goals (Thompson 1967; Ouchi and Harris 1974). The formal structure defines status relationships among organization members. It influences the relationship between an organization and its environment by specifying external communications channels. And the organization chart provides a simple map (for both observers and participants) of major aspects of the agency's work.

Changes in organization structure—reorganizations—can also be important in the life of an organization.[1] They provide one means by which the chief executive can assert changes in policy direction. (In the federal context this is one of the few major actions the agency head may effect rapidly without significant intervention by the larger bureaucracy or Congress.) However, planning for them is time-consuming; attention to reorganization reduces the resources available to attend to other important issues. Reorganizations also provide a means to demonstrate that an agency is responsive to particular constituencies or problems. However, if reorganizations occur too frequently, they may come to be viewed as demonstrating not responsiveness but lack of direction.

The appropriate structure for NIE had been debated and analyzed by Levien, the Planning Unit, and witnesses at the congressional hearings on NIE's creation. During the first year of NIE's existence, designing an appropriate organization structure—along with questions of personnel recruitment and program plans—was viewed as an important means to establishing and maintaining a high-quality agency. During its first two and a half years, NIE was unable to find the "right" structure. Between August 1972 and November 1974 an initial structure and four "reorganizations" were announced; on the average, NIE operated about six months under each.[2]

We explore three questions in this chapter:

What structural change was involved in each announced reorganization?

Why were so many reorganizations announced?

What were the consequences of reorganization?

To answer these questions we briefly examine each of the announced reorganizations. Unlike the material in chapters 5 and 6, this chronology extends beyond Glennan's resignation, because a reorganization accompanied his leave-taking and was not completed until some months later. We examine the reorganizations from three explanatory perspectives. The first perspective emphasizes the new and developing nature of NIE; because it is a new organization, we would expect some evolutionary structural change. The second perspective views structural instability as a reaction to pressures generated by forces internal and external to the institute. And the third perspective views reorganizations as the manipulation of important symbols.

Organization Structure Chronology

1971

| February | Levien report suggests organization structure |

1972

January	NIE Planing Unit publishes "An Initial Structure for NIE"
February	Rand publishes five alternative structural plans
June	Nixon signs NIE legislation
August	(NIE receives 84 people and $110 million worth of programs from OE)
September	First operating structure announced by Elliott
November	(Glennan sworn in as first NIE director)

1973

March	First reorganization announced by Glennan
April	Proposed organization structure discussed at senior staff retreat
May	Second reorganization announced by Glennan
October	(Senate Appropriations Committee recommends $75 million for fiscal year 1974)
December	(Five Priorities announced)

1974

January	Third reorganization, featuring Five Priorities, announced
April	(House denies supplemental request)
May	Creation of Executive Committee announced
August	(Glennan resigns)
November	Fourth reorganization announced by Elliott
	(Conference Committee recommends $70 million for fiscal year 1975)

NIE's Five Organization Structures

It is difficult to describe the intent and effect of each of NIE's reorganizations without overwhelming the reader with endless details. We will rely upon two kinds of summary characteristics in describing and analyzing each organization structure: substantive characteristics (the content or focus of activity in major work units) and structural characteristics (the size, shape, and hierarchical position of major work units). There are four major substantive building blocks that appear in some form in all the organization plans (plus the director's office, planning, and administration). One is "research"—those activities that support or carry out fundamental inquiry (such as a research grants program or an internal research program). The second is "directed programs"—those activities devoted to large-scale directed attacks on particular problems (such as the voucher project or the Mountain Plains career education program). The third is "practitioner-oriented" programs—those activities devoted to conventional school concerns (such as curriculum development and teacher training). And the fourth is "dissemination"—those activities devoted to conveying R&D knowledge to potential users. There are also four major structural characteristics: number of people reporting to the director; number of levels in the hierarchy; number of promotions or demotions; number of groups affected.

Even though these characteristics are useful in summarizing the details of any reorganization, it should be understood that within the institute no organization plan was considered only in these terms. Each reorganization was accompanied by a more or less elaborate justification for it—ranging from bureaucratic expediency to rational analysis to political necessity. Each reorganization was the subject of extensive speculation by institute staff before its announcement. And each was assessed for clues about who had become more or less important and what work was being more or less rewarded.

NIE's first organization structure, an admittedly temporary one organized by Elliott during the summer of 1972, was pragmatic and "flat" (see fig. 7.1 for NIE's first organization chart). It consisted of eleven hierarchially equal units, each of which reported to the acting director. This structure simply accommodated all the people and programs transferred from OE and the Planning Unit with as little disruption as possible. Each of the major programs inherited from OE was housed in its own unit; the Planning Unit staff was housed in a "New Initiatives" unit (headed by Silberman), which was to continue program planning, and a "Laboratories and R&D Centers Transition" unit, which was to manage the evaluation of that program.

NIE's first "permanent" organization structure was announced by Glennan in March 1973. Although discussion and analysis of an appropriate structure had been under way since Glennan arrived in November 1972, that analysis had not yet yielded the right structure. It was a much more mundane reason that impelled the announcement. The HEW Office of the Assistant Secretary for Administration was insisting that NIE produce its official organization chart. Every HEW agency had to have one; NIE was delinquent.

Glennan's announcement in March 1973, made only four changes to the flat, eleven-unit initial structure (see fig. 7.2 for NIE's second organization

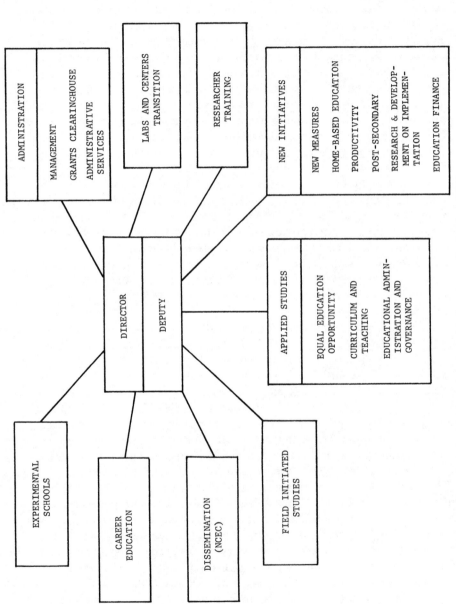

Figure 7.1. National Institute of Education organization chart, September 1972.

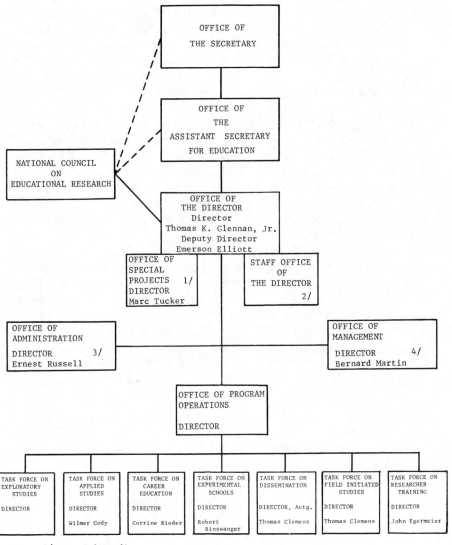

1/ Special studies

2/ Includes public information, congressional relations, science advisor, advisor to the Institute, EEO officer.

3/ Includes contracts & grants, finance, personnel, general services, staff resource center.

4/ Includes budget, management analysis, organization development, and planning.

Figure 7.2. National Institute of Education organization chart, March 1973.

chart). It transformed the former Laboratories and Centers Transition unit, which had finished its "transition" responsiblities, into the "Office of Special Projects" and moved it to the director's office. It dissolved the New Initiatives unit (Silberman, by this time, had left NIE). It created an "Exploratory Studies" unit to house many of the bright young social science researchers who had begun to arrive at NIE. On paper the biggest change was to insert a new layer in the hierarchy ("Office of Program Operations") between the director and all the program units. In fact, no one had been hired to direct that office, and so all the program unit heads continued to report directly to Glennan.

The changes brought by this reorganization were minor. No actual reporting relationships were changed. There were no promotions or demotions. The focus of activity was changed for only one unit (Special Projects). And only the four or five people who had been working for Silberman found themselves in new situations. But the agency was growing; by March 1973 it employed 169 people. The staff in the director's office was increasing; the task forces were getting larger; several key managerial posts were vacant. As a result, the number of people reporting to the director had increased from fifteen in September 1972 to twenty-four in March 1973.

Even as the March 1973 structure was announced, the analysis and deliberation over the proper structure continued. A paper commissioned by Glennan in the fall of 1972 sounded three of the themes that were to characterize the entire period of debate until NIE's second "permanent" structure was announced in May 1973. These three themes were the need to reflect NIE's legislative mandate in the organization structure, the need to provide an attractive home for research personnel, and the need to derive the structure through rational analysis. In emphasizing this last point, the paper asserted:

> NIE must make decisions on plans and structure on the basis of rational and coherent thought, not on the basis of the likes, dislikes—comforts and discomforts of management—no matter how competent those managers may be. [Ward, 27 November 1972]

A second paper, written in January 1973, reiterated these themes in a series of eleven criteria by which any proposed organization structure should be evaluated (Perkins, January 1973). Not unlike the requirements for the associate director for the Office of Programs position described in chapter 5, several of these criteria were incompatible with one another. It would be difficult to imagine any one organization structure that could meet all of them.

In May 1973 Glennan announced NIE's second "permanent" organization structure (see fig. 7.3 for NIE's third organization chart). At the time of its announcement, this was considered the "right" structure. The major change it created was the dividing of the "Office of Program Operation," which had

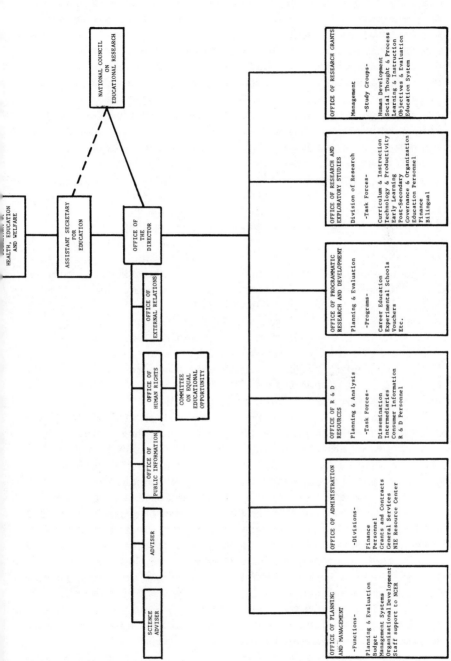

Figure 7.3. National Institute of Education organization chart, May 1973.

been created in the previous structure, into four offices. One would house the research grants program; one, the laboratories and centers project officers and the researchers; one, the large directed programs; and one, dissemination, training, and special projects.

In this reorganization, two new work units were created (one in the Office of Research and Exploratory Studies and one in the Office of Administration). One previously existing unit—the Applied Studies Task force—was dissolved. Nine fewer people were reporting to Glennan after the reorganization, and the degree of hierarchy in the organization was increased. Previously all work units (except the four divisions in the Office of Administration) were one communication link away from the director. After 17 May, four work units were one link away from the director and fourteen groups were separated by two links. Nine individuals who previously had formal direct contact with Glennan were moved "down" into the organization. In this reorganization only one unit leader, the head of the dissolved "Applied Studies" unit, relinquished a significant number of staff; this is the only significant "demotion" as measured by staff size. The effect of the reorganization on personnel within work units (below the level of unit leader) was not large. Aside from some minor changes in the Office of Administration, all the shifting of personnel took place within Research and Exploratory Studies. Most of the members of the former Exploratory Studies Task Force became members of the Research Division and reported to an associate director rather than to Glennan. Most members of the former Applied Studies Task Force were dispersed among the various task forces within the Exploratory Studies Division. By this time the agency employed 303 people (216 professionals). Approximately 70 people (50 professionals) reported to different supervisors as a result of the reorganization.

In summary, the May 1973 reorganization directly affected between 20 and 25% of the institute's personnel, almost all in the Office of Research and Exploratory Studies. The second level of the hierarchy was expanded. However, because of vacancies in the associate director positions, the continued existence of the "inner circle," and the near absence of change in unit staff sizes, the changes in status affecting unit heads were few.

During the summer and fall of 1973 a number of events occurred that would influence NIE's next permanent organization structure, announced by Glennan in January 1974. Throughout the late spring and summer the institute continued to hire personnel; the agency employed 375 people by July 1973. Two new work units were created and new programs were transferred from OE and OEO. In the fall of 1973, NIE received its first budget cut. In December NIE announced its Five Priorities.

In January 1974 Glennan announced NIE's third permanent organization structure, designed to feature the Five Priorities (see fig. 7.4 for NIE's fourth organization chart). Four of the five priorities (Education and Work, Local

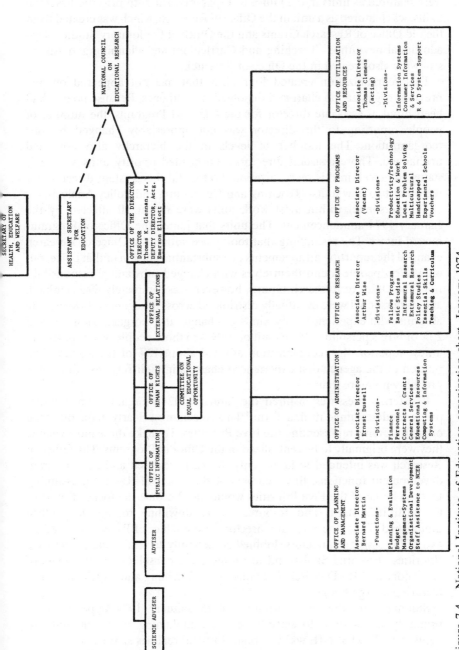

Figure 7.4. National Institute of Education organization chart, January 1974.

Problem Solving, Productivity and Technology, and Diversity and Pluralism) were featured as units in the Office of Programs. The fifth priority, Essential Skills, was featured as a unit in the Office of Research, which was created from the old Office of Research Grants and the Office of Exploratory Studies. Two additional new units—Teaching and Curriculum and Planning and Analysis—were also created in the Office of Research.

This reorganization created four units that had not appeared on any previous organization chart and dissolved two old ones. Because no one had been hired as associate director for the Office of Programs, the number of people reporting to the director was not appreciably changed by this reorganization. The number of levels in the hierarchy also remained unchanged. Those assistant directors who headed priority units saw their status enhanced in this reorganization. So too did the assistant directors for the other two new units—Teaching and Curriculum and Policy Analysis.

The personnel within most work units were not at all affected by the January 1974 announcement. The units that joined the Office of Programs moved intact. The reshuffling that took place within the Office of Research changed the reporting arrangements of a substantial portion of that office, but only a few people found themselves with changed substantive responsibilities. The Office of Research Grants, however, was completely disassembled, and its personnel were eventually distributed across the agency. If we include all units who experienced any kinds of change, the reorganization affected 20% of NIE's personnel. If we limit ourselves to those people who reported to a new superior, the reorganization affected about 12% of the agency. The portion of the agency that experienced changes in their responsibilities was probably no more than 8%.

If external pressures inspired the January 1974 reorganization, internal pressures determined its final form.[3] This is seen most clearly in the dispersal of the programs representing the Five Priorities. To make these most visible, they were originally to be centralized in the Office of Programs. The Office of Research was intended to house only the basic research and new program development functions. But members of the Office of Research, assuming that the home of the Five Priorities would also become the focus of most of the institute's status and resources, were unwilling to see their office diminished. Thus, the associate director for the Office of Research, aided by two of his assistant directors, lobbied successfully to retain one of the Five Priorities—Essential Skills—and to promote the consolidation of a mass of laboratory and R&D center programs into a Teaching and Curriculum unit featuring a large budget.[4]

Summarizing, the reorganization of 25 January 1974 appears to be primarily a response to outside forces complaining of an inability to "understand" what NIE was all about. Internal realities shaped and limited the form of the organizational changes that were implemented. The number

of changes in the reporting relationship among senior staff were few; the
degree of hierarchy in the organization was not changed; only a small portion
of the agency was in any way affected, and most changes that took place
involved what became the Office of Research.

In May 1974 Glennan announced the creation of an Executive Committee.
This group, consisting of the director, the deputy director, and the five
associate directors, was to convene regularly and assist the director by
deliberating over current issues.[5] The hopes associated with the creation of
the Executive Committee could hardly have been more comprehensive. As
Glennan described it:

> I envision this committee as aiding me in devising the guidance to the
> program areas that will lead to the generation of the policy proposals I
> submit to the National Council on Educational Research. The Associate
> Directors should thus become not only a major instrument for formulating
> Institute policy but also, in their management roles, a major means of
> communicating this policy to the Assistant Directors. The major concern of
> the committee will be programmatic and resource allocation issues. I
> expect it will also consider NIE's administrative and management policies
> as well as our relations with external groups. [Glennan, 6 May 1974]

Glennan was not alone in his hopes for the Executive Committee. Many of
the senior personnel within the institute saw it as a panacea:

> —should make our life easier because in the past we've had to deal with
> such a wide range of decision makers. This way we can reach everyone just
> by going through [the Executive Committee].

> —I think the Executive Committee enhances Glennan's and Elliott's
> leadership—they won't have to spend so much time talking to everyone
> around the Institute to find out what's going on.

> —[the Executive Committee] will be *very* significant. It will in fact, run the
> programs . . . as a result of the establishment of the Executive Committee I
> no longer receive fund requests or personnel requests, which relieves my
> desk of a lot of the daily mail.

> —Over time [the Executive Committee] must [give] the Associate Directors
> a degree of independence . . . authority must accrue to the Associate
> Directors.

The first operations of the Executive Committee were not without their
difficulties (the role of the Executive Committee in decision making is
discussed in chap. 8). Nonetheless, its creation was significant. It became an
important symbol of authority. It was not immediately clear what would be
the relationship between the committee and the director; it was clear,
however, particularly to the more aggressive assistant directors, that the old
days of going directly to Glennan for special dispensations were on the wane.

Over the summer of 1974, important internal and external events occurred
that would lead to changes in the January 1974 organization structure and the
Executive Committee. The NCER gave Glennan a somewhat unenthusiastic
vote of confidence in July. Glennan's relations with the appropriations
committees and some constituents failed to improve. Glennan resigned on 28
August, effective 1 November. NCER chairman Haggerty resigned in
September. The Division of Research in the Office of Research was quietly
disbanded. Five million dollars was awarded to the institute, to fund work on
Compensatory Education.

As a consequence of Glennan's resignation, Elliott once again became
acting director, on 1 November 1974. One week later he announced a
reorganization[6] (see fig. 7.5 for NIE's fifth organization chart). This reorganization abolished the three "offices" created in the previous structure. In their
place were six units: the (revised) Five Priorities plus dissemination. This
reorganization increased the size of the second level of the hierarchy by three
positions. A number of people enjoyed increased visibility as a result of this
reorganization. The heads of "Education and Work" and "Organization and
Management for Change" were "promoted" and joined the Executive
Committee. The former adviser for human rights moved from a staff to a line
position (heading "Education Equity") and acquired increases in both staff
and fiscal resources. Unlike the case in previous reorganizations, several
leaders experienced losses in relative stature in this reorganization. Each of
the former "office" heads was, in effect, demoted. Within work groups fewer
than thirty people reported to a different supervisor as a result of the
reorganization.

Elliott accompanied his announcement of the reorganization with a
four-part justification for it.

It is my intent that we:

—bring our aspirations more in line with our capabilities, Congressional
intent, and reasonable expectations for appropriations;

—orient our thinking more toward problems we are addressing than to
styles of management;

—base our actions on existing council policies, modified, as we will
recommend to the council, to reflect more recent experience and statements of Congressional intent or constituent interests; and

—address our primary attention to the good of the Institute as a whole.
[Elliott, 7 November 1974, p. 1]

The first and third points stressed the importance of aligning the institute
with the preferences of influential groups external to NIE—Congress,
constituent groups, and the NCER. Several of the newly featured units were
attractive to outsiders. "Organization and Management for Change," "Education and Work," "Dissemination and Resources," and the "Teaching and

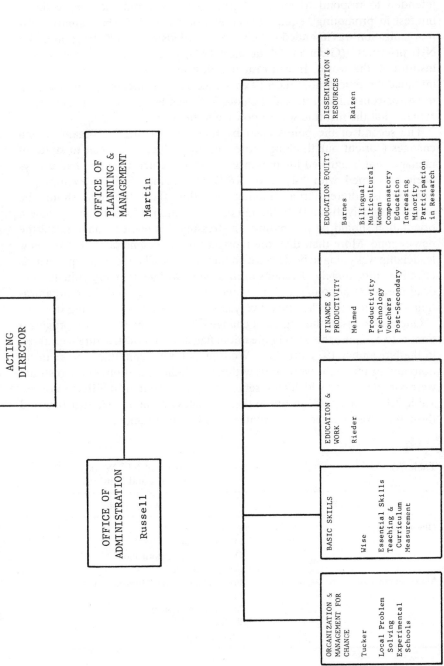

Figure 7.5. National Institute of Education organization chart, November 1974.

Curriculum" component of Basic Skills each had at least one sizable or vocal
constituent group associated with it. The Educational Equity unit title was
intended to respond to minority group pressures and the congressional
interest in promoting "equal educational opportunity." The January 1974
reorganization was intended to "give increased visibility and attention to the
NIE priorities" (Glennan, 24 January 1974, p. 2); that is, to explain the
institute to the world. In contrast, the November 1974 reorganization was
intended "to reflect more recent experience and statements of congressional
intent or constituent interest" (Elliott, 7 November 1974, p. 1); that is, to
explain that the institute was responsive to the world.

The second of the points cited by Elliott explaining his organizational
changes ("orient our thinking more toward problems ... than to styles of
management") signaled his presence as the new chief. Glennan had always
been concerned with "styles of R&D management" (i.e., developing a
program is different from running one, thus these functions should be
organizationally distinct). In the fall of 1974, Elliott believed that a problem
orientation should be paramount. In stressing this point he announced the
new regime. More than that, the reorganization demonstrated that the new
leadership was going to be decisive on tough issues. Changes were specified as
effective immediately. Responsibilities were assigned to individuals, and
deadlines were announced. A new man was in charge, and the reorganization—NIE's fourth in less than two years—was a means of asserting it.

One way to assess the degree of change introduced by the four reorganizations is to compare the units in the initial flat, eleven-unit structure with those
in the November 1974 structure. We thus put aside announced reorganizations and examine the work units within which the operations of the institute
were conducted and which represented daily reality for most NIE employees.
Table 7.1 lists the work groups in the original, summer of 1972 structure and
those that existed after the November 1974 reorganization.

Table 7.1   Comparison of NIE Work Units:
                                       Summer 1972 and Winter 1974

Summer 1972	Winter 1974
Office of Director ⟶	Office of Director
	Director's staff
	Office of Public Information
	Science Adviser
Management Task Force ⟶	Office of Planning and Management
	Planning
	Management Systems
	Budget
	NCER Support

Summer 1972	Winter 1974

Administration Task Force ⎯⎯→	Office of Administration
	  Staff
	  Finance
	  References Center
	  Contracts and Grants
	  Computing and Information Systems
	  General Services

Career Education Task Force ⎯⎯→	Education and Work Task Force
	  Staff
	  Planning, Research, and Evaluations
	  Non-Traditional Alternatives
	  School Based Career Education
	  Adult Career Education

Dissemination Task Force ⎯⎯→	Dissemination and Resources Task Force
	  Staff
	  Information Systems
	  Consumer Information and Services
	  R&D Systems Support
	Organization and Management for Change Task
	    Force

Experimental Schools Task Force →	Experimental Schools Program

Lab and Center Transition Task
  Force ⎯⎯⎯⎯⎯⎯→
	Local Problem Solving Program
	Finance and Productivity Task Force
	  Productivity Program
	  Technology Program
	  Vouchers Program
	  Post-Secondary Program
	Basic Skills Task Force

Applied Studies Task Force ⎯⎯→	Teaching and Curriculum Program
	  Essential Skills Program
	  Measurement Program
	Educational Equity Task Force
	  Bilingual
	  Multicultural
	  Women
	  Compensatory Education
	  Minorities in Research

New Initiatives Task Force—
  Disbanded
Field Initiated Studies Task
  Force—Disbanded
Researcher Training Task
  Force—Disbanded	

In table 7.1 the solid arrow indicates a unit that evolved continuously, little affected by the announced changes in organizational structure. In the first six groups listed (through Experimental Schools) the core staff was stable and the responsibilities of the unit remained the same through the end of 1974. The Laboratory and R&D Center Transition Task Force became, over time, the Local Problem Solving Program; its core staff remained the same, but its responsibilities changed.[7] These seven stable groups taken together always have represented a clear majority of both the personnel of and funds distributed by the institute. The Technology and Voucher units transferred to NIE nine months after the initial structure was announced. After arriving, they remained stable in both mandate and personnel.

A somewhat special case is the Applied Studies Task Force (where most of the transferred laboratory and R&D center work was originally housed). The responsibilities of this group were dispersed and then reassembled in the Teaching and Curriculum program. Two of the three original units that were eventually disbanded (New Initiatives and Field Initiated Studies) were involved with "research"—either supporting fundamental inquiry outside the institute or initiating studies inside. It is this function that bore the brunt of all the reorganizations. The Exploratory Studies Task Force appeared in March 1973, replacing New Initiatives. In May 1973, the Office of Research and Exploratory Studies consolidated Exploratory Studies and Applied Studies, and reordered existing work units; Field Initiated Studies became, intact, the Office of Research Grants. In January 1974, the dissolution of Research Grants was announced and the new Office of Research absorbed most of its personnel while simultaneously reshaping some of the work groups which came from Research and Exploratory Studies. By November 1974 some research work groups were gone (e.g., Handicapped Research), some had come and gone (e.g., Institutional Effects, Social Influences), some had come and stayed within programmatic units (e.g., Essential Skills, Measurement), and some had just emerged (e.g., Increasing Minority Participation in Research). Most of the research efforts that survived the November 1974 reorganization were located in the Educational Equity Task Force.

We have noted that a minority of NIE's personnel were affected by any single reorganization; here we see that the same people tended to be reorganized on each occasion. In fact, through all the "structural changes" a large majority of the work groups (responsible for the vast majority of the institute's budget) were unaffected. Over its first two and a half years and four reorganizations, NIE's underlying structure was very stable. Only one part of the agency—"research"—repeatedly took the brunt of reorganization.

Three Perspectives on Reorganization

In an effort to explain NIE's structural behavior we approach it from three different perspectives. First, we examine the data as a management scientist might, looking for relationships between size, growth, and structure. Second, we adopt the view of the political scientist, relating structural change to the variety of forces impinging on the institute. Third, we borrow from the artist and psychologist and examine the symbolic nature of structural change. These are complementary perspectives, not competing ones.

Reorganization as a Response to Organizational Growth

Organization theorists have long considered organization growth to be an important variable influencing structural change.[8] To some degree, growth in the size of NIE's staff does seem to have influenced its structure. Table 7.2 summarizes NIE's growth statistics and structural changes over two and a half years. We note the rapid increase in the size of NIE's staff in its first eighteen months. Between 1 October 1972, and 31 March 1974, NIE's work force expanded at an average annual rate of 136%, or 7.4% per month.[9] As the number of employees reached about 200, the number of work groups reached about 30, and the number of office heads reporting to the director increased to 12, a new layer of management was introduced. Thereafter the number of office heads reporting to the director remained stable, even though growth in the number of employees continued. These data suggest two early phases of growth: an initial phase when the size of the second hierarchical level of leadership was determined, and a second period when the bureaucracy was "fleshed out" below this second level. People moved in and out of the second level of leadership, but the size of the group remained fairly stable after May 1973. However, we also note that the number of major offices and the number of work groups fluctuated over time. This stemmed from a seeming inability to decide how to deal structurally with the "research" activities.

Note that the net number of work units created or eliminated by a particular reorganization is typically small compared with the change in the total number of work units between reorganizations. In other words, units were continually being created and eliminated (mostly created) within major offices; more of these actions took place between than as a result of reorganizations. This suggests that structural change is a process resulting from the stresses of rapid growth; this growth induces important structural changes outside formal reorganization announcements. Another fact bearing on this issue is the small number of people directly affected by any reorganization. When one considers that, at the very least, 77% of NIE's personnel were in no way directly touched by a single reorganization (they worked with the same people, received no changes in responsibilities, and reported to the same individuals), the strong degree of fundamental organizational stability we have described is underscored.

Another important influence on the organization structure is the effect of a halt in growth. The last reorganization occurred in an environment of budget and staff size constraints. Under these conditions, a redistribution of resources and status in which someone gets more almost certainly must

Table 7.2

Comparing Five Organization Structures

Organization Characteristics	Organization Structure				
	Summer 1972 (as of 10/1/72)	March 1973 (as of 1/31/73)	May 1973 (as of 6/30/73)	January 1974 (as of 3/31/74)	November 1974 (as of 11/7/74)
Total NIE Personnel	120[a]	169	303	436	400[c]
Total budget of current fiscal year	$110 M ('73)	$110 M ('73)	$110 M ('73)	$75 M ('74)	$70 M ('75)
# of hierarchical levels	2	2	3	3	3
# of people reporting to director					
Total	15	24	18	22	18
Total less Office of Director	10	12	7	9	8
# of major offices specified[b]	—	3	6	5	8
# of work groups[b]	11	22	47	39	36[c]
# of units created	—	1	2	4	1
# of units disbanded	—	1	1	8	4
# (%) of employees directly affected	—	6(4%)	70(23%)	85[c](20%)	(<10%)
# of leaders whose status was:					
enhanced	—	1	2	5	7
diminished	—	—	1	—	3

[a]Including people on loan from other agencies and from the Planning Unit.
[b]Appearing on organization charts or personnel rosters.
[c]Estimated.

require that someone else receive less. So we find that the November 1974 reorganization involved demotions for a significant number of people for the first time.

In summary, because growth expanded the number of work units within NIE, it was necessary to create an intermediate level of management between the director and the operating units. Relatively few units were created as the result of reorganizations; rather, these formal announcements confirmed the creation of units that emerged as a result of growth. As long as the organization was growing, there was little cost (in terms of the status of unit leaders) associated with reorganization.

Reorganization as a Response to External and Internal Forces

This analysis focuses on the fact that NIE was pressured by a complex of forces but possessed few alternative responses to cope with them. One class of forces called for organizational action. Over time the nature of these forces changed from internal to external pressure for reorganization. Internally, the initial concern for rationality and the fact of rapid growth both created such pressure. The initial structure and the first reorganization were viewed only as holding measures, to be replaced by a structure derived from the careful consideration of alternative designs. Rapid growth simultaneously provided an accumulating pressure—top management could not maintain direct communication with the expanding number of work units. After the second reorganization, the pressures motivating action became increasingly external. The budget cut and the announcement of the Five Priorities in the fall of 1973, and later the continued criticism from Congress and constituents, were believed to require some sort of structural response. The first three organization structures can be viewed as an attempt to relieve internally generated pressures by a structural solution. The last two reorganizations were attempts to relieve externally generated pressures by the same solution. In the first case, the medicine might have cured the illness. In the second case, however, it was little more than a palliative. It is not a cure—perhaps there is no cure—but it might relieve the pain for a short while.

A second class of forces helped determine what form the reorganizations would take: the pulling and hauling among influential individuals within the organization. In every instance these came to play a role, in some cases overpowering the initial motivation for change. The first reorganization was intended to certify the initial structure, but the Special Projects group became attached to the director's office. The second reorganization specified an Office of Programs, but each major program continued to operate independently, reporting directly to Glennan. The third reorganization was intended to highlight the Five Priorities in one unit, but in order to "share the wealth" they were spread across the institute. The fourth reorganization, as first conceptualized, placed Local Problem Solving and Experimental Schools within the Finance and Productivity Task Force; protests led to the creation of a separate unit for them.

In an operation with a high degree of "democratic" decision-making, one would expect leaders who are politically adept and persistent to succeed, and some of the younger managers are cases in point.[10] On the other hand, eliminating units whose performance is perceived as less than adequate, or whose leadership has been less aggressive, is not necessarily easy. When goals and technology are unclear, the decision to eliminate a program can be based on little more than personal taste. There are few objective criteria that can make the decision clear-cut. Furthermore, eliminating units produces unhappy people. These two factors offer no incentive for a director to dismantle any but extremely weak units. A system with these features thus tends to protect work units and provide the microstructural stability we have observed.

Reorganization as Magic

Special powers are associated with the idea of reorganization. NIE top management repeatedly employed it to solve major problems even though there was no evidence that it had helped in previous difficulties. Personnel throughout the institute took the reorganization announcements seriously, even though most of them were never directly affected. Particularly in the later reorganizations, we see an interesting form of schizophrenia on the part of NIE staff. There was the belief that the institute was in trouble and that reorganization was appropriate action. But at the same time there was effective resistance to significant structural change.

This behavior suggests that the idea of reorganization has important symbolic characteristics.[11] In this regard, the director of NIE could be viewed as a politician facing two publics. One consisted of the Congress, education constituents, and the greater Washington bureaucracy, who sought assurance that NIE was responsive to their criticisms. They had neither the time nor the inclination to examine closely the organization's response to criticism. The fact that a reorganization had been announced automatically served as a partial assurance.[12] This public wanted only to know that some significant action had been taken to correct perceived shortcomings; reorganization was on the list of significant actions.

The second public was the personnel of the agency. To this public, criticism from outside was threatening—a budget cut is more than a symbolic threat. But anything that jeopardized status within the organization was also a threat. The most reassuring solution was one that alleviated external pressures without creating internal anxiety.[13] If no such solution existed, the director would attempt to satisfy the external public with minimal disruption to the internal public.

In many ways this is what NIE leadership did. It attempted to make both publics happy. When external pressures mounted, a decision would be made to reorganize.[14] The nature of the changes would be discussed among NIE leaders until a satisfactory compromise was struck—one that qualified as an honest-to-goodness reorganization, yet minimized internal tensions.

Conclusion

None of these perspectives by itself provides a satisfying explanation for NIE's behavior. Together, however, they provide some of the richness that the complexity of the story requires. The motivations for structural change were real. Organizational growth, desire for rationality, and, later, external criticism required structural action. As top management went about designing appropriate responses, they were not constrained by technological factors associated with education research but were confined by political factors internal to the institute. As external criticism persisted, the need to reorganize recurred, while the resources available to the institute contracted. While trying to minimize internal upset, it was difficult to make the later reorganizations much more than symbolic.

By the fall of 1974, the reorganizations had created unintended effects. Instead of reassuring outside observers, the repeated reorganizations created the impression of instability and lack of direction.[15] Take, for example, the last reorganization: it was in this announcement that the NIE, mandated to carry out research in education, eliminated its Office of Research.

Eight   Decisions

Introduction

In the classical model of organization decision-making, decisions are viewed as the output of a single rational actor who weighs the consequences of all alternatives and chooses the course of action that brings the greatest good to the organization (Allison 1971, pp. 10–38). More recent interpretations suggest that for organizations with an ambiguous mission operating in a complex environment, the decision-making process is a collection of interested parties, deadlines, standard operating procedures, solutions looking for problems, and problems looking for solutions (Cohen, March, and Olsen 1972). The way major choices are made influences every facet of the organization. It affects the adequacy of those decisions and the extent to which they are taken seriously by people both inside and outside the organization. It creates beliefs about who is "important" and what behavior is "rewarded."

In this chapter we examine three decision processes begun during NIE's first year. The first is an effort to produce a conceptual framework for education R&D that would provide intellectual guidelines for the agency's activities—the paradigm search. The second is the development of a procedure to be used in planning the agency's program activities—the planning process. The third is the creation of the annual budget. The paradigm search and the planning process received a great deal of attention from NIE top management and their support staff.[1] These first two decisions were seen as important not only for their content but also because the process of reaching decisions was to set the tone for all future operations. And the budget request, of course, was crucial to the agency's continued existence and the way it conducted its business.[2] These three issues illustrate the full range of two dimensions characterizing all NIE decision processes: the degree of conceptual abstraction and the degree of interaction with the environment. The paradigm search was the most abstract and least involved with NIE's external environment; the planning process was intermediate on both dimensions; and the budget was most concrete and most closely related to elements outside the agency.

Each issue had its own distinctive features. But they also possessed some similar characteristics. First, all three issues were interrelated: The paradigm was to determine program categories for the budget justifications; the planning process was to yield budget estimates for individual programs;

annual budget preparation deadlines were to provide scheduling benchmarks for the planning process. Second, each process had to compete with the other two and with myriad other issues for the attention of the institute's small senior staff. There were not enough top people available to assign any of them full time to any one of these processes. Yet, because all three issues were viewed as extremely important, most senior staff wanted to contribute to or review all of them. Third, all three processes were begun with the high degree of optimism characteristic of most new organizations.

The dynamic process exhibited by all three can be characterized briefly. Top management described the issue and set comprehensive, usually ambiguous criteria for its resolution. Staff were asked to prepare a proposal. Top management and senior staff discussed the proposal and identified inadequacies in it. Through the period of preparation and discussion, internal and external events altered the definition of the issue. Staff were asked to prepare a new proposal based on the new definition, and the cycle began again. In some cases a decision was made only after an amazing number of cycles had occurred. And in most cases closure on an issue was compelled by external deadlines rather than by internal staff satisfaction.

In this chapter we describe and analyze each decision process in its own self-contained section. The advantage of this presentation is that it highlights how the character of each process changed over time. The disadvantage is that it obscures the extent to which, at any particular time, numerous activities were under way that affected the given process.

We attempt to answer four questions:

How did managerial models of "appropriate" decision-making affect the decision making process?

How did organization constraints affect it?

How did the processes change over time?

What were the consequences, for the staff and for the agency as a whole, of these processes?

Decisions Chronology

Although chapter 8 discusses each of the three major decision processes separately, we present a single chronology to demonstrate the extent to which all three processes overlapped.

1972

October	Budget (B): $110 million recommended for fiscal year 1973 by Conference Committee
November	Paradigm Search (PS): Paradigm search begins (Glennan is sworn in as NIE director)
	PS: Meeting with Rand staff

| December | PS: | First five frameworks identified |
| | PS: | "Reality test" applied to revised five frameworks |

1973

January	Planning Process (PP): OPM staff begin devising a planning process
	PS: Active development ceases
March	PP: First draft distributed
	B: $162 million (fiscal year 1974) requested from House Appropriations Subcommittee
	PP: Second draft distributed
April	PP: Third draft presented at senior staff retreat
	PP: Meeting of NCER nominees; Haggerty expresses interest in NCER participation in planning process
	PP: Fourth draft completed
May	PP: Fifth draft completed
June	B: $142 million recommended by House Appropriations Committee for fiscal year 1974
July	B: $162 million requested from Senate Appropriations Subcommittee for fiscal year 1974
September	B: $50 million recommended by Senate Appropriations Subcommittee for fiscal year 1974
	PP: Drafts 6 and 7 completed
October	B: $75 million recommended by Senate Appropriations Committee for fiscal year 1974
November	PS: Twelve priorities presented at NCER meeting
	B: $75 million recommended by Conference Committee for fiscal year 1974
	PP: Haggerty outlines method for allocating funds
	PS: Small group meetings held to develop Five Priorities
December	PS: Five Priorities presented to NCER
	PP: Drafts 8 and 9 distributed

1974

January	PP: Executive Committee idea emerges
February	B: $25 million (supplemental) requested from House Appropriations Subcommittee
Feb.–March	PP: Drafts 10, 11, 12, and 13 completed
March	B: $25 million (supplemental) requested from Senate Appropriations Subcommittee
April	B: $0 (supplemental) recommended by House Appropriations Committee
	B: $130 million requested from House Appropriations Subcommittee for fiscal year 1975

May	PP:	Martin releases "budget call" with fiscal year 1976 planning sequence
	B:	First Executive Committee meeting to develop fiscal year 1976 budget
	B:	$0 supplemental recommended by Senate Appropriations Committee
	B:	$0 supplemental recommended by Conference Committee
June	B:	Eighteen pounds of fiscal year 1976 planning papers received by OPM
	B:	$134.5 million requested from Senate Appropriations Subcommittee for fiscal year 1975
	B:	$100 million recommended by House Appropriations Committee for fiscal year 1975
	B:	Glennan announces tentative fiscal year 1975 and 1976 allocations
	B:	$80 million voted by full House for fiscal year 1975
July	B:	Fiscal year 1976 allocations presented to NCER as a "staff exercise"; no approval granted
August	B:	$65 million recommended by Senate Appropriations Subcommittee for fiscal year 1975
		(Glennan resigns)
September	B:	$0 recommended by Senate Appropriations Committee for fiscal year 1975
		(Haggerty resigns)
November	B:	$70 million recommended by Conference Committee for fiscal year 1975

The Paradigm Search

The First Year

The search for a conceptual framework for NIE's R&D program was part of a greater planning effort stretching across a long period of time, beginning with the Levien Preliminary Plan and extending beyond NIE's first year. When Glennan became director in November 1972, he inherited a bookshelf of documents from the Planning Unit and lists of initiatives NIE might sponsor that had been suggested by various groups. It was evident that NIE needed an intellectual structure for organizing all the ideas and proposals.

The search for an organizing framework became known as the "paradigm search." The paradigm would serve many purposes. It would supply a set of shared terms and categories to facilitate internal communication. It would provide a means for identifying topics ripe for R&D funding. It would be useful in explaining the institute's activities to the outside world, particularly in organizing and explaining the budget. It would also be useful in developing the institute's organization structure. One of the strong criticisms of OE was that it had never developed a coherent rational justification for its R&D activities. The paradigm would remedy that problem for NIE.

In November 1972, the paradigm search commenced. John Mays assumed major responsibility for the effort; Glennan, Elliott, and Martin also participated almost daily. Two members of Martin's staff were assigned to the task. The first frameworks were generated out of a review of the "literature" on R&D agendas in education and the particular preferences of several of the involved individuals.[3] One framework, championed by Mays, focused on "research styles"—basic research, applied research, development, and dissemination. Another, supported by Martin and others, emphasized classes of problems—inequities in educational finance, lack of equal educational opportunity, and so on. A third organized education by age groups—preschool, elementary school, secondary school, postsecondary education, and adult education (see table 8.1 for various paradigms generated during the search).

A senior staff meeting was held in early November 1972 to describe the initial paradigms. The consensus was that no one framework was even remotely satisfactory. The research styles proposal suffered from difficulties of definition. The problem areas overlapped. The age breakdown was somewhat arbitrary and too tied to the existing organization of American educational institutions.

So the search widened. NIE asked Roger Levien for assistance.[4] Levien and NIE organized a small two-day conference whose purpose was "to present for Tom Glennan's consideration a series of ideas and proposals on the substantive nature of NIE's program for [fiscal year] 1973 and [fiscal year] 1974" (Martin, 20 November 1972). The five organizing frameworks that survived or emerged from the meeting were the focus of much attention through early December. Martin's staff members elaborated the various frameworks and solicited comments on their modifications from a small number of respected colleagues (the "inner circle" described in chap. 5). They were discussed at the regular staff meetings. At special staff meetings, to which most of the senior staff was invited, they, along with specific program proposals, were the only agenda items.

These special staff meetings were an important substantive and social forum during NIE's first year. These meetings usually were held in the late afternoon and continued until the exit of people (to dinner or other compelling alternatives) emptied the room. All task force leaders were invited. Although most of the task force leaders who had transferred from OE did not often attend these meetings, the "younger managers" usually attended or sent first-line subordinates. Invitations to the meetings were

Table 8.1   R&D Frameworks Generated by
                                       "The Paradigm Search"

Early November 1972
    Research styles: Basic, applied, development, dissemination
    Problems: Inequities in education finance, lack of equal education opportunity
    Age groups: Preschool, elementary, secondary, postsecondary, adult

---

Late November 1972
    Research styles: Basic, applied, development, experimentation and evaluation, implementation, policy analysis, state-of-art survey, dissemination
    Subject matter: Curriculum, tests and measurements, technology, teacher training, school management
    Target populations: Ethnic minorities, women, disadvantaged, urban, rural, private schools, parochial schools
    Systems perspective: Objectives and evaluation, learning processes, educational systems
    Existing divisions: Directed studies, field initiated studies, special emphasis (programs), R&D resource development, dissemination

---

Mid-December 1972
    Research styles: Systematization of knowledge, research, policy analysis, consumer information, intellectual backup for national movements, component development, model development
    Subject matter: Curriculum, evaluation, tests and measures, technology, teacher training, school management and educational systems, objectives and goals
    Target populations: Ethnic minorities, women, disadvantaged, urban, rural, private schools, parochial schools
    Age groups: Early childhood (0–2), childhood (6–11), junior high (12–14), youth (15–21), adult
    Existing divisions: Directed studies, field initiated studies, special emphasis programs, R&D resource development, dissemination

---

Early November 1973
    Education of the disadvantaged
    Multicultural education
    Learning
    Basic skills
    Technology applications to education
    Educational personnel
    Choice, decision-making, and accountability
    Measurement
    Economics of education
    School to work transition
    Postsecondary education
    Strengthening the R&D system

December 1973
    Essential skills
    Productivity
    Relationship between school and work
    Local problem solving
    Diversity and pluralism

---

limited, but curious passers-by, usually former members of Glennan's staff at OEO, were occasionally invited to sit in. The meetings were informal and spirited. Glennan, not a man of few words, participated energetically and set the tone. John Mays usually described the work done since the previous gathering and initiated the debate, which was unstructured in both participation and content. In part this was because operational criteria for a suitable paradigm were never specified. Hence all proposals were worthy of equal attention. But in addition most of the people who attended these meetings enjoyed analysis and debate. They were having a good time. The problem was a difficult one, unmastered in any previous attempt. Its intellectual significance was unassailable. There was no externally-imposed deadline by which a paradigm had to be accepted. These factors and the firm belief that a comprehensive search would yield an optimal framework combined to keep the matter from closure.

After two weeks of senior staff debate in December 1972, Martin asked his staff to use each of the current frameworks to organize the existing lists of new program proposals and all the inherited programs. He called this exercise "the reality test." After two days of work by two people it was clear that none of the frameworks provided a satisfactory way to display NIE's work; in every paradigm, a large percentage of the institute's activities had to be categorized arbitrarily. Martin pointed out the difficulties uncovered by the "reality test" at the next paradigm search meeting in late December. He noted that closure on a framework was necessary if it was to be used in the development of the fiscal year 1974 budget testimony. And he pointed out that his overworked staff had little more time to devote to the search. Elliott, who was chairing this meeting, presided over a discussion that by now was familiar.[5] One person supported one framework; someone else, another. Arguments that had been heard before were offered and countered. No coalition formed to promote a compromise. Elliott did not impose a choice; Glennan did not strongly favor any of the alternatives. No framework was chosen.

No formal end to the search was proclaimed. Indeed, it continued in somewhat different forms as the institute set about the more pragmatic tasks of funding proposals and creating an organization structure. However, the desire for a deductive comprehensive framework was never satisfied.

The first-year paradigm search exhibited two characteristics common to most new organizations: a lack of appreciation for history, and a highly optimistic view of the possibilities for the new organization.[6] NIE's top management and staff did not attempt to analyze and learn from the experience of OE's Bureau of Research or NCERD. Several former members or associates of NCERD who testified at the Brademas hearings had warned against attempting to be too rational, too comprehensive. Their warnings were either unheard or unheeded. Nor was the counsel of friends of NIE considered. Several observers of NIE, themselves "good people"—the kind welcome in the new institute—suggested that attempts to apply a scientific model to education R&D were folly. At an Educational Staff Seminar meeting attended by Glennan and other senior NIE staff, Professor Sheldon White of Harvard University characterized education as a field "in the age of alchemy" and therefore not amenable to highly scientific organization.[7] David Cohen, another Harvard researcher, suggested that, unlike the research fields it was trying to emulate, education did not have a foundation of theory on which to base experiments; rather, educational R&D is based on "hunches." But a comprehensive deductive model remained the standard of excellence among the NIE senior staff.

A third characteristic of the paradigm search is that it served functions other than its manifest one. It indicated who the director thought was important. It demonstrated to NIE personnel the acceptable style for decision-making and the standards for adequacy of major proposals. Glennan clearly exhibited his preference for "democratic" decision-making. An individual was valued more for an ability to present a convincing case than for past experience in the field or for formal position in the institute. High standards of intellectual rigor were applied to proposals; optimal solutions, derived from examination and analysis of a set of comprehensive alternatives, were sought. The norm emerging from this process was that it was better to have no decision than to have a suboptimal one.

The Second Year

The paradigm search of November and December 1972, characterized by a high degree of abstraction and generality, yielded no "acceptable" framework within which to organize NIE's R&D activities. During October and November 1973 external pressures and internal discontent impelled yet another attempt to develop an organizing framework. The context within which this effort took place, however, was much different from that of the first year. By this time NIE had suffered its first budget cut and had "discovered" that it had few political allies. The NCER had met five times and was pressuring Glennan for a coherent rationale for the agency's work. A permanent organization structure had been announced and many senior positions had been filled. Friendships and internal reputations had been established. Cuts in inherited programs had been made; managers of both the remaining programs and new programs were solidly embedded in the agency's structure.

Against this background the NCER met on 5 November 1973 to hear Glennan describe twelve high-priority areas for NIE support. These had been pulled together from Planning Unit and Rand proposals, from suggestions made by program leaders (essentially their "bids" for a portion of any new money), and from ideas that had won general acceptance across the institute (for example, everyone agreed that reading and testing were important targets for NIE money). The list had been generated in a piecemeal way and showed it. The NCER refused to approve it. They asked Glennan to reduce the number of priorities and to make sure they had clear anticipated outcomes and strategies. The NCER wanted the new list in four weeks.

Although the next month's activity involved some of the same participants as the paradigm search a year earlier, the two processes were quite different. First, there was now an externally imposed deadline (the December NCER meeting) and a strong signal (the budget cut) that the external world would not wait patiently while NIE searched for the perfect framework. Second, previous NIE efforts to produce an all-encompassing, rational framework had failed; NIE leadership knew they had failed and was disinclined to run around the same track again. Third, there had been up to a year's thinking and planning in the program areas by members of the institute staff. Glennan had watched these plans develop, had been consulted on their merits, and felt more or less comfortable with them. Finally, the earlier paradigm search had been undertaken for Glennan, not by him. Now he was feeling pressure from both inside and outside the institute to be more involved and more decisive. As he described it,

> People had come up to me and said, "Glennan, you've just simply got to take more charge. You're being too nice to people. You're trying to listen to too many people. Do something. You're the one that's got to make the decision." [Glennan, 7 December 1973, p. 4]

The day after the November NCER meeting Glennan announced in a staff meeting that he wanted "to get a small group of people together" to pare down and consolidate the twelve priority areas. He chose five or six people to brainstorm for two days. Glennan characterizes the group as "people who I'd worked with, who I thought had some sense of what I wanted, or maybe had been pushing me to do these kinds of things" (7 December 1973, p. 4). By the end of the second day the group had delineated five priority areas: Essential Skills, Productivity, Relationship between School and Work, Local Problem Solving, and Diversity and Pluralism.

The Five Priorities were a combination of areas "everyone" agreed were important and areas in which work was already under way. The first two priorities, Essential Skills and Productivity, met both criteria. They had been identified as important by every planning document from the President's Message of 1970 onward. In addition, NIE had sponsored a summer institute on reading four months earlier that had generated support for Essential Skills in some academic circles[8] and the management commitment of a Harvard scholar who had come to NIE as a fellow. NIE's investment in "productivity" included the education technology programs inherited from OE. Additionally, the manager of that program had previously directed an interagency study committee on productivity in the social sector. The Relationship between School and Work was primarily a recognition of ongoing work—the Career Education program. (It is also possible to find references to initiatives that might belong in such an area in some of the early planning documents.) The Local Problem Solving priority probably came closer than any of the others to growing from systematic, comprehensive analysis. Tucker and his staff had worked for months on an assessment of the characteristics of the R&D and dissemination systems. They had become convinced that the capacity for reform and renewal of local school districts had to be improved if the products of R&D were ever to be utilized in the schools. The Local Problem Solving priority was the result of that analysis and conviction. Diversity and Pluralism was a catchall priority. It provided a place for a number of inherited programs, such as the Voucher Experiment and Experimental Schools. It also offered consolation to any "humanists" who might feel that all the other priorities overemphasized cognitive outcomes and questions of efficiency. And it provided a home for and a way to justify any interesting ideas that might come up later.

Four- or five-page descriptions of each priority area were sent to all senior staff for comment. Significantly, Glennan wrote three of the five descriptions himself; he had not contributed any written materials to the first year's paradigm search. The memorandum accompanying these descriptions adopted a tentative tone.

> My desire is to go to the Council in December with our program organized around a set of themes (priorities) such as these. . . . I hope you will take time to give some serious thought to these materials, recognizing that they are preliminary efforts. . . .
>
> 1. Do these represent a reasonable and defensible set of priorities?
>
> 2. How should the basic statements of purpose be worded?
>
> 3. Are there serious problems with the statement of the problems to be dealt with?
>
> 4. Are there significant activities that you feel the institute should undertake that are not included? [Glennan, n.d., pp. 1–2]

With Glennan out of town, Elliott chaired a senior staff discussion of the papers on 13 November 1973. During that meeting, the major point of argument was whether there should be one priority or several. The senior staff who had come from universities (none of whom had worked on the first year's paradigm search) argued for a single "broader, more elegant, more conceptually adequate way to state [NIE's] goals" (Martin, 13 November 1973, p. 2). The program managers (for example, people from Experimental Schools, the Voucher Experiment, and Career Education) argued for several priorities. That night Glennan read Martin's summary of the staff meeting and the written comments from his senior staff. He was pleased with the comments and decided then and there to announce that NIE had five priorities. As he recalled, "It was really, I thought, useful and good criticism, and it was my judgment—which I essentially made right there—that we would stay with the five [priorities] rather than the one" (Glennan, 7 December 1973, p. 9). In the space of seven days, the Five Priorities had been delineated, discussed, and decided upon. The institute had a decision, although not everyone realized it at the time. As one assistant director recalled:

> Most of us walked out of that meeting [i.e., the two-day Five Priorities meeting] saying, "Well, that was another interesting session. What's going to happen tomorrow?" There had been a whole long run of meetings to make decisions which were never heard from again. And I think most of us believed that as soon as we walked out that door there would be at least eight more priorities entering it and sixteen more the day after. What absolutely astonished us was that Tom [Glennan] made them stick. He really did.

Over the next week the five descriptions were rewritten. They were presented to the council and approved on 3 December 1973.

Why then was a decision made in 1973 that was not made in 1972? To an outsider, the Five Priorities might have looked like a very curious collection. Indeed, John Brademas (D–Indiana) later complained:

> They do not appear to be the results of systematic and critical evaluation. For the overriding question with respect to the priorities, of course, is "Why were these particular priorities chosen?" Are there not others equally important, or even more so? [Brademas, 25 March 1974, p. 5]

A number of factors interacted to produce this decision. External pressures had grown and an external deadline had been imposed. Up to a year's planning for specific programs had been accomplished inside NIE. Although there were certainly sharp differences of opinion among senior staff, there also had developed a collective memory, a shared set of experiences and assessments. Glennan himself was totally involved in this effort. Finally, no one suggested any other priorities—the comprehensive and deductive criteria had been foregone. All staff comment centered on the five areas as they were presented. This might have been a function of the short amount of time allowed for comment. Or some people might have believed that suggesting other priorities was unnecessary because no decision would be made—that this was another empty exercise. Others might have believed that any decision was better than no decision—that suggesting other priorities would jeopardize that decision. Or people might have believed that these priorities truly represented areas of institute competence. Certainly they aligned with the things the agency was doing; these particular priorities thus threatened none of the programs and required no major new implementation effort.

The Planning Process

The First Year

In early 1973 Bernard Martin initiated the development of a set of procedures to be used in planning the agency's R&D activities—the planning process. HEW requires all of its agencies to create a planning system through which the department can be apprised of future agency activities. Even if HEW did not have this requirement, Martin believed NIE needed a planning process in order to develop its budget justifications in a systematic way. The planning process would also demonstrate NIE's commitment to systematic management. In NIE's early months, Elliott and Martin frequently talked of developing systems and procedures that would differ from those considered typical of federal government agencies. Personnel promotion procedures, a management information system, contracts and grants procedures, and an internal evaluation plan were to be developed from the ground up, with NIE's specific needs and constraints in mind. The planning process was one of the first attempts at developing a bold new system. No model was singled out for replication, nor was the development of the planning process to focus much on the existing practices of other government agencies; the NIE was going "to be something different."

Unlike the paradigm search, the criteria for the planning process were initially well specified. Three major criteria were equally important: (1) the procedures were to accommodate the realities of external deadlines and internal resource limitations; (2) they were to be comprehensive; and (3) they were to emphasize openness, actively soliciting interaction with individuals and groups outside NIE.[9] In spite of the relatively clear charter associated with the planning process, it was not free from ambiguities. When the project began, the NCER had not been appointed. Yet the planning function had to specify a role for the NCER. Additionally, the process would be used in an organization whose structure had not yet been decided upon and for activities whose comprehensive paradigm had not yet been found.

In January 1973 Martin's staff members who were charged with developing the planning process began their work. On 9 March 1973 they released the first draft of the planning process to the Office of Management professional staff. This fifty-seven-page document described the construction of an "Institute Plan" that would result from a long and complex set of procedures including "research design reviews" of internal projects by the director, "program package reviews" for the NCER, the development of a "Director's Plan," a "Council Plan," and finally the "Institute Plan" (Hansot, 9 March 1973). Reaction to this first draft was negative. The process appeared too complicated; some features, such as the Council Plan, seemed unnecessary;

and the proposed system seemed to require too much top management time to operate.

A second draft, responsive to these criticisms, was distributed on 23 March 1973 to all of those who would be attending a senior staff retreat the first weekend in April. Martin noted that, though he was "getting more comfortable" with the proposal, it still appeared somewhat cumbersome. The staff members incorporated Martin's required revisions and made further attempts at simplification in the third draft of the planning process. Like its predecessors, this third draft, dated 29 March, was more than fifty pages long and demanded a considerable amount of time and effort from a conscientious reader.

The retreat convened Sunday night, 1 April 1973. Table 8.2 provides a profile of the thirty-seven people who attended, key participants in all the major decisions made during NIE's first year. It was a young group (more than half of its members were less than thirty-six years old). It included a disproportionate number of people from the Office of the Director, Office of Management, Office of Administration, and Office of Exploratory Studies. Most of its members (thirty-two) had worked in the federal government, but not in OE, immediately before their employment by NIE.

After introductory comments by Glennan, one of Martin's staff members presented the planning process. Most of the subsequent discussion and criticism was concerned with minor detail, such as the amount of time allowed for program reviews. However, toward the end of the discussion, the planning process was dealt a surprising blow. Glennan declared that he was uncomfortable with the "openness" of the proposal because it would require too much effort in gathering public comment. Martin's staff had established extreme openness as a cornerstone of their proposal, based on previous statements by Glennan. They were stymied.

In April and May Martin and his staff produced drafts four and five of the planning process. They stipulated that public comment would be solicited by individual programs and that new initiatives would come in large part from NIE staff committees. Further, in deference to Patrick Haggerty, just nominated as NCER chairman, the NCER would play a more significant role in the review of program designs. Draft five was discussed at a senior staff meeting on 18 May 1973. At that meeting Glennan and Elliott voiced no clear support for the proposal. They suggested that, because congressional approval of the NCER nominees was expected soon, it might be best to wait for council approval before committing the institute to a set of procedures.

Nearly five months had passed and five drafts of procedures had been developed. Each proposal had been altered incrementally to eliminate features displeasing to various interested parties. There was still no clear sense, however, of whether the product was improving, what an acceptable product might look like, or who would decide when the proposal was

Table 8.2   Summary Characteristics of Participants in NIE Senior Staff Retreat: April 1973

	Age					
	<30	30–35	36–40	41–45	>45	Total
Number	4	16	9	6	2	37
Percentage	10.8	43.2	24.3	16.2	5.4	100

	Previous Employer							
NIE Office	OE	OEO	HEW	Planning Unit	Other Government	University	Other	Total
Director	1	5	1	2	3		1	13
Management	1		1		1		2	5
Field Initiated Studies	(1)ᵃ							(1)ᵃ
Vouchers		1						1
Career Education			1		1			2
Experimental Schools	2							2
Dissemination	1							1
Exploration Studies	1	3				2		6
Administration		1	1	1	1			4
Research Training	1							1
Applied Studies				1	1			2
Special Projects				1				1
Totals	7	10	4	5	7	2	3	38

ᵃOne person was the acting head of both Field Initiated Studies and Dissemination at that time.

"finished." There was agreement on the need for a set of procedures, but there was no indication that a decision was nearer at hand than it had been at the beginning of the undertaking.

Theories for Indecision

The NIE senior and support staff are at least as well educated, as thoughtful, and as talented as those of most Washington agencies. The case cannot be made that their somewhat bewildering behavior, their willingness to write, read, or discuss draft after draft after draft of papers on agencywide issues was caused by a lack of intelligence or formal training. Rather, the evidence we have explored suggests that a number of factors combined to prevent decision processes from reaching closure. In brief,

1. The reward structure evident through the decision processes did not provide incentives for closure—indeed, it provided incentives for prolonging debate.
2. The director did not convey any preference for particular outcomes.
3. Coalitions in support of particular proposals did not form.
4. A lack of specific expertise among the most influential participants and disdain for the experts who were available prolonged the processes.
5. The agency could operate without settling some of the agencywide issues.
6. These agencywide issues were handled in a grander, more dramatic fashion than were program issues. The process itself was pleasurable for many of the most important participants.

In an organization with agressive managers and support staff, inconclusive decision processes can be generated by competition for recognition and promotion. This would occur if the competition was based not on program achievement but on the exercise of process-oriented skills. If the competitors perceive the game as one in which the ability to debate skillfully is paramount, and if there are two or more competitors of roughly equal ability, we would expect lengthy processes.[10]

The decisiveness and intentions of leadership can also generate these processes. If the chief does not know what he wants, decision processes are likely to take longer as alternatives are provided for his perusal. It is reasonably clear that Glennan did not have a stable outcome preference in mind in either the development of a planning process or the paradigm search. It is not clear, however, that in either case his sole concern was with the outcome. The means to the outcome were also important. That is, through the discussions on the agencywide issues Glennan could promote analysis, criticism, and team-building.

If we assume that the director were concerned primarily with process and only secondarily with prompt outcomes, then we might ask why others, particularly Elliott and Martin, did not in some way exercise their influence to either speed up the processes or make sure they sustained themselves to some conclusion. One might have expected coalitions to form around existing alternatives; through bargaining, a consensus would have been achieved. However, stable groups did not coalesce around a point of view and attempt to pursue it to adoption. It might have been that the points of view expressed in debate were not sufficiently compelling to warrant efforts at coalition-forming. This seems unlikely in that individuals did frequently support one or another position. Perhaps the structure of incentives did not favor the formation of coalitions. The perceived rewards for artful debate may have outweighed the returns to diplomacy. Furthermore, the active argument that ensued upon the presentation of any new proposal may have discouraged individuals from coalescing around it. It is possible that there was not enough energy available to engage in extended coalitional activity. There were, at any one time, a number of urgent matters confronting each of the influential decision-makers. Thus the ability to take initiative and persist over a long period was limited. Because of the large number of staff involved in the decision process, a successful coalition would have to bring together seven or eight persons. The energies required to do so might have been considered by all participants as too great. Perhaps there was no agreed-upon currency of exchange; people might have been willing to form coalitions, but were unable to do so because there was nothing to trade. Finally, there might have been, in effect, a coalition of the whole that objected to virtually any strengthening of agencywide management. It is possible that program managers were opposed to anything that might endanger their programs and thus they almost instinctively countered attempts to change existing systems or impose new ones.

If coalitions were not a feature of NIE's decision processes, neither was deference to in-house experts. The opinions of recognized experts can aid closure by providing a reference against which alternative proposals are measured. But the NIE senior staff was not filled with recognized experts in important policy areas. Many of these people were relatively new to the federal government, and some of them were new to the field of education. Furthermore, the opinions of some of the experts who did reside within the institute—senior people transferred from OE—were not held in high esteem by top management.[11]

There was no pressing operational reason for closure on such issues as the paradigm search or the planning process. Owing in part to the procedures that came with the inheritances from OE and OEO, many of the vital day-to-day programmatic functions were taking care of themselves—people were hired, requests for R&D proposals formulated, contracts and grants negotiated, projects monitored, and reports written. Even the preparation of budget requests, an agency-level function closely tied to the planning process, could be (indeed was) performed in the absence of procedures top management felt were important.

The final factor delaying closure might be called the pleasures of the process. Events can be symbolically important because people want them to be so. The importance of the event is found in its certifying effect (those who participated are acknowledged as important), in the resources allocated to it (staff work, the biggest conference room, the time of people with significant titles), and in the alleged gravity of its subject (planning and long-range issues). The purpose of these events is to put on a satisfying show, and this need not involve actually making decisions. So it may have been with the processes we have described. Decisions at the program level were being made; they were made in an informal fashion in small groups that included some top managers (see the discussion that follows concerning budget decisions). Because these decisions were taken care of, the agency could deal with higher-order affairs in a symbolic fashion. The style in which they were conducted provided exciting confrontations and stimulating ideas. The continued pursuit of these pleasures may have been a factor in prolonging the debate.

The Second Year

Those working on the planning process were drawn away from this task in the late spring of 1973. Though little staff work was done on the process between late May and mid-September a number of events with significance for the planning process did occur during this period. First, the NCER held three meetings in Washington during the summer. Among the many things conveyed to the institute in these meetings was the council's view of its role in the planning of NIE activities. A number of NCER members expressed specific preferences related to planning and the planning process. Haggerty went so far as to present Glennan with a book he had written about the development of Texas Instruments Incorporated, which stressed the use of particular planning systems (Haggerty 1965). Second, during the summer of 1973 the fiscal year 1974 funding level for the institute was uncertain. At that time a substantial increase over the fiscal year 1973 funding level seemed likely (from $110 to $162 million), but NIE did not know how much money it would have. Thus, the institute was unable to concentrate on fiscal year 1975 budget development, even though its first formal 1975 documents should have been ready for submission to HEW in September. It seems likely that if the preparation of fiscal year 1975 budget-planning documents had not been delayed, there would have been greater immediate concern about the development of the planning process. Third, the members of Martin's staff who had worked on the first five drafts had either left the institute or been assigned to other tasks. A new staff man took over responsibility for the planning process. By early September 1973 personnel were available, the initial preferences of the NCER had been heard, and final appropriations for the fiscal year 1974 budget were soon to be announced. The planning process once again moved to center stage.

During September 1973, drafts six and seven were written. They addressed many of the issues addressed in earlier drafts but changed the focus of the process somewhat. While the spring drafts emphasized global issues, generating external comment and preparing "the Institute Plan," the fall draft featured more parochial issues—careful review of internal programs and specific decision points for the director. In an effort to meet previous complaints, draft seven specified that all senior staff would be present at reviews of ongoing programs. And it stipulated that the director, not his deputy or any of the associate directors, would make final program-funding decisions. The NCER role was unspecified but included "annual Council reviews of overall institute activities" (Williamson and Hansot, 24 September 1973, p. 14). And the sensitive issue of soliciting external comment was sidestepped by assigning that responsibility to the Office of External Relations.

During most of October and November the NIE leadership and Martin's staff were swamped by work more pressing than the planning process. Several things occurred during this period that were to influence subsequent work on the planning process. The Five Priorities were announced. Future planning processes would have to accommodate their existence. The budget cut and the growing possibility that the institute would request a supplemental appropriation to recoup at least some of its "lost" resources injected grave uncertainty into the scope of activities the planning process must cover. Related to both the Five Priorities and the budget cut were the actions of Haggerty. In late November he outlined to Glennan a method by which the NIE's fiscal year 1974 expenditures, originally planned to be $162 million, could be cut back to $75 million, organized around the Five Priorities and arranged to provide the groundwork for a supplemental request, if this proved advisable. Haggerty's proposal called for factoring each program and other planned expenditures into "decision packages," described simply as "a package of activity on which an independent decision can logically be made" (Haggerty, 23 November 1973, p. 2). The packages would then be ranked under each priority, and a $75 million cutoff point would be applied to the list. An examination of what would and would not be funded using that cutoff point would help the institute determine if it needed more funds, and if so, how much more. Haggerty referred to the approaching due date for the annual NCER report to the president and suggested, "It is really difficult to imagine a report which would be satisfactory at the present time if it were not based on the kind of analysis [I have] suggested" (Haggerty, 23 November 1973, p. 5).

These factors—the announcement of the Five Priorities, pressure from HEW for data on the fiscal year 1974 supplemental budget request, and Haggerty's ideas on planning—led to a new round of interest in the planning process in late November 1973. About this time Glennan shared with Martin's staff his thoughts on a reorganization that would place planning and conceptualizing responsibilities in one office and program operating responsibilities in another—the "thinkers and doers" model, similar to a structure he had used at OEO. He requested that this structure be described in a planning process paper that would concentrate on developing material pertinent to the fiscal year 1975 budget.

And so the third round of writing planning process drafts began. On 5 December 1973, Martin's staff circulated draft eight, entitled "Structuring FY75 Planning in the Priority Areas: Some Preliminary Thoughts." The cover memo pointed out that budget categories should be related to the Five Priorities and that, once again, the institute was behind schedule in budget preparation.

By allocating funds against the established organizational units of the Institute rather than priority areas we neither require nor provide incentives for interrelating the work of the various units. We need to think through how we can structure these incentives.

We are late in the planning cycle even for FY75. If we fail to obtain substantive information now regarding FY75 proposals we jeopardize our ability to be on top of a substantive agenda when we have to go to Congress. [Williamson and Hansot, 5 December 1973]

Draft eight described a general strategy for organizing work on the Five Priorities, based on Glennan's "thinkers and doers" model. The issues that had been the primary focus of earlier planning process documents occupied only two of the document's six pages; they were upstaged by the description of the reorganization. The proposed planning sequence reflected the "decision package" language of Haggerty much more than it did the "program review" orientation of the first seven drafts. This draft was sent to a sample of influential senior staff members, clearly labeled "for discussion only."[12] No one was pleased with the implied reorganization. The reaction was tactfully conveyed to Glennan as, "rather strong negative initial reactions" (Hansot and Williamson, 11 December 1973, p. 8).

Martin's staff made one last effort to distill features of a process incorporating the concerns expressed in the criticism of draft eight, the preferences of Haggerty and Glennan, and the "realities," or external deadlines, that Martin continually stressed. Draft nine is the last document in the December series. The planning process was ignored until late February 1974.

The period between mid-December and mid-March was filled with preparations for congressional testimony regarding NIE's fiscal year 1974 supplemental budget request and the development of fiscal year 1975 budget allocations. During these weeks four items arose that would affect the next round of planning process drafts. First, although abandoning the "thinkers and doers" reorganization that intrigued him earlier, Glennan decided that an executive committee could help with the important decisions of the institute, particularly resource allocation decisions. The Executive Committee, under consideration from January 1974, would have to be included in any new set of planning procedures. Second, Haggerty continued to emphasize his interest in the institute's planning procedures.[13] Third, by the end of February it was evident that the requested supplemental appropriation was by no means a certainty. Prudent managers throughout the institute were reviewing their financial commitments to contractors and grantees. The "commitment base," or amount of money "morally" committed to a contractor in a future year, became a matter of great concern as the prospect of tight money became more serious. An up-to-date planning process would have to isolate the part of the planned budget that was felt to be already "committed." Fourth, in March Martin had to prepare the fiscal year 1975 budget. Hence, he had less time to devote to the planning process.[14] At the same time Martin had to turn his attention elsewhere, Elliott began to take a more active interest in the planning process.

Drafts ten and eleven of the planning process appeared during the last week in February 1974. They featured Haggerty's concept of "decision packages"; explicit recognition of a program's "commitment base"; and program review by the Executive Committee (Williamson, 25 February 1974). On 8 March the author of these drafts shared his impatience with Elliott and Martin:

> I recommend that we come down on whether the process I have proposed or some specific alternative is the direction we want to go, check with the associate and assistant directors, make whatever elaborations and revisions are necessary and then implement the plan. When I look at the calendar for FY76 planning, I don't think we have the luxury for much picky deliberation and unless there are basic flaws with the concept I think we should move. [Williamson, 8 March 1974]

Drafts twelve and thirteen were written during the second week in March 1974.[15] They specified thirteen sequential steps that began in January of each year and produced a budget submission to OMB/HEW by 15 September including a process to accommodate changes in the NIE budget that occurred as OMB and Congress made modifications. Elliott extensively criticized draft thirteen, but he also indicated that "this is close to right sequence." ASPE reacted to this draft with, "beginning to look like respectable staff work."

Because of intrusions involving the fiscal 1974 and 1975 budgets, it was not until late April that attention to the planning process was again evident. With this round of action came at least the semblance of a conclusion. On 1 May 1974, Martin sent all office and program heads the fiscal year 1976 "budget call," describing the procedures that were to be followed in developing the fiscal year 1976 budget and including a memo titled "Fiscal Year 1976 Planning Process." This memo was essentially a condensed version of the early March proposals. Although some of its features were designed specifically for fiscal year 1976, this document represents the formal declaration of an official NIE planning process.

The essential features of the planning process were as follows:

Office of Planning and Management (OPM) submitted to associate and assistant directors "high" and "low" target figures within which each program plan (including a goal, the specific objectives sought and strategies to be used) and decision package was to be developed.

Assistant directors and other program heads submitted program plans and decisions packages to OPM.

OPM prepared a draft "Institute Plan" including analysis of activities across programs and an initial rank ordering of decision packages across the institute.

The Executive [Committee] received program plans and the OPM draft Institute Plan and specified revisions.

OPM made the revisions, and solicited comment on the revised plan from assistant directors.

OPM submitted comment to the Executive Committee and the committee made its final review.

OPM notified senior staff of the "first round of decisions" and completed materials for a presentation to the NCER.

The Institute Plan was presented to the NCER.

As the budget was reviewed by HEW, OMB, and Congress, adjustments to the initial plan were made by adding and deleting decision-packages on the ranked list. [1 May 1974, pp. 3–5]

Most of Martin's planning process memo was concerned with the definition of terms (program plan, goal, social experiment, strategy) and the presentation of sample forms to be completed. Notably present were terms introduced by Haggerty ("decision package," "rank ordering"); a powerful role for OPM (which Elliott felt was appropriate); important duties for the newly formed Executive Committee (of interest to Glennan); and a clear reference to the "realities" imposed by HEW and OMB (about which Martin felt strongly). Notably absent were a clear indication of how outside constituents were to be involved (an issue sensitive to Glennan); a specification of the relative authority of the associate directors, director and deputy director (about which there were disagreements); and the notion of formal "program reviews" (toward which some assistant directors were hostile). (In the "budgets" section of this chapter we analyze the role of the planning process in the preparation of the fiscal year 1976 budget.)

Fourteen separate complete drafts of the planning process were produced in sixteen months. This endeavor consumed a significant amount of the energy of the senior staff—not only the analysts who actually wrote drafts but also all the managers and staff who read and commented on them. The analysts were exhausted and demoralized by the task. By June 1974 Martin had to admit:

> I'm not sure I now have any single person on the [OPM] staff, with the exception of myself perhaps, who finds the substance of a planning process interesting and exciting ... I don't think there's anyone on the staff who jumps into these questions with great excitement. [14 June 1974a]

How Could a Decision Process Like This Have Come About?

How can we explain decision-making processes like these, which seem so inefficient and irrational, occurring in an organization attempting to operate in an efficient and rational manner? The interweaving of three factors—internal political considerations, a turbulent environment, and a significant number of inexperienced, analytically oriented senior staff members—yielded the vacillating, somewhat cyclical behavior we have observed.

The internal politics focused on three issues. One was the philosophy and style to be exhibited by the planning process; a second was the appropriate role for OPM; and the third was the relative authority of the director and associate directors. Initially, the stylistic issue involved two points of view. Glennan favored an informal, collegial, highly discursive form of planning and decision-making. Competing with this notion were the preferences of Elliott and Martin, who wished to emphasize highly systematic, sequential planning procedures that recognized the constraints ("realities") imposed by the greater federal bureaucracy. When the NCER was finally established, a third point of view with an influential spokesman was introduced. Haggerty, also in favor of highly structured planning procedures, felt strongly about a particular set of elements (decision packages and rank ordering) that would emphasize resource allocation instead of program content.

During the course of development of the planning process, each of these points of view enjoyed better and worse times, depending at least in part on the relative bargaining position of its supporters. When an important NCER decision was nearing, Haggerty's leverage was enhanced; when an HEW or OMB request for budget information arrived, the Elliott/Martin position enjoyed favor; in the absence of either, the director's position temporarily enjoyed an advantage. The planning process that eventually emerged, one that was highly structured and included Haggerty's terminology and Glennan's Executive Committee, featured elements drawn from the preferences of each of the major actors.

The second issue, the role of OPM in the planning process, was a dynamic one. Originally most of the senior staff seemed in agreement; OPM was to be a facilitator, criticizing and aiding personnel in the operating units who developed initiatives and planned programs. By 1974, however, some members of the top management began thinking about a more substantial role for OPM. Because Glennan's attempt to install the thinkers and doers structure had been unsuccessful, there was no identifiable organization unit within NIE responsible for finding and developing proposals to fill gaps in NIE's program structure. OPM was a natural candidate for the job. Martin, however, was reluctant to take on this role, or at least to take it on as rapidly as Glennan and Elliott would have liked. In the planning process finally implemented, OPM was charged with the broader mandate—Glennan and Elliott prevailed—but in fact only a very limited amount of "policy analysis" was performed for the fiscal year 1976 cycle.

The third major internal political issue, the relative authority of the associate directors and the director in budget allocation decisions, was not resolved in the 1 May 1974 paper. Beginning in late 1973, this was a point of debate among both the OPM staff members developing the process and top NIE management. At that time the discussion was somewhat abstract because only one associate director of an operating division had been hired. By 1 May 1974, it was known who would fill the two vacant associate director positions, and the authority issue had become a very real one.[16]

If the institute's internal politics were somewhat stormy, the environment external to NIE was a hurricane. Here we need stress only that by NIE's second year the cumulative effect of this unkind environment was leaving its mark. It kept a constant press on the institute and, at the very least, made continuous uninterrupted work on the planning process—or anything else at the institutewide level—difficult.

Another contributor to the vexing behavior we have observed is the characteristics of the senior staff. As we have discussed elsewhere, those developing the planning process as well as those who criticized and influenced it were, for the most part, young and inexperienced. Furthermore, the senior members of the staff, including the director and some of the important analysts, were newly arrived from positions that demanded careful, objective analysis preparatory to decisive action; one of the very evident features of the institute over the period we have observed is an insistence on deliberation, with a strong emphasis on intellectual discourse. Martin characterized this persistent behavior, "There has been a disinclination to make a decision and a fascination with the nature of problems rather than with their potential solution" (Martin, 14 June 1974a).

The interaction among these three factors is straightforward. The initial attempt to create a planning process (January through April 1973) was drawn out by the deliberative style of top management and opposing views on whether a discursive or structured planning process was appropriate. The arrival of the NCER pushed aside the process. In September the development was resumed but now had to acknowledge Haggerty's preferences. Almost before any real momentum could be generated, the budget cut occurred, and attention again was diverted to an externally generated crisis. In December the third round commenced, spurred by Glennan's interest in reorganizing around a planning style comfortable to him. This effort was interrupted by external pressure regarding the fiscal year 1974 supplemental request and fiscal year 1975 budget planning. In late February round four began. This series of drafts introduced the Executive Committee feature and disputes over the role of OPM and the authority of the associate directors. Continuity was again broken as attention turned to allocating the fiscal year 1975 budget. Finally, in May, under externally imposed pressure to develop the fiscal year 1976 budget, political differences were compromised or neglected, and an official planning process was announced.

Budgets

Fiscal Year 1974

We have described two important decision-making processes in which NIE's top management participated; closure was not reached in either case during the institute's first year. If there is one decision a federal agency must make, however, it is how much money to request from Congress for the coming year.

As we noted in chapter 4, the way NIE received its first appropriation ($110 million for fiscal year 1973) was peculiar because the passage of NIE's authorizing legislation was not in phase with the federal budget-making cycle (see Appendix 5 for a general description of this cycle). To a lesser extent, preparing the fiscal year 1974 budget was also out of phase with the standard cycle. NIE did not begin developing its fiscal year 1974 budget request until November 1972. When it did begin, it was under a variety of constraints. During the development of the fiscal year 1974 budget there was no NCER, no permanent organization structure, no planning process or agreed-upon intellectual framework for the institute's activities. There were few staff members available to work on the budget. There were a number of implicit program "promises" that would have to be accommodated in the allocations.

Writing budget documents is specialized work, requiring experienced manpower. As of November 1972, there were only two budget staff members in the Management Task Force; these were John Christensen, the acting chief budget officer (formerly the first assistant to the chief budget officer in the Office of Education and one of the youngest people ever to hold a senior position of this type), and one junior assistant. The top management of the institute, whose attention was spread over a large variety of important issues, did not systematically devote time to the budget task. Many of the tasks they were performing, such as program reviews and the paradigm search, no doubt provided helpful information relative to the development of the budget itself, but in terms of senior staff energy and attention, these tasks were in competition with the budget. Constraints were also associated with the dollar amounts that could be allocated to individual budget categories. Many of the transfer programs had "commitment bases" that extended beyond fiscal year 1973; these provided effective "floors" for these individual programs (Christensen, March 1974). In addition, Congress had been informed, in the fiscal year 1973 budget documents, of preliminary plans for expenditures for some programs in fiscal year 1974 (see table 8.3 for these estimates).

If there were seeming constraints on several important aspects of the budget, there were no apparent constraints on the optimism of those developing it. Table 8.3 contains information only on programs that could be discussed during the fall of 1972, namely, the large inherited programs, even though they had not yet been fully reviewed by NIE. Exactly how each of these numbers was generated is not clear. They emerged from modifications to estimates made by the Planning Unit. Neither the Planning Unit work nor the modifications (made primarily by Elliott) were based on thorough investigations of the programs involved; there had not been sufficient time to perform these. Rather, a strong sense of optimism, some rules of thumb, and some existing estimates seem to have generated the numbers—which represent approximately a 25% increase in requests for the major inherited programs. Table 8.3 contains no information on new initiatives, and we cannot, through direct budget statements, estimate the expectations that might have been associated with fresh NIE undertakings. Nonetheless, it is clear that NIE was optimistic about fiscal year 1974 expenditures when it began to develop the budget, and this optimism was to continue throughout the process.

In contrast to the paradigm search and the development of the planning process in which the entire senior staff met frequently to review the proceedings, the 1974 budget development occurred primarily in small-group meetings. The key figures drawing the budget together were Elliott, Martin, and Christensen; they met with increasing frequency during the fall and winter to consider various ways of describing the elements of the budget and various ways of obtaining estimates of these elements from program leaders. Glennan's presence at these meetings became more frequent as the congressional budget hearings neared. Although special meetings of top staff were held during the fall of 1972 to discuss the paradigm search, personnel

Table 8.3   Estimates of Fiscal Year 1973 and
                                                 Fiscal Year 1974 NIE Expenditures (In
                                                 Thousands of Dollars)

Program	FY 1973	FY 1974	1973–1974 increase (%)
Dissemination	15,750	27,125	72.2
Experimental Schools	30,000	40,800	36.0
Career Education[a]	11,515	15,150	31.6
Laboratories and R&D U.C. Centers[b]	35,900	34,800	−3.1
Subtotals	93,165	117,875	26.5
Handicapped research	2,600		
Training	2,600		
Unsolicited research	—		
D.C. Schools Project	2,250		
Salaries and expenses	6,820		
New initiatives	2,565		
Total budget	110,000		

[a]Note that Career Education was $16,629,000 in FY 1972.
[b]This program was shifting from institutional support to the purchase of individual lab and center products, and many projects were dropped in the process.

Source: FY 1973 Budget Justification Backup Material, 6 October 1972.

recruitment, and new programs, the budget was discussed by the total senior staff only as one of many items in weekly staff meetings.

Of greatest concern to Glennan, Elliott, Martin, and Christensen was the identification of the "bottom-line" figure. This is the number OMB and HEW were most interested in. It would also reflect the strategy the institute would pursue through the appropriations process, that is, either ask for more than expected in anticipation of a routine cut by the Congress or make a realistic request and depend upon compelling testimony to achieve it. Throughout the fall of 1972, Glennan informally discussed the total request level with individual assistant directors and members of the inner circle. These discussions typically included a consideration of existing agency commitments, tentative new initiatives, the current budget, perceived signals from Congress or other external sources, and the results of prior discussions with other individuals within the agency. Out of each of these discussions emerged a new, usually higher, total request level.

Discussions with assistant directors about allocating funds internally among the program units were only loosely coupled with the latest thinking on the total request. Individual program heads were expected to make the case for their internal allocation on the basis of a carefully conceptualized rational program design. Because such designs had not yet been formally constructed, these conversations were always speculative. Several of the program heads had never participated in the creation of a budget justification; their inexperience could not have reduced the uncertainties of the project.[17]

Periodically throughout the fall and winter of 1972, Martin and Christensen collected the latest information and combined the various program and total agency figures into a consistent presentation. This inevitably required adjustments to the total or subparts or both. The synthesis was discussed with Glennan and Elliott and possibly other senior staff members and quickly became part of the information base feeding the current round of budget discussion.

It is not difficult to see how a system of this type yielded higher rather than lower budget requests. Because those with program responsibility were involved in the determination of both program and total agency budget requests, they had access to estimates of the amount of resources currently allocated to each program. This information became one of the factors influencing the next discussion on a program allocation between the director and an assistant director. The assistant director would then seek an increase in the resources allocated to his or her program based on knowledge of increases allotted to other programs. Given a rational argument for the increase, the director had no compelling reason not to permit it. The usual procedure for so doing was to raise the total agency request. The more iterations a process like this cycles through, the higher the likely budget request. A deadline or other constraint on the period of time available might limit the number of cycles; alternatively, more elaborate internal communication channels, as might be found in an organization with an elaborate hierarchy, might increase the time required for each iteration. Within NIE, however, no deadline other than the House hearings was respected, and one of the most evident attributes of Glennan's style was direct and frequent contact with his senior staff, facilitated by the flat organization structure. Ultimately, NIE submitted a budget request for $162 million to the House Appropriations Subcommittee on 9 March 1973. This was a 47.3% increase over its fiscal year 1973 mark and was presented only four months after the fiscal year 1973 budget was approved.[18] The presentation of this budget set off a series of events that took place primarily outside the institute. The fate of the fiscal year 1974 budget was discussed in chapter 4. We need note only that the fiscal year 1974 budget was not considered to be resolved internally until early in calendar 1974.

Having described the process by which the fiscal year 1974 budget was developed, let us consider alternative explanations of how this system emerged. First, consider the case of a director who wanted to develop support among a cautious staff for an unspecified but substantial increase in budget authority. Staging competition among program heads would certainly achieve this; however, the evidence does not convincingly support this explanation. The projections cited in the fiscal year 1973 budget indicate that substantial growth was anticipated well before Glennan became involved with fiscal year 1974 budget development. Clearly, those within NIE were expecting and were supportive of major increases in budget authority. More significantly, this model attributes superior deception skills to Glennan. His personal style radiates openness and honesty to the extent that it is difficult to conceive of his engineering a major covert undertaking to increase staff enthusiasm for a large budget.

A second explanation suggests that an experienced and respected bureaucrat could set the total agency request at an "appropriate" level, and a system such as we have described would serve to supply the details. In this case Elliott, exploiting his contacts throughout the federal establishment and rules of thumb developed over the years at OMB, would determine the gross agency request. There are many reasons why estimates based on personal experience and information available to NIE might yield a higher budget request. The $110 million for fiscal year 1973 was a sizable budget; yet this amount was based only on the transfer of OE programs, not on the fuller, more coherent research program that fiscal year 1974 funds would support. The most visible guidance for resource growth came from the 1971 testimony before NIE's authorizing committee. In these hearings R&D in education was envisaged as similar in size to that of NIH and NASA. And new agencies in recent history, such as OEO, had had records of rapid growth. Although these factors support a tendency to a higher request, they do not explain why the total request would change as the budget developed or why a highly iterative process would be desirable to supply support for it. In an environment in which time and staff were short, one might expect a more efficient means of allocating an established total budget among programs than the one used.

A third explanation suggests that the director wanted to build a budget favoring the "good people" rather than prespecified programs. Perhaps Glennan wanted to allocate his resources in those places where he believed the chances for a successful outcome were greatest. Given that top management was concerned about the quality of the institute's personnel, and given that Glennan had not been with NIE long and thus may not have reached a judgment on the quality of individuals on his senior staff, an iterative process that featured contact between the director and the program heads seems reasonable. In this case the total budget outcome would derive from an assessment of appropriate levels of expansion for each senior staff member. Those perceived as more competent by top management received more budget authority. This model would predict frequent contact between the director and program leaders, and this was definitely the case. Were it being fully implemented, however, we would expect to have seen a systematic pattern in this contact. What evidence we have indicates that the director discussed budget affairs with program heads along with other concerns. More than a systematic assessment, the pattern of contact reflected the minicrises, task fulfillment, and social preferences one would expect in any organizational environment.

A fourth explanation suggests that the budget process resulted from the disarray one would expect in a new agency. A flat organizational structure existed while the "right" structure was being developed. All senior staff members were very busy. Top management and senior staff had not worked together long and had not agreed informally on the objectives of the organization. This disarray, together with NIE's ambiguous legislative mandate and the absence of the NCER, meant that the budget had few substantive restraints. Top management, as it cycled through the process of greasing the squeakiest wheel, would arrive at the budget issue and initiate discussion with the senior staff. Replies from program heads would take place as they could be fit in among other pressing issues. The total budget estimates that emerged would reflect an almost random set of exchanges between the director and the program heads.

In fact, combining elements of each explanation best answers the quandary. The director probably did want to see the agency grow vigorously. The deputy director did try to apply his experience to the budget development. The "good people" probably were encouraged to participate in the process more than others. And the chaos and optimism that characterized the first months of NIE's existence surely was reflected in the budget process.

The Fiscal Year 1974 Supplemental Request

In October 1973, NIE's fiscal year 1974 budget was cut to $75 million; before the end of the month NIE had decided to return to Congress with a request for additional fiscal year 1974 funds. The supplemental request appears to have resulted from a strong desire on the part of the institute to recoup "lost" resources, reinforced by the encouragement of the Office of the Secretary of HEW (see chap. 4 for the role of HEW officials in this decision). First, the institute believed it had $76 million worth of current program commitments. Although some paring might be achieved, more than $75 million would be necessary if any new program development were to be undertaken (Glennan, 30 October 1973, p. 7). And it seemed essential to begin new programs because the implied mandate of the institute was to improve federally sponsored educational research, not to run programs inherited from OE. Second, a generous supplemental appropriation would help erase the negative impressions generated by the appropriations hearings. Third, and more subtly, not to request a supplemental appropriation would be admitting in effect that the arguments of NIE's congressional detractors had some merit. On 30 October 1973, Glennan wrote a lengthy memo to the secretary of HEW discussing the budget cut and the state of the institute, and giving a prescription for action. As Glennan saw it, "It is important for us to restore our credibility promptly, and with forthrightness to put aright the misperceptions voiced by Senator Magnuson" (Glennan, 30 October 1973, p. 2). He concluded by specifying several necessary "elements of support." The first was "A well documented request for a supplemental appropriation to be sent to the Congress—probably for about $50 million" (Glennan, 30 October 1973, p. 8).

As noted in detail elsewhere in this chapter, many important events unfolded in the wake of the 1974 budget cut. The NCER held meetings, constituent groups were active, new senior personnel joined the staff. During this congested period in the early winter of 1973 the decision was made to appeal for $25 million.[19] The problem then was to make a compelling case for this money. To this end, a conference of senior staff was convened in Annapolis, Maryland, in early January 1974.

Three aspects of this conference make it notable. The first is that it was necessary to generate a justification. Even though top management was convinced that it required more money to implement new programs, it did not have a clear sense of what those programs were. The second is the forum chosen to create the justification. The fact that a conference of more than thirty staff members was selected as the means of arriving at a plan to present to Congress is consistent with the decision-making style we have previously observed. The third aspect was an unexpected outcome of the conference— the disillusionment of NIE staff. The fact of the gathering, rather than any specific point discussed, bothered participants. It seemed to violate much of what they believed in and had publicly supported—namely, the deliberate, careful development of important initiatives. In contrast, the conference was called to develop, in two days, ideas that would soon be widely advertised. One of those in attendance summed it up: "What went on out there was just wrong . . . that's not the way you build a program" (Hansot, 14 June 1974).

In January the institute's top management, assisted by the staff of the HEW deputy assistant secretary for budget, incorporated the conference ideas in a formal budget presentation. The HEW staff reviewed both the written and oral work and helped select specific language and develop the general lines of argument. The justification was complicated by the fact that NIE had delayed payment on some ongoing programs until fiscal year 1975 to fund new initiatives in fiscal year 1974. Thus, of the total $25 million request, about $16 million was slated for deferred payments, and about $9 million was requested for new activities. Although only about half of the request was slated for the Five Priorities, the bulk of the fifty-two-page justifying document described the allocation in those terms (see table 8.4 for program allocations described in the supplemental request). The justification was almost totally devoid of examples or anecdotes, describing programs only in abstract terms.

Table 8.4   NIE Budget Allocations by Program
                                           Described in Request for Supplemental
                                           Appropriation: Fiscal Year 1974

Program	Amount	Percentage
Productivity[a]	$ 411,000	1.7
Education/Work[a]	2,000,000	8.0
Problem Solving[a]	2,930,000	11.7
Diversity[a]	7,950,000	31.8
Experimental Schools	(2,950,000)	(11.8)
Educational Vouchers	(3,000,000)	(12.0)
Multicultural	(1,000,000)	(4.0)
Handicapped	(1,000,000)	(4.0)
Essential Skills[a]	886,000	3.5
Teaching and Curriculum	6,668,000	26.7
Basic Policy Studies	1,655,000	6.6
Dissemination	2,500,000	10.9
Totals	$25,000,000	100.0

[a]Indicates one of the five priorities.   Source: NIE FY 1974 Supplemental Budget
                                                  Justification, p. 10, 26, 37, 47.

On 27 February 1974, Glennan, accompanied by his senior staff and the deputy assistant secretary for budget, went before the House Appropriations Committee. In his brief opening comments, Glennan gave four reasons for requesting the supplemental appropriation:

At the time of the original fiscal year 1974 appropriations hearings, the NCER had not yet been appointed and thus official policy had not then been established.

The review of inherited programs had been only recently completed.

The NCER had reviewed NIE's programs and established the Five Priorities.

$75 million was not enough to run the existing programs for fiscal year 1974. [House Appropriations Subcommittee, 27 February 1974, pp. 248–49]

Neither this committee nor the Senate Appropriations Subcommittee was impressed by this rationale. As noted in chapter 4, they refused to grant NIE any supplemental funds.

Fiscal Years 1975 and 1976

The development of the fiscal year 1975 budget followed essentially the same deliberative and choice-making pattern described for the 1974 budget and the supplemental request. This is not surprising, because some of the important circumstances of the institute were much the same in the fall of

1973 as they were in the winter of 1972. No consensus on an appropriate budget level to plan for had been achieved by Glennan, Elliott, Martin, and influential assistant directors. Though an organization structure had been adopted in May 1973, many of the important positions within it were still vacant. A formal planning process had not yet been implemented. Until late in the process, no explicit organizational goals existed. NIE requested $130 million in March 1974. As has been noted in chapter 4, the final appropriation, not decided in Congress until November 1974, gave NIE $70 million.

The planning and budget development systems associated with the fiscal year 1974 and 1975 budgets were loosely structured at best. Neither of these budgets fared well before Congress. Something different was required for fiscal year 1976.

> The fiscal year 1976 is a uniquely important one for the institute. It will show our priorities clearly for the first time since the inherited commitments should largely have been honored. More importantly, the 1976 budget and the program it represents will be the basis upon which the institute will be examined during the reauthorization hearings. [Glennan, 21 May 1974, p. 1]

These portentous words opened a 21 May 1974 memo from Glennan outlining his plans for creating the fiscal year 1976 budget. As reflected in Glennan's memo, two organizational factors seemed to provide a basis for optimism as the institute launched a new round of budget preparation. First was the presence of the Executive Committee, which had initially convened on 3 May. It was Glennan's hope that the Executive Committee would provide a decision-making forum in which statesmanship and a concern for the institute as a whole would replace, or at least dampen, the entrepreneurial zeal of assistant directors whose perspective seemed limited to the immediate welfare of their own programs. Second, the planning process was in operation. Admittedly, it was rudimentary compared with the sophistication of many of the early drafts that outlined that process. But it did provide for a period of time during which program and organizational units could reflect on future priorities and then submit written plans and cost estimates that could serve as the building blocks of the 1976 budget submission.[20] However, the 1976 budget process would face a number of difficult obstacles, including short deadlines; unexpected congressional cuts in the 1975 budget; external pressure; substantive dilemmas concerning the desirable future course of NIE work; and the inherent complexity of transforming a committee into a decision-making body.

Each step in the fiscal year 1976 budget-making process was squeezed by a tighter deadline than the step before. On 1 May 1974, Martin asked NIE's associate directors, assistant directors, and other program heads to begin fiscal year 1976 program planning (Martin, 1 May 1974). Because the planning process faced immediate deadlines imposed by HEW, program units had only thirty days to complete their plans. During this same period many of the units were already heavily burdened by the requirements of completing contract and grant arrangements so that fiscal year 1974 funds could be disbursed by 30 June, the end of the current fiscal year. The deadline for submission of program plans to Martin's office (OPM) was 3 June. The plans were accumulated into three massive notebooks, together weighing eighteen pounds. The eight-member OPM staff had eleven days in which to "analyze" these plans before presenting their analysis to the Executive Committee. The Executive Committee, in turn, had three days to review the plans and the OPM analyses and make preliminary budget allocations.

The consequence of the short deadlines was that each set of participants (program staffs, OPM staff, and Executive Committee) felt that it had considerably less time to discharge its responsibilities than the complexity of the proposals and the gravity of the budget submission warranted. In addition, a sense of physical exhaustion came to pervade the institute. As Glennan later declared, "We have allowed ourselves to be driven by our deadlines" (Glennan, 25 June 1974).

Uncertainties concerning the fate of the 1975 budget clouded the planning for the fiscal year 1976 budget in two ways. The fact that program heads did not know how much money they would have to spend in fiscal year 1975 made it difficult to plan 1976 activities. But, additionally, the process of wrangling over the fiscal year 1975 budget introduced tensions and sensitive issues into the fiscal year 1976 planning. First, program staff complained that there was no "coherent strategic approach" guiding the process of allocating funds to program heads (Martin, 29 March 1974b; Werksman, Binswanger, and McDaniels, 15 April 1974). One of the manifestations of this lack of a strategic approach was that projects already under way ("the commitment base") were not reexamined during the budget process. Therefore, in effect, the complaint was that program managers with expensive transferred projects were successfully hoarding money. Program managers also protested that they had not been sufficiently consulted about budget priorities. And they complained that the budget-planning process was carried out in the context of unrealistic expectations concerning appropriations.[21] These issues exacerbated the 1975 budget allocation process. But, because work on the 1975 and 1976 budgets was going on simultaneously, they also confused the 1976 process.

The simultaneous confrontation of 1975 and 1976 budget-planning problems was heavily influenced by external pressures from groups demanding that they get their share of the budget. The chief state school officers were pressing for a congressional directive that $30 million of the fiscal year 1975 budget be spent on dissemination and largely channeled to state departments of education. The NIE Executive Committee was prepared to make some commitments to dissemination in exchange for constituency support of the

$130-million budget request but wished to spend less than $30 million and also sought to avoid a specific congressional directive (NIE Executive Committee Minutes, 13 May 1974, p. 2). The House Appropriations Committee did specify that $12.9 million be spent on dissemination and that figure appeared in the internal 24 June allocation of a $100-million budget. However, when the House cut the appropriation to $80 million, the dissemination budget suffered (see table 8.5 for 1975 and 1976 budget figures). The institute was also under pressure from minority groups, particularly the Task Force de la Raza, a group of representatives from the Chicano community (NIE Executive Committee Minutes, 13 May 1974, p. 1).[22] And the leaders of the laboratories and R&D centers also maintained a high level of interest in the budget proceedings. In early July in the aftermath of the 1975 budget cut by the full House, an internal OPM memorandum outlining drastic cuts in laboratory and R&D center support was leaked to the directors of several of these institutions. Amid the resulting furor, a meeting was hastily convened between Glennan and CEDaR representatives. On 18 July 1974 Glennan insisted that no decisions about funding cuts had been made and that CEDaR had misinterpreted the internal memorandum (Glennan, 31 July 1974, p. 16). One consequence of external pressure was that programs not defended by an active lobby—Essential Skills, Productivity, Vouchers, Experimental Schools, and Local Problem Solving—tended to bear a disproportionate share of the reductions necessary to move from a $90 million commitment base to an $80 million budget for 1975. In contrast, Dissemination, Multi-cultural Studies, and Teaching and Curriculum, each defended by an active external constituency, fared better. Naturally those units most affected by the 1975 cuts were disposed to seek substantial increases for their 1976 budget allocations. But with no aggressive lobbies for support, it was difficult to make a strong case.

In addition to tight deadlines and external pressures, the 1976 budget process was still carrying the weight of unresolved, vaguely stated "policy issues." Glennan set forth six of these in his May memo to the NCER:

> 1. Is the institute dealing adequately with the statutory policy that NIE work provide "to every person an equal opportunity to receive an education of high quality"?
>   . . .
> 2. What should be the balance between Research, Development and Utilization/Dissemination? . . .
> 3. What should be the balance among the priority areas?
>   . . .
> 4. What is the institute's policy toward curriculum development to be? . . .
> 5. What should the institute's policy be on institutional support [of laboratories and R&D centers]? . . .
> 6. What should distribution of efforts be among age groups?
>   [Glennan, 21 May 1974, pp. 2–3]

Table 8.5   NIE Budget Allocations by Programs: Fiscal Year 1975–76 (In Thousands of Dollars)

Program	(1) "Commitment Base" for FY 1975 (6/24/74)	(2) $100-Million Budget for FY 1975 (6/24/74)	(3) Initial Budget Allocations for FY 1976 (6/24/74)	(4) $80-Million Budget for FY 1975 (7/7/74)	% Ch of (Over
Research					
Essential Skills	915	915	10,800	823	−
Teaching Curriculum	23,411	23,967	15,000	20,345	−
Basic Studies	1,475	1,320	10,000	1,191	−
Policy Studies	2,597	2,597	3,500	2,442	−
Multicultural	2,903	2,903	9,000	2,714	−
Measurement	−	−	3,080	−	−
Women's Studies	−	−	1,000	−	−
Programs					
Productivity	9,875	9,876	14,000	6,237	−
Education and Work	17,284	15,956	21,000	13,545	−
Local Problem Solving	2,911	2,311	8,000	1,568	−
Experimental Schools	7,998	7,898	6,050	4,000	−
Vouchers	4,400	4,400	4,140	2,900	−
Practitioner Research	−	−	5,000	−	−
Dissemination and Resources	4,850	12,850	30,000	6,025	+2
Administration	11,950	12,900	14,000	11,300	−
Office of Planning and Management	165	165	275	200	+
Office of Human Rights	−	−	360	−	−
Science Adviser	−	−	100	−	−
Office of Public Information	−	−	340	−	−
New Activities	−	1,942	−	6,710	−
Totals	90,734	100,000	155,645	80,000	−

Source: OPM memoranda for dates indicated.

Each of these issues can be seen as simply the reflection of the institute's immediate political problems. Yet each also had an older history within the institute. These same issues had haunted the paradigm search and the debate over the Five Priorities.

The mid-June deliberations of the Executive Committee had been planned to be the decision-making high point in the creation of the fiscal year 1976 budget request. Yet those deliberations were largely an exercise in frustration and futility. As Glennan would later recall:

> As is usual, there was a whole set of things that got in and screwed the process up—the appropriations process particularly. . . . The meetings were frustrating in many ways because the problem was so large and we really had so little way to put a handle into this whole thing. [Glennan, 31 July 1974, pp. 1, 5]

One major problem that interfered with the Executive Committee process was, as the senior staff feared, that the fiscal year 1976 planning process had been carried forward under totally unrealistic budget forecasts. The total "low" budget requests for fiscal year 1976 had totaled $156 million. Given the House cut to $80 million for fiscal year 1975 in late June it became clear that even the low budget figure was wildly unrealistic. A factor contributing to the $156 million total was that individual programs did not critically reexamine their "commitment bases" as Glennan had wanted them to. Instead, the programs justified expenditures already under way and went on to propose additional spending (Glennan, 31 July 1974, p. 2).

A host of other problems also plagued the process. The Executive Committee was overwhelmed by detail. In addition to the three heavy notebooks of individual program submissions, Martin provided a sixty-three-page memo presenting the results of OPM's hastily completed analysis of the program submissions. The Executive Committee simply did not have the capacity or the time to deal with even the OPM memorandum (Glennan, 31 July 1974, p. 5). In addition, immediate questions concerning fiscal year 1975 allocations were imposed on the Executive Committee. This imposition further reduced the already inadequate time for discussing fiscal year 1976 plans. It also projected the Executive Committee into immediate internal political wrangles over the allocation of 1975 funds. As a result, the associate directors had difficulty in approaching the budget discussions as "statesmen" with an institutewide perspective rather than as leaders of portions of the institute with obligations to advocate the programs headed by their assistant directors (Glennan, 31 July 1974, pp. 28–29). Reduction of the statesmen role then led to uncertainties about whether the Director or the Executive Committee should make the final allocational decisions (Martin, 15 October 1974).

Furthermore, the criteria for decision-making were, as usual, highly ambiguous. There had been rhetoric to the effect that the best conceptualized programs would receive the lion's share of fiscal year 1976 funding. However, the decision criteria finally employed strayed from "quality" and were more consistent with external political reality and a felt need to be "fair" to various assistant directors. As Glennan described the mid-June Executive Committee allocation process:

> We ended up with an allocation of '75 funds and an allocation of '76 funds. They were not terribly thoughtful allocations because they essentially said: Well, — — program needed a chance. The submission wasn't worth it, but it was an important area and they needed the resources to try to get on with the job, and so we gave them some. — — submissions were very good, but she was too spread out, and it already had enough of the resources in the institute, so we wouldn't give her nearly as much as she wanted; and we gave her some. It turned out to be a very uninspired set of allocations. [Glennan, 31 July 1974, p. 6-7]

After the Executive Committee meetings, Glennan announced tentative fiscal year 1975 and 1976 allocations that were based on the assumption that the House Appropriation Committee's recommendation for $100 million for fiscal year 1975 would be approved by Congress. Seventy-two hours later the Labor–HEW appropriations bill reached the floor of the House. That evening Congresswoman Green's amendment to slice $20 million from the budget was approved by the House.

Several top NIE leaders were out of town that weekend; when they returned on Monday they began to pick up the pieces of their shattered budget allocations. NIE's budget officer and a staff analyst were asked to undertake cuts in the 24 June allocations, then only one week old. They faced the 12 July deadline when budget recommendations had to go to the NCER. The fiscal year 1975 totals had to be reduced to $80 million. In light of the House vote, Glennan and Elliott insisted that the target figure for the fiscal year 1976 had to be reduced from $155 million to no more than $130 million.

The fiscal year 1976 budget process had begun as a "bottom up" process with recommendations coming from the program units. Now, within a few days, the OPM staff had to apply a "top down" correction by cutting both the fiscal year 1975 and the fiscal year 1976 allocations by more than 15%. On 8 July the OPM team gave the Executive Committee their recommendations for drastic cuts. Their two prime tools were reductions in the "commitment base" across the institute and deep slashes in the funding of laboratory and R&D center projects. (This latter recommendation was the one leaked to the laboratory and R&D center directors.)

The associate directors on the Executive Committee were in a difficult position. They were being asked to approve heavy reductions in the programs managed by their assistant directors. The acceptance of the cuts was made even more difficult by the fact that the cuts had only the crudest rationale and, in Glennan's words, "bore no relationship to the quality of the program [being cut] or anything like that" (Glennan, 31 July 1974, p. 12). Two associate directors were new and relatively unfamiliar with their programs. Finally, the assistant directors were to have only thirty-six hours in which to appeal the reductions. The Executive Committee unenthusiastically endorsed the OPM recommendations.

The newly reduced budget allocations were reported to the NCER on 12 July. Glennan presented them as a "staff exercise," not as a final recommendation (Glennan, 31 July 1974, p. 13). The council view was that there was no point in discussing the allocations until the director was prepared to make a firm recommendation, and thus they took no action (Glennan, 31 July 1974, p. 15).

The major efforts on planning both the fiscal year 1975 and the fiscal year 1976 budgets were supposed to have been completed by July 1974. But neither budget was yet resolved. On 7 August 1974, Glennan issued "planning and budget" guidance to the senior staff for fiscal year 1975 under the assumption that NIE would receive $80 million. These allocations would again have to be revised downward in December after final congressional approval of only $70 million. In the same memo Glennan directed that OPM work with the new director of external relations (now called the adviser for government and public affairs) in arranging to obtain the views of "external constituency groups" on the fiscal year 1976 budget. In fact, a new round of planning for fiscal year 1976 had been opened.[23] Glennan concluded his 7 August memo by stating, "We should all strive to improve our performance in both giving clear tasks with reasonable deadlines and in accomplishing those tasks" (Glennan, 7 August 1974, p. 10). Such an admonition may have impressed the NIE staff as ironic.

The budget processes are unique among the issues discussed in this chapter in that they clearly display some learning on the part of key individuals. Through the course of three sets of budget hearings, Glennan did improve his testimony before Congress (as noted in chap. 4). The written justifications, though not lucid by fiscal year 1975, were improved over earlier efforts. Attempts to communicate formally with Congress and constituents did accelerate after the original budget cut. And budget pressures did bring closure on the planning process issue as top management learned that some order was required in the development of budgets. Through the budget process, the institute as a whole also learned: by fiscal year 1976 it was clear that education R&D was not destined for billion-dollar-per-year prominence in the foreseeable future.

Conclusion

The paradigm search, begun as an internally motivated attempt to employ the scientific model, produced no framework in the first year. In the second year, reestablished in response to external criticism, the search yielded the Five Priorities. They were not established deductively, but rather grew from work the institute was already sponsoring. The development of the planning process, begun primarily as an internally motivated attempt to improve upon conventional government procedures, yielded fourteen drafts from more than a year's work. The "official" planning process was ultimately filled with compromises and ambiguity. Although the budgeting process was most constrained by external deadlines, even it seemed to cycle endlessly, as a result of the cuts imposed by Congress. Each cut meant, in effect, that the process had to begin again.

Evident in all three processes is the desire to implement a rational model of decision-making. In each case, vaguely defined optimal criteria existed initially; alternatives were generated; the alternatives were debated in light of the criteria. Yet decisions did not come promptly. Rather than consider alternatives simultaneously, the NIE system examined them sequentially. As each alternative cycled through its iteration, events external and internal to the institute continuously reshaped the criteria against which the solution was judged. The development of alternatives, the desire for and belief in deliberation, and the press of events led to situations in which the alternatives under consideration were out of phase with the criteria used to evaluate them. The processes we have described came to closure only when an important external deadline required it—in the case of the budgets and the Five Priorities—or when staff exhaustion and a deadline impelled it—in the case of the planning process. In each case the final decision was made despite a desire for further deliberation. In each case the final decision was the result of a single top manager's (sometime with staff help) making somewhat arbitrary judgments.

As decision processes continued without closure, they became receptacles into which were dumped the latest important issues. Attempting to resolve the latest issue within the particular process inevitably changed the focus of the decision. Certain issues were never resolved (e.g., the relative authority of the director versus the associate directors, the policy role of the NCER). They tended to appear and reappear in all the decision contexts.

Across time, the spirit of the three decision processes changed. Initially, the institute was optimistic, and closure on issues was impeded by an insistence on achieving optimal solutions to ill-defined and changing problems. Later, corresponding roughly to NIE's second year, the internal optimism waned somewhat, and internal "pulling and hauling" became a greater obstacle to closure. Initially the institute had the initiative; it wanted to "be something different and better." Later the initiative was lost and the institute had to operate in a reactive manner, attempting to overcome a backlog of internal and external problems.

The deliberative and cyclical style characteristic of these undertakings was not atypical. Other systems and procedures for the conduct of agencywide business fared similarly.[24] This same unwillingness or inability to come to closure extended to agencywide discussions of programmatic substance as well. More than one observer of NIE has been impressed with the fact that the agency was quick and accurate in identifying its problems but unable to implement solutions to them. One of the top leadership trio accurately characterized the decision-making problem:

> [The institute has a] fascination with the problems and complexities of educational R&D and a disinclination to elicit from those problems and complexities some set of ideas that people believe in. ... Decisions are made by the force of events, not by conviction, and thus [they] can be easily changed by the next set of events. [Martin, 14 June 1974a]

Despite a lack of closure on major issues, the agency was able to continue its daily operations. One might thus conclude that the agencywide issues—ones such as the paradigm search and planning process, if not the budget—were not vital to the agency's well-being. From an operational perspective this might have been true. However, the agency's inability to reach closure on issues of proclaimed importance did come to affect both external opinions about the agency and staff morale. Toward the end of NIE's first year, staff began referring to NIE's "analysis paralysis." This was initially a facetious term. By the end of the second year, however, "analysis paralysis" was a serious entry in the NIE lexicon. We explore its consequences, in terms of staff morale and agency reputation, in chapter 9.

Nine   Belief and Action

Introduction

The foregoing history of NIE may be viewed as the result of three streams: actions, external events, and beliefs. The first stream consists of actions taken by or occurring within the research bureau of the Office of Education and its successor, the National Institute of Education: the reorganizations, the fall of old leadership and the ascendancy of the new, the declaration and revision of goals, the allocation and reallocation of resources, the attempts to establish cordial relations with the rest of the world. The second stream consists of events in the outside world that had an impact upon NIE and its predecessors: the ebb and flow of constituent support, the congressional process of passing legislation and appropriating money, the arrival and departure of presidents and cabinet secretaries, the creation of rules and deadlines by other elements in the bureaucracy.

The third stream is the most difficult to specify. It is the partly stable, partly shifting set of beliefs adhering to and infusing the past decade of federal effort in education research and development. This stream includes beliefs about why education R&D should be conducted, what can be expected as products, the appropriate federal role, how the federal enterprise should be managed, and who should manage it. It also includes performance assessments of both individuals and organizations supporting or conducting education R&D.

In previous chapters organizational actions and external events determined the unfolding of the story; the relevant systems of belief have been a discontinuous thread running through the accounts. In this chapter the belief structure becomes the center of attention; actions and events play the contextual role.

Our emphasis on beliefs is not surprising. We began our study of NIE in the aftermath of its first budget cut, in October 1973. The small national community associated with the institute was already alive with concern and explanation of "what went wrong." Our initial intention, in retrospect a sublimely naive one, was to discover the "lessons" that might be learned so that, whatever the mistake might have been, we could warn against its repetition. However, our inquiry did not uncover uncontroverted evidence, but rather found inconsistent and conflicting beliefs about what had happened. These beliefs had been shaped by differential exposure to actions and events, differential exposure to those individuals who were busy promulgating interpretations of the institute's current and recent experience, and each individual's normative vision of what should have happened. These beliefs thus became the source of our problem, not the source of our solution. We became interested in how these beliefs had arisen and in their impact upon the apparent decline of the new institute.

Our model of the development of belief in a new agency is a simple one. If an agency is treated positively by the external world, it will come to believe it is "successful." Furthermore, it will believe that agency actions led to the rewards and therefore will continue similar actions. If an agency is treated negatively by some part of the external world, it will search for evidence of success in other quarters. If the countervailing evidence is strong, the agency will come to believe it is successful. If the countervailing evidence is weak or nonexistent, the agency will come to believe it is a "failure." Furthermore, it will believe that agency actions led to the negative treatment and will attempt to change them.

In this chapter we attempt to specify the major themes in the developing set of beliefs about NIE. We explore the concepts with which NIE began its existence—beliefs about education R&D and expectations for the new agency. We examine the effects that external events and assessments had on NIE's developing belief structure. And we examine how beliefs shifted over time. We try to answer two questions:

How are beliefs generated? reinforced? changed?

How do beliefs affect the actions of a new agency?

Axioms and the Initial "Lessons"

The brief history of education research and development inside both OE and NIE reveals two major unchanging tenets of belief about the federal education R&D enterprise. These are the axioms of progress and management.

The axiom of progress appears in two forms in the R&D agency's environment and in the agency itself. In the staff offices, congressional committees, and other organizations that constitute the R&D agency's evaluative environment, there is a firm belief that R&D should yield tangible "improvements" in schooling within a few years. A corollary belief is that education R&D should be able to develop a strong constituency among school practitioners. The connective reasoning is simple. School practitioners want improvement. If R&D leads to constructive reform, it will be appreciated by teachers and administrators. If teachers and administrators value R&D, they will give it their political support. Because of such reasoning the absence of practitioner support is viewed as sure evidence that education R&D "isn't working." This external expectation of progress—manifested by strong practitioner support—has never been satisfied. Within the education R&D agency, the expectation of progress is translated into an expectation of growth and prosperity for the agency itself. That expectation was fulfilled in OE for a brief period during the mid-sixties but has been steadily frustrated since that time.

The second axiom is a persistent belief that the R&D process can be managed from the federal level. Belief in the feasibility and desirability of federal management has gone beyond modestly imagining that federal officials are capable of determining whether a proposed project is desirable or whether an existing project should be continued. Rather, federal officials have spoken and acted as if they were able to prespecify the directions and objectives that individual research and development projects should pursue and achieve. And, even beyond that, they have often adopted the posture that individual projects could be orchestrated in a way constituting a coherent, comprehensive agencywide attack on selected problems in American education. These two more sweeping notions constitute what we term the "belief in management."

Although there have been perturbations in the expectation of progress and the belief in management, by and large these axioms have affected policies concerning federal R&D in education for the past decade. Within the general framework of these axioms, more specific beliefs developed about NIE. During the period of planning for NIE, these beliefs were derived from an examination of the "failure" of OE and the "success" of agencies supporting science R&D. After NIE's creation, these beliefs were shaped both by the external context within which the agency operated and by the internal actions that marked the agency's development.

At the time of NIE's creation, it seemed evident that three strategic concepts were vital to the achievement of purposive management and tangible progress in education R&D.

1. NIE must be isolated from political forces and must avoid surrender to or seduction by special interest groups.
2. NIE must be different in style and substance from its predecessors. To fulfill this mandate the institute must emphasize the hiring of "good people" who are not representative of the OE bureaucrats who formerly managed the R&D efforts.
3. NIE must develop a coherent and comprehensive plan for research that is not decreed by either political pressure or administrative fiat, but rather is derived from careful identification and rational analysis of the major problems facing American education.

NIE began with these concepts. Had the agency experienced early success (e.g., budget increases), these concepts would have been credited and assumptions about their efficacy would have been reinforced. But two and a half years of "failure" for NIE led to the erosion or reversal of each of these beliefs.

External Events

Events external to an agency can affect the development of belief about the agency in two principal ways. Indirectly, they can influence the prevailing mood or atmosphere of the environment in which the agency exists. Directly, external events can reach into the agency itself by providing rewards or punishments, reassurances or threats. In the case of NIE, external events did little to contribute to a positive belief structure within the agency.

The late 1960s were marked by a growing public disenchantment with education. By the time NIE was created the extravagant claims made for federal education programs of the early 1960s had been pronounced unrealizable. The high aspirations had been shaken by works such as those by Coleman et al. (1966) and Jencks et al. (1972) and by evaluations of social and educational interventions such as Head Start. Those who persisted in their belief in the possibility of progress and manageability in federal education R&D programs had to confront less confidence and more cynicism, on the part of Congress and the public, concerning the ultimate utility of their work. Furthermore, science and R&D in general, even as supported by the more prestigious agencies like NSF and NIH, saw their prestige and share of the federal dollar diminishing. And the national political and economic crises of the early 1970s did nothing to foster an optimistic environment for any new agency. The growing exposure of the Watergate scandal in 1973 and 1974 tended to debilitate the White House and, by extension, had something of a paralyzing effect on the entire federal government. These factors set the largest context within which belief about NIE would develop.

A second level of external events had a more direct effect upon the agency, although they did not occur because of NIE, nor did the institute have the power to prevent them. The departure of Moynihan from the White House and the replacement of HEW Secretary Richardson by Caspar Weinberger deprived the institute of two important figures who had played key supporting roles in creating it. With Moynihan's departure, there were no remaining White House staff members who either understood NIE or cared about it. Richardson's absence meant that there was no one with a personal stake in the survival of the new agency at the highest levels of HEW.

A third category of external events was directly tied to the agency, although still not under its control. Paramount among these events were the two budget cuts and the denial of the supplemental budget request. Also important were the eight-month delay in the appointment of the NCER; a lawsuit against the agency charging that it was operating illegally; and the revelation of an OE contract-backdating scandal involving contracts transferred to NIE.[1]

Although the external events described here were unpleasant for NIE, by themselves they need not have unduly affected the internal belief system. Had there been countervailing positive external assessment from prestigious or powerful constituent organizations or condemnation directed toward Congress, the negative events need not have seemed so dire.

The External Assessment

No doubt NIE was mentioned occasionally at Washington lunches and Capitol Hill cocktail parties; we do not know what was said there. But it is possible to examine what was said by the press; this may serve as a partial measure of "social belief" about the agency during its first two and a half years of existence. NIE has been the topic of articles, editorials, and letters to the editor in both the mass-circulation newspapers and the more specialized education and scientific press.

In a sample of general press articles about NIE, including every article in the *New York Times* and the *Wall Street Journal* through December 1974 the headlines convey a deterioration when viewed over time (see table 9.1). From "gets a lesson" to "scuttling," the verbs and the picture grow gloomier. Of course one may argue that the national press overplays the crises; nevertheless it does represent one consistent and highly visible source of external assessment. The education press devoted more attention to NIE, but their reports were hardly rosier.

The explanations proffered by the press probably served both to reflect the conventional wisdom about NIE's shortcomings and to generate further speculation along the same lines. In both the general and the specialized press the first budget cut was the trigger for a series of stories that depicted NIE in increasingly desperate straits. The *New York Times* interpretation was that NIE's difficulties stemmed primarily from a lack of political wisdom inside the agency. After the first budget cut in 1973, the *Times* offered its political explanation: "a criticism heard on all sides—the the Institute and its Director, Thomas K. Glennan Jr. had done an atrocious job of Congressional relations" (*New York Times*, 22 October 1973, p. 64). Closely related to this explanation was the observation that the agency could not make a good case for funding education R&D—Glennan's testimony was "vague"; educational R&D itself is "poorly understood" and "a mess." The *Times* did identify some factors over which the agency had no control that affected its political fortunes: the delay in the appointment of the NCER; the fact that the Nixon administration was proposing cuts in "a host of other popular programs" while asking for increases in NIE; the fact that NIE was "one thing the President wants" while Congress was growing increasingly hostile toward him. But the implication, on balance, was that if NIE improved its political tactics, the factors over which it had no control would recede in importance.

Table 9.1   Press Headlines about NIE: 1973–74

General Press

"New education agency to consolidate US research"
  (*New York Times*, 27 January 1973)
"Educators seek to enjoin agency" [describing the NCEC lawsuit]
  (*New York Times*, 15 March 1973)
"Institute of education gets a lesson in how not to win more money from Congress"
  (*New York Times*, 22 October 1973)
"Researchers under fire: Lack of political clout in Congress threatens once-glamorous National
    Institute of Education"
  (*Wall Street Journal*, 28 June 1974)
"No damn fools" [Letter to the editor from Daniel P. Moynihan]
  (*Wall Street Journal*, 8 July 1974)
"Charges by former employee cloud education agency future"
  (*Oregonian*, 20 September 1974)
"Congressional fund cuts imperil educational research institute"
  (*New York Times*, 30 September 1974)
"Scuttling research" [editorial]
  (*New York Times*, 30 September 1974)
"Congress may kill 1972 education project"
  (*Baltimore Evening Sun*, 1 October 1974)
"White House reports changes of officials"
  (*New York Times*, 7 November 1974)

Education Press

"NIE: Learning about Congress the hard way"
  (*Education Researcher*, November 1973)
"Glennan quits NIE: group's future in doubt"
  (*Publishers Weekly*, 9 September 1974)
"Will Glennan's resignation brighten NIE's future?"
  (*Chronicle of Higher Education*, 19 September 1974)
"NIE: Another appropriations crisis"
  (*Education Researcher*, November 1974)
"Scuttling education research"
  (*Change Magazine*, November 1974)
"Why the debacle at NIE? Departing director answers"
  (*Phi Delta Kappan*, November 1974)

The *Wall Street Journal* explanation closely paralleled that of the *New York Times*. NIE had gained no political support in Congress: its presentations were "pedantic and often unintelligible"; its "youthful" staff was offensive to important outsiders; Glennan alienated Magnuson because of his "inability to give glib, understandable explanations of what the agency is up to." The *Journal* also mentioned the possibility that not all of NIE's problems were its own fault.

Some of the agency's trouble was probably unavoidable. "Their misfortunes exceed their mistakes," says Michael Timpane, a Brookings Institution researcher. The institute inherited from the Office of Education a passel of controversial projects that were bound to produce political headaches. [*Wall Street Journal*, 28 June 1974, p. 36]

The only "misfortunes" mentioned were connected with transfer programs and made up less than 6% of the article, however. Clearly the media were not reporting good evaluations that might lead to the development of positive beliefs about NIE. Nor were they, by and large, attributing NIE's difficulties to events over which the institute had no control.

The media were not the only source of external negative assessment. In its second year of operation NIE began hearing criticism from two important sources that previously had been supportive—the Office of the Secretary of HEW and Congressman John Brademas. The charge was that NIE was sloppy and unresponsive. Elliott noted, "We find in our dealings with the Office of the Secretary of HEW . . . a feeling that we're uncooperative, or that we don't do things, or do them inadequately" (Elliott, 11 June 1974). This assessment was shared by John Brademas:

Individual inquiries and their disposition are an important kind of image-bearing communication. I have been distressed to receive at least a half-dozen legitimate complaints of delays, lost proposals, and outright refusals to return calls from outside individuals. Several letters I have personally referred have been handled without adequate attention to their substance, and more important, without attention to the impression such lapses create in Congressional staff, members and the public. [John Brademas, 25 March 1974, p. 8]

By mid-1974 the external judgment of NIE failure was widespread. Two factors account for the ubiquity of negative external assessment. First, there had been no expectation that events would so bedevil the institute. The entire process of creating the institute, both in the executive branch and in the authorizing committees of Congress, had been infused with rhetoric asserting that NIE was "the answer"; that a new agency would overcome and eliminate the disappointment of the past. Accompanying this rhetoric was the widely shared anticipation that the NIE budget would grow within a few years to between $250 million and $1 billion per year. While the degree of anticipated budget growth was somewhat ambiguous, no one anticipated a reduction in funds for the institute. Budget levels were a simple index of NIE success; that index was plummeting, not rising.

Second, there was an initial absence of countervailing propaganda asserting "success" for NIE. Each of the constituent groups concerned with the institute had reason for major dissatisfaction with it. They were the source of complaints rather than praise. The institute itself, the most likely source of countervailing propaganda, failed to produce it in the first year. Internally,

NIE management was committed to a phaseout of many of the projects transferred from OE. Yet the transferred programs represented the vast bulk of NIE's operations. Initially, the institute's leaders were incapable of boasting of programs about which they had either little information or profound private doubts.

After the October 1973 budget cut, the institute's leadership began to discover virtue in those inherited programs that had proved popular with their varied constituencies. When pressed for evidence of "success" in NIE programs, the institute's leadership pointed to legacies from OE such as Individually Guided Education and Multi-Unit Schools developed by the Wisconsin R&D center. The Mountain Plains Career Education project in Glasgow, Montana, which was dear to the hearts of Senators Mansfield and Magnuson, was praised in NIE's congressional testimony even though the same project had been scorned inside the agency during the first year.

These changes in behavior were not motivated solely by political considerations. To some extent the institute staff found that their initial contempt for anything bearing the stamp "Made in USOE" was unjustified. Some of the OE projects did address real problems, served some tangible group, and/or had competent leadership. Some were improved during their first year in NIE. The NIE management saw themselves as becoming both better informed about their OE inheritance and more realistic politically. Yet the adverse external assessments continued unabated.

Internal Beliefs: "The Problems"

Although the institute staff largely accepted the gloomy views arising from Congress and the press, there was one competing explanation for NIE's reversals. As we described in chapter 4, some believed that NIE's misfortunes were the result of accidents and the mistakes of others. The first budget cut, in this perspective, was the consequence of the inebriation of one key congressional figure or the forgetfulness of another. NIE was unpopular with Congress because a phone conversation was ended abruptly by an NIE staff member or because NIE had fired the friend of a powerful Senator. This "accidental" interpretation was championed by some. It was partially accepted by others who simultaneously believed that the institute itself had committed some substantive blunders. The top leadership of NIE entertained both explanations and was unsure how much credence to place in either one.

But as the misfortunes before the appropriations committees continued and as it became clear that neither the full House nor the full Senate was more friendly than the appropriations committees, the utility of the "accidental" explanations declined. The persistence of NIE's misfortunes in Congress made it increasingly difficult to accept an "accidental" theory. Further, as believers in the management axiom, the NIE staff assumed that, whatever the problem, there were management strategies that could ameliorate or solve it.

NIE staff had attended to internal problems and processes from the inception of the agency. However, the growing belief in the judgment of failure intensified those concerns. Before the budget cut, most staff members could have constructed a list of both pros and cons about NIE operations. Yet, in the aftermath of the cut and the continuing negative external assessments, the list of deficiencies and problems became more significant than the list of assets because the search was on for causes of failure.

Two major, related categories of problems grew in importance as viewed by NIE staff: problems of mismanagement and problems of indecisiveness. The problems of mismanagement seemed to center on a misuse of personnel and the absence of management systems.

> Wasting human talent by any person is morally wrong—and bad management. You must fully employ everyone on the payroll. [461]

> Those offensive *systems*, for program development, planning, communicating, etc., must be established as soon as possible. [131][2]

In many new organizations all participants share an overwhelming workload; this was not true at NIE. Although some staff members were working sixty or seventy hours a week, others were complaining of boredom and neglect. It was not that there was not enough work to go around but rather that top management did not delegate the work equally across the institute. For members of the "inner circle" and some of the senior management and their aides, the work load was appalling. But the former OE staff member was rarely asked to take on a special assignment or to work late night after night. The "good people" were asked to overextend themselves; other people were left to their own devices.

> A new agency should learn to integrate the experiences of established, knowledgeable civil servants with the enthusiasm and verve of personnel who are new to the government bureaucracy. [117]

> The Office of the Director must concern itself with agency morale and fostering good relations among staff members—not playing favorites, making snap judgments regarding people's talent (writing people off) etc. The Director and Senior Staff should adhere closely to established hierarchical structure and steer clear of kitchen cabinets, etc. [524]

Although many of the overburdened staff initially found their work exhilarating, over time they began to tire and their frustrations grew. Unit leaders, along with Glennan, Elliott, and Martin, who were busy with their own work, found little time to assess the unreasonable demands they were imposing on others. One overworked staff member commented dejectedly,

> It's just that no one seems to care. As long as you get the work done, they don't worry about what you have to put up with. [135]

One consequence of this fatigue was a growing disinclination to respond to demands and deadlines:

A major problem is not being able to predict or control your environment. The extent to which days are interrupted, major policy decisions that you're trying to work through get turned aside, because something comes in with a "Red Special" and you have to respond to it immediately. One day I had, at 3:30, three things with "Red Specials" on them all due at 4:30, and they had arrived at 3:30. That kind of thing, when you can't predict and when you can't control, you can begin to guess the sorts of things that does to people. [344]

They do not inform people of things that are coming up that they are going to have to do until the time is upon them. I have been asked to do things on Monday morning that they had to have Monday evening that they had known about for at least two weeks. And I consider it an imposition. . . . I've sort of reached a point now, sometimes it's hard to carry that out, where when someone tells me the deadline is such and such I ignore it—I don't ignore it but I don't take it seriously. I feel, well, if it's not in Monday they'll live 'til Tuesday. [448]

As was noted in chapter 8, many of the management systems and procedures that might have expedited much of the routine work had not been developed by the time staff responsiveness began to slacken. Whether or not these systems and procedures would in fact have made the institute run more smoothly, their absence was seen as an indicator of "bad management." Furthermore, the problems of mismanagement were undoubtedly exacerbated by the series of adverse external events. By the time the institute had coped with one external event, another presented itself. With each new crisis the routine work of organizing the new agency had to be put aside. Over time the ability to "catch up" dwindled as personnel resilience lessened.

Institute staff not only were tired of being overworked or underworked, they were also confused.

It is very difficult to establish any kind of an organization if there is no direction. [369]

This is the most confused agency I have worked at. [254]

These comments reflect the deep frustration that became evident in the institute over the "indecisiveness" of top management. This theme is not new in this study. Previous chapters have emphasized the sense of chaos that emerged from decision-making processes in the institute. In many cases decisions simply were not made. Proposals and memos cycled through the system while, simultaneously, the nature of the problem to be solved became redefined, thus rendering obsolete the most recent proposal for solution. In a few cases, such as the five priority areas, or questions of organizational structure, decisions were made only to come "unstuck" or to be seriously "modified" within a few weeks or months. These effects led to a sense of drift within the institute, and that sense became linked with the judgment of failure. Many NIE staff members came to believe that decisiveness was the key to ending NIE's travail.

Two theories arose among NIE staff to account for mismanagement and indecisiveness, both concentrating on the alleged shortcomings of top management. The first asserted that the leaders of NIE lacked management experience. Elliott and Martin had previously managed no more than a handful of people. Glennan's staff at OEO had never been even 25% as large as NIE's staff in 1974. Thus, some NIE staff members perceived each of the top three leaders as "staff" people who lacked the proper experience to become "line" managers. Further, there were few obvious examples of broad managerial experience elsewhere in the institute. The second theory emphasized the lack of commitment, rather than the inexperience, of top management. Several NIE staff members believed the leadership failed to display a deep personal commitment to a particular set of issues or problems in American education. For example, there was no evidence of an overriding management concern with a target group such as the poor or ethnic minorities; no special concern for a particular level of education such as the secondary schools; no burning attraction to a particular reform such as open classrooms or decentralization; no deep affiliation with a group of practitioners such as teachers. This theory argued that a particular moral commitment or group affiliation would have provided a basis for decisions on the nature of projects NIE should undertake and thus lay the basis for decisive management.

Internal Beliefs: The Later "Lessons"

From the prevailing analysis of internal problems, the institute learned some "lessons" about the strategies necessary for achieving purposive management and tangible progress.[3] These lessons did not contradict the axioms that intentional federal management of education R&D was both feasible and desirable. Rather, they represented a new phase in views about how success could best be achieved.

There were three components to the shifting portion of institute beliefs:

1. The institute must develop effective political and congressional liaison. As part of this effort, support for institute programs must be built among existing educational constituencies.
2. The institute must hire more experienced managers. If necessary, these managers should be drawn from the ranks of veteran civil servants.
3. The institute must exhibit a well-understood plan of action. If necessary, these decisions should be somewhat arbitrary and should be imposed by top management.

Congressional and Constituent Relations

The necessity for good congressional and constituent relationships seems to be the most pervasive lesson learned by the NIE staff as of June 1974. "Set up external relations immediately and hire someone who is known on the Hill" (108). "Don't expect a long honeymoon with Congress" (128). "Good congressional relations should be NIE's top priority" (132). "Any agency—especially a new one like NIE—must put effort into gaining confidence by the Hill" (144). "Even a new organization, in its so-called honeymoon period, has to pay very close attention to congressional priorities and perceptions" (232). Two years after the agency opened, the political lesson had been well learned.

Experience

Glennan, Elliot, and Martin all came to believe that they had made mistakes in their personnel selections.

Martin: There's not enough gray hair around here. [15 October 1974]

Elliot: Rather than move with confidence, inexperienced staff says, "Let's find out more about this area." [11 June 1974]

Glennan: I've always enjoyed young people and never emphasized experience in the people I've hired. A lot of our difficulties are because we haven't had that experience. [Our people] don't know how to set up the system, manipulate it for their own ends. Experience really pays off in terms of their ability to live with uncertainty . . . to deal with adversity, to take the long view. [March 1974]

This belief in the virtue of experience was not limited to top management. A number of the professional staff believed one of the key "lessons to be learned" from the NIE experience was that a new agency needs "competent civil servants" and should not have "inexperienced managers." Some of the comments were terse: "Do not hire so many inexperienced managers" (108); "Experience and maturity at all levels are essential." (131). And others were not:

Scholars on limited contract were brought in for leadership roles, and little advice was sought or listened to from the "bureaucrats"—a disparaging term. A bureaucracy is necessary. It is certainly inevitable. But knowledge-able *civil servants* (my term, not theirs) were not only not utilized, they were automatically and systematically cut off from these "scholar-directorships." [228]

A number of people came to believe that Glennan himself was not experienced enough to guide the agency. One group believed his lack of familiarity with education programs and problems was a disadvantage. Representative of that viewpoint are the comments:

The Director's background should be closely allied with the purpose of the agency, in this case educational research. [318]

You can't build a strong agency on the basis of a major leadership cadre
that contains little substantive expertise about educational research. [474]

Do not pick an operations research analyst (with no real program
management expertise in education) to run an education organization.
[273]

Another group believed his lack of political experience was a liability.

The Director...should have national stature and ability to understand the
political nature of a new Federal agency and its necessary compatibility
with Congressional committees. [328]

A Plan of Action

As did the appropriations committees, the institute staff shared a perception that NIE did not have a coherent strategy. Beginning with the Levien
report of 1971 and extending through the "paradigm search" of 1972–73 and
the planning effort for the fiscal 1976 budget conducted in early 1974, the
institute had searched for a powerful and persuasive intellectual rationale that
would provide guidance both on the goals it should seek and the strategies
required to reach them. As had a similar quest conducted within OE in the
late 1960s (Gideonse 1970), the NIE effort ended in frustration and
indecision. A perception emerged within the institute that policy was being
buffeted by external pressure and internal politics.

Although a comprehensive plan of action appeared to be an unattainable
mirage, the internal thirst for such a plan remained unquenched. With the
failure to create a comprehensive plan through analysis and debate, a belief
grew that it was the proper function of top management to impose one. The
declaration of the Five Priorities, the sole managerial gesture in this regard,
failed either to still external criticism or to ease internal disquiet. Yet, at the
end of the first two years, the institute remained convinced that a satisfying
strategy was attainable, somehow, and that in its discovery lay part of the
solution to the institute's troubles. "NIE should have a sense of 'mission,' a
policy which will be kept for a length of time to create stability" (132). "Set
clear and easily understood objectives at the outset—create a sense of
purpose" (348). "Set goals that are clear and with which people can identify.
... Have clear goals at unit and staff level so that some sense of coherent
mission is present and some sense of accomplishment is possible" (418). "It is
better to take the initiative and go with what you think is right rather than to
take a reactive, responsive position" (524).

In view of the earlier history of educational research and development
within the Office of Education, the later "lessons learned" by NIE are ironic
indeed:

> 1. Whereas OE had been criticized as "too political," NIE
>   came to view political support as supremely important.

2. Whereas OE had been criticized for allowing unimagina-
tive bureaucrats to control research, NIE came to believe
that it required more experienced civil servants.
3. Whereas OE had been criticized for seizing upon objectives on an opportunistic basis and for lacking a comprehensive, coherent, stable research agenda, NIE came
to be frustrated in the search for such an agenda and to
yearn for explicable objectives even at the cost of a
measure of arbitrariness in the decision-making process.

Although NIE officials may not have realized it, the circle had closed.
Important "lessons" learned by the OE critics before they had come to
manage NIE had been replaced by a different set of lessons during the
institute's first two years. Within the context of the unchanging expectation
for progress and the persistent belief in the possibility of managing R&D, the
accepted wisdom concerning the means to these ends had gone through a full
cycle in only two years.

The Rush to Judgment

One of the important features of the history of education research within
both OE and NIE is the rapidity with which initiatives were undertaken and
then judged to be either seriously deficient or completely bankrupt. NIE is
only the most recent victim of this rush to judgment. Among earlier casualties
were the laboratories and R&D centers, OE's "mission orientation," and
NCERD. Yet one might wonder why any conclusions concerning NIE,
whether judgments of failure or success, need have emerged within eighteen
months of its creation. After all, the 1971 legislative hearings had emphasized
the wisdom of taking the "long view" of the success or failure of research and
development. This counsel of patience was disregarded.

The reasons for the rejection of patience are difficult to isolate. However,
one relatively straightforward ingredient is the annual appropriations process. Operating in a busy environment, pressed to make allocational decisions
among myriad competing claims, the appropriations committees must act as
if their actions are well founded. Thus, they find comfort in simple
impressions of the quality of various agencies and programs. The institute
inadvertently drew attention to itself by seeking a rapid increase in appropriations and thus implicitly demanded a judgment by Congress. Congress
might have been content to ignore a new agency that sought only modest
budget increases. But attention was necessarily directed to the institute when
it asked for a 50% budget increase at the same time that the administration
sought to cut back other education programs.

Second, in some respects the institute was "older" than its date of creation
implied. While there might have been some willingness to suspend judgment

concerning an agency only one year old, NIE's major programs had been initiated earlier in OE, and the appropriations committees felt justified in demanding results or program termination.[4]

Third, the appetite for summary judgment extends far beyond the appropriations committees. The entire bureaucratic and legislative community in Washington is busy, yet desirous of appearing knowledgeable.[5] It is assumed that events have explanations. Those who aspire to be "insiders" (and it is hard to find federal officials who don't wish to be insiders) had best know an explanation for events or rapidly construct one. The first NIE budget cut cried out for an explanation. The resulting explanations constructed a link between the cut and the quality of the affected agency even though evidence on the latter point was fragmented and partial.

Finally, the institute was heavily populated with "policy analysts" whose professional preoccupation is the gauging of program "outputs." The presence of such analysts within the agency probably contributed to the institute's tendency to introspection and self-examination.

Conclusion

NIE's initial belief structure had been generated from the expectations surrounding its creation. There was optimism and confidence that good people, unsullied by special interest group demands, could rationally deduce a plan that would lead to success for education R&D. Over time a series of failures led to a reassessment of the *means* to success. The belief structure was altered. But the assumption that success was achievable through intentional action went unchallenged. The axioms remained.[6]

Changes in the belief structure also had consequences for further organization action. As people came to believe that the agency was not well managed, they became less willing to respond to what they perceived as "meaningless" deadlines. Thus, when the leadership did attempt to reduce management sloppiness, the staff responded sluggishly. As people came to believe that top leadership was indecisive, they became less willing to take seriously, and act upon, the latest decisions made by top management. These reactions on the part of staff simply exacerbated the problems and therefore reinforced the changing beliefs.

Ten

Conclusion: Observations on Organizing an Anarchy

Introduction

Between 1970 and 1975 the National Institute of Education evolved as an idea, was created as a new federal agency, and came close to extinction. We have viewed this short history as one episode in the continuing federal effort to support education R&D, as a case study in the development of a new organization, and as a means for increasing our understanding of many organizations in the public sector. Our detailed description of NIE, in chapters 1–9, has three components:

—A consideration of the political processes involved in the birth of a public agency and an examination of the flow of events in NIE's environment. NIE was not the result of an immaculate conception; its creation served some concrete political, bureaucratic, and personal objectives only loosely related to education research. It was caught in a context that had some importance for it, but over which it had almost no control.

—A detailed exposition of the pattern of bureaucratic development and action in the agency. NIE had to hire people, spend money, establish procedures, prepare budgets, make reports, and get organized.

—A description of the development of belief about the agency. NIE was an ambiguous stimulus. Over time people inside and outside the agency developed opinions about it and conflicting impressions of what was happening there.

Many of our speculations about public sector organizations are implicit in the case study analysis. We do not attempt to review all of them here. Rather, we try to identify some themes having broad significance for understanding the implementation of public policy through bureaucratic mechanisms. They are organized as comments on two broad sets of issues:

What can be expected from federal efforts in education R&D?

What should managers keep in mind when creating and organizing a new agency?

What Can Be Expected from Federal Efforts in Education R&D?

There are only a few readily available tools for the redirection of the federal education R&D effort.[1] Preeminent among them are shifts in budget levels, reorganization of the bureaucracy, installation of new leadership, and declaration of new goals. In the past decade the federal government has run through this repertoire of responses to the "failure" of education R&D. The primary result has been the growth of disillusionment. Every suggestion for reform in federal sponsorship can be quickly countered by citing recent evidence that such a reform does not work. Reorganizations do not work; new leadership has little, if any, effect; new goals have insignificant impact; and vastly increased funds can not be won from the Congress unless and until evidence is produced that reorganizations, new leadership, and fresh goals do, in fact, work.

The record of the past decade—the reorganizations within OE, the creation of NCERD, the creation of NIE, and the changes in NIE—leads us to suspect that there are no dramatic differences in short-term effectiveness among different organizational structures, different leaders, or different official goals. Memories are too long and the proclaimed failure of every excuse for hope is too recent. A rapid cycling through the entire repertoire of "reforms" has bred frustration and threatens persistence in the very slow, inherently uneven, and difficult-to-manage federal education R&D enterprise.

NIE's original conception is as deeply implicated in any failures as is its subsequent implementation. The axiomatic beliefs (described in chap. 9) in both the likelihood of tangible progress resulting from education R&D and the possibility of a strong, centralized management of the R&D process underlie this cycle of reform and despair. Simply stated, the basic tenets of "progress" and "R&D management" are inconsistent with the realities of schooling and research in the United States. The inconsistencies arise from two basic factors. First, education research does not closely resemble its alleged analogues in the natural sciences. Second, education research must be managed with a sensitivity to the decentralized aspects of American schooling.[2]

Changes attributable to education research are rarely achieved through a tangible product or device. Education research often plays the comparatively modest role of recording events, identifying problems, weeding out factors of lowest relevance, and illuminating alternative solutions to limited problems. The theoretical basis for curriculum design is much weaker than the theoretical basis for missile design. There is only a distant relationship between translating physical science research into the practical work of engineers and translating education research into school practices. Further, education R&D has no impact on many important causes of educational difficulties, such as malnutrition in children and racial discrimination.

There are severe limits on the diffusion of educational innovations even when new procedures and devices have produced encouraging results in small-scale studies. The highly decentralized nature of American education means that disseminating information about new practices and providing technical assistance to help implement them is a massive task in a school district with many schools, much less in the nation as a whole. Equally important, pressures against any particular reform can come from one or more of the large number of potential veto groups that exist within the community of teachers, administrators, parents, and taxpayers. School administrators learn to prefer the known shortcomings of present practice to the political dangers of attempting the new and unknown.

The conventional argument for federal direction of education R&D is that because state and local school districts cannot fully "capture" the benefits of education R&D (other localities or regions will benefit from research they did not support), these levels of school governance will underinvest in such research. For this reason, education R&D is an appropriate activity for the federal government to support. However, this argument is reasonable only to the extent that the agenda of desirable research topics at the federal level overlaps those at state and local levels. Certainly, everyone wishes to have surer methods of teaching reading, for example. But there is much less agreement across localities on the desirability of learning more about vouchers, ethnic studies, or sex education curricula. Even with regard to widely approved research topics, such as reading, there are local variations in particular emphasis—for example, regional interests in teaching bilingual children to read. There are also factional splits in the research community as to which basic strategies for teaching reading hold the best prospects for further investment. These variations in the incidence of educational problems, splits over basic educational values, and disagreements over research approaches give rise to political pressures upon any agency that supports education research.

The crucial political question at the federal level is that of constituencies. It is most unlikely that an R&D program operating under a consistent overall strategy, even if such a strategy could be conceptualized, could satisfy the requirements of divergent constituents. Further, the optimism about building a political constituency for R&D assumes the infusion of substantial new money to attract participants into the coalition. Yet one condition for winning new money is to have the coalition already formed. Education research is supported primarily by federal funds, and the record indicates that new federal funds can be obtained only in the context of a broad increase of funding for education programs, as was the case in 1965. Therefore, without a change in federal views toward education, and a corresponding shift in national budgetary priorities, the prospects are dim for either a new coalition or substantial new money for education R&D.

The foregoing factors help explain the fragmentation, duplication, modest size, and marginal impact upon practice that characterizes, and will continue to characterize, American research and development in education. In summary, education R&D will not yield insights or products that will continuously improve American schools. It is questionable whether an enterprise as diverse, value laden, and technologically underdeveloped as education R&D can be managed at the level of the prespecification of results or the coordination of diverse efforts. And, in terms of public priorities, it has not been demonstrated that education R&D deserves constant growth or that the R&D enterprise would benefit from unceasing expansion.

In place of the beliefs in rational management and tangible progress, we assert the following:

1. Education is important, but not supremely important as compared with other governmental endeavors.

2. Innovations can improve education, but probably not dramatically.

3. Research and development can aid in creating sensible innovations, but they are not always a major factor in such stimulation.

4. It is possible to achieve some sense of direction in a growing R&D enterprise, but in weak technology fields such as education, it does not require much growth to swamp any capacity for managing the system.

5. Education research serves competing values and varied audiences. It cannot be conducted within a single conceptual framework, or according to a single long-range plan.

6. Education research and development is worthy of investment but not necessarily at levels dramatically different from the present.

Education R&D is not a panacea. But it need not be abandoned. Research and development do help to discover problems; they help in formulating useful ways to view problems; they sometimes suggest ameliorative steps. These are not heroic contributions. But as long as education R&D does not espouse heroic goals, it can honestly seek modest returns in exchange for a modest investment.

Research and development inevitably involve the risk of failure. It is vital to recognize that failure is not always the result of incompetence. Nor is failure always attributable to lack of leadership, lack of money, or the structure of the organization. Education research has made a small amount of progress. It is capable of some progress in the future. But at the moment the enterprise desperately needs a period of stability. A vastly disproportionate amount of energy has been invested in crusades to change leadership, funding, and structure. But the value of such changes is small even under optimum conditions and vanishes entirely when such reforms are implemented in the naive belief that they will achieve quick substantive results. Within the institute the inclination to reorganize, to seek vastly expanded resources, or to seek a comprehensive conceptual framework should be resisted. Outside the institute, the inclination to charge wholesale incompetence or to put the agency to death should be resisted. What is required now is internal persistence, external monitoring at a low level of intensity, and a sympathetic ear to the results the institute may gather.

The education R&D enterprise can best accommodate conflicting political pressure if the advocates of different research problems and different research strategies can turn to one or more of a series of federal, state, and local agencies that are prepared to support education research. In turn, each of these agencies should sponsor efforts in a variety of directions without being consumed with guilt at their failure to achieve a single, overarching plan for using research to improve education. Although these diverse efforts will undoubtedly continue to find most of their financial support coming from federal dollars, we hope that state agencies and local institutions can be persuaded to use a small fraction of their own budgets to support research in education as well.

The pursuit of modesty, diversity, and stability fails to set the heart beating faster. But, in this case, it may serve to sustain life and lead to productivity.

What Should Policymakers and Managers Keep in Mind When Creating and Organizing a New Agency?

Those who decry the lack of planning in government might well have been encouraged by the early history of the National Institute of Education. Although the planning period was not perfect, there was a genuine commitment to formulating organizational goals and structure before the agency was created. The determination to analyze alternatives and to plan carefully before acting also characterized the early days of the agency's existence. Yet the planning, even though performed by able analysts, was of little use once the institute began to accumulate experience. Indeed, we have suggested that the commitment to planning was itself the cause of significant mischief.

The conventional model of planning relies upon assessing the experiences of other people in other places to produce "learning." Hence, in the NIE case, planners could look to NSF, NIH, and NASA experiences to "learn" what to do; the OE experiences to learn what not to do. But this kind of learning (and hence the planning based on it) is necessarily thin.[3] The planners know little of the myriad people, procedures, processes, constraints, opportunities, and accidents producing the artifacts they study. This ignorance is even more striking in de novo planning—in which few useful analogies exist, even thin ones.

This point is of general importance. As a practical matter, a new bureaucracy must act. The press of events simply cannot be resisted while plans and analyses are constructed. But more important, a new agency must act in order to learn—to understand its strengths, limitations, and context. There is little a new agency can learn until it has experiences that can be subjected to its own processes of interpretation. Action precedes understanding.[4]

But action is no guarantee of understanding. First, the answer to the question, "What happened?" is often arguable. And, second, even given a single, stable interpretation of what happened, it is often difficult to discern why it happened. In this latter respect, managers often mistakenly view events and their "causes" as being closely coupled. As the history of NIE illustrates, there are many instances in which planning is only loosely connected to action, decisions are only distantly linked to problems, reputation is not correlated with activity, and belief is disconnected from policy.[5]

Nevertheless, to a significant degree the construction of a new bureaucracy is an intellectual problem that requires trying to make sense out of events as they occur. It is not a passive problem like putting together a jigsaw puzzle on the dining room table. Rather, it is an active problem in which the table moves, the pieces change shape, and, not infrequently, the lights go out. We have no recipe or cookbook to offer those confronted by the dilemmas of constructing a new bureaucracy. But we can suggest some questions managers may find helpful in making sense of an institution's formative stages.[6]

1. What Are the Political Terms of Creation?

Managers can incorrectly attribute historical inevitability and significance to a new organization. They often interpret the act of creation as a sign that important people are interested in the organization and consider it significant. Intimations of future resources and expressions of confidence are taken to be redeemable pledges. But it is often the case that a significant part of the coalition that creates a new agency loses interest once the symbolism of creation is exhausted. The initial patrons of the new bureaucracy wander away or are assigned elsewhere.

The creation of a new agency is no sure testament to its importance. Nor is it a sign that people agree on its goals. Enthusiastic expressions of high expectations may well mask either the absence of any operational definition of agency goals or the presence of serious conflict over them. A new bureaucracy can imagine itself to be a well-protected tiger cub even as a monsoon soaks its feathers. Who has a deep and lasting stake in the success of this organization? What rewards do they seek for their support? Who wrote the "minority reports" opposing the creation? On what basis could opponents and skeptics be persuaded to be friends? These are questions that the managers of new organizations must place at the top of their list for exploration in the early days.

2. What Are Limitations of the Models of "Success" and "Failure" Embedded within the New Agency's Historical Context?

The models of success or failure are inevitably oversimplified and thin. Therefore the manager can usefully inquire into the substantive and stylistic cues that generated them. What "reforms" have been tried in the past? Do these reforms tend to come and go in a cyclical fashion? If so, where are we on the cycle? What bureaucratic and political constraints have impeded previous attempts at success? Not only are the models oversimplified, but they are not necessarily shared in a consistent fashion by everyone important to the fate of the new agency. Managers should assume everyone has some model of the agency but should not assume those models bear any relationship to the one held by the manager.

3. Given My Inheritance, What Can I Aspire to Improve?

Managers are often determined to create a new organization of unique style and productivity. They pursue perfection, not marginal improvement. The pursuit of perfection presents at least two risks. First, it impedes action and therefore learning from the consequences of action. Early in an agency's life it can afford to experiment with organizing and managing its work. Its environment and staff are usually willing to tolerate initial experimentation (or chaos). But if managers eschew any action in order to plan for the perfect action, they lose the opportunity to experiment and therefore to learn from their own early experiences. Over time, the demands for a coherent explanation of the agency's work will inevitably grow more insistent; toleration for experimentation will decline.

Second, without major improvements in its underlying technology (not only "hardware," but also people and procedures), it is unlikely that a new organization can be dramatically more productive than its predecessors. NASA could not have placed a man on the moon in 1969 without benefit of the technology that matured during and after World War II. Yet most new agencies do not fall heir to a legacy of new technology. (It is unlikely, for example, that Amtrak will significantly exceed the performance of the private railroad management that preceded it.) Nor do they have access to a substantially different workforce or system of procedures than did their predecessors. Even though it may be desirable to alter some standard operating procedures inherited from the past, a requisite for these modest changes is to have the vast bulk of other standard procedures in place and operating smoothly. No organization can simultaneously establish entirely new patterns in organizational hierarchy; job descriptions; methods of recruiting, hiring, and promoting; techniques of budget preparation and planning; means of letting and monitoring contracts; and sweeping changes in its relationships with its environment without courting disaster. The stability of some established procedures is the foundation for changing others. And, in this regard, the skills, experience, and intuition of established bureaucrats are invaluable allies in the change process.

Change is often desirable; sometimes it is possible; but no "new" organization starts with a clean slate. Pursuing perfection impedes learning and incremental change.

4. How Can I Intervene in the External Generation of Demands and Evaluations?

A new bureaucracy must cope with a larger bureaucratic and political community that may have little enthusiasm for the organization's creation or its continued good health but that will inevitably make demands on the new organization. In some instances, those who create demands can be persuaded to insist that the new agency do what the agency managers privately wish. Thus, the managers of a new agency may have a chance to educate their superiors and colleagues about how to make the agency respond. Of equal importance, managers should consider means to affect the impressions that will rapidly form about the adequacy of the new agency. What people think about an organization is not simply the concern of gossip-column readers. It forms the basis of how people act toward it. Hence, influencing people's beliefs about a new organization can also affect their actions with respect to it. In effect, we suggest that leaders of organized anarchies must depend not so much on their power to compel as on their ability to conjure. We use the term "symbolic leadership" to denote the ability to affect the beliefs about or perceptions of the new organization in the eyes of others.[7]

Two factors contribute to the possibility for symbolic leadership: ambiguity of organization goals or expectations and ambiguity of experience. Constituencies experience some uncertainty about what they want. Lobbyists are as interested in taking credit for what has happened as they are in determining what will happen. Elected officials are generally interested in demonstrating that "progress" is being made while having an incomplete set of a priori notions on what constitutes progress. Thus the initial, ambiguous charter for the new organization is subject to some definition by management.

Furthermore, the outputs of a bureaucracy are complex, subtle, and often hard to detect or evaluate. Those who evaluate a new organization are sometimes willing to equate the testimonials of good performance proferred by management with the testimonials that should be expected. (Those who have never seen a game of tennis can be persuaded that one scores points by putting a large rubber ball through elevated hoops.) To the extent that a new bureaucracy can be defined by its leadership as a new game, creativity in defining rules for winning and losing is possible.

There are some simple procedures to affect the indexes for evaluation. One is to assemble a group of commentators who will be prone to rate the new bureaucracy a success rather than a failure and to disseminate their findings widely. Another is to declare intentions to reach goals that have already been attained and, subsequently, to discover one's success.

One possible objection to these tactics is that such behavior is simply charlatanism. To be sure, there is the spirit of sleight of hand in our counsel. But there is also the recognition that interpretations of organizational performance are often a matter of superficial impression and social contagion. Therefore, leaders have the obligation to intervene in the development of interpretations and in their contagion in relevant social networks.

5. What Can We Be Proud Of?

Confusion, conflict, exhaustion, and missed opportunities inevitably accompany new organizations. For some, these elements are essential ingredients of their charm. A new agency can accept large doses of these difficulties and still thrive. What it cannot suffer for long is an active sense of demoralization. Adequate standard operating procedures are a good antidote for demoralization. But equally, if not more, important is an excuse for pride. It is easy for top management, caught up in the heady and portentous activities of the new agency, to forget that subordinates may have little sense of the significance of their actions. Managers must be sure that subordinates can complete the sentence, "What we are proud of around here is . . ."[8]

Even the problems of new agencies can be turned to advantage. If there is confusion, the new agency can be proud that it is open to new ideas. If there is conflict, the new agency can be proud that, in the democratic tradition, competing voices are heard and respected. If there is redundant effort, the new agency can be proud of its "fail-safe" procedures. If there is exhaustion, the new agency can be proud of the dedication of its staff. Just as managers should create positve interpetations for external consumption, they should promote inspiring messages for internal purposes as well.

6. What Are the Disadvantages of Bureaucratic Growth?

Managers usually respond to incentives for organizational growth. Such incentives arise from both the selfless and the selfish motivations of leaders. On the one hand, increased quality of service to the public is often associated in the manager's mind with an expanding budget and staff. One the other hand, a simple and widely used index of a manager's success, and hence career potential, is the number of dollars and employees under his or her direction. But there are disadvantages as well as advantages to agency growth. In political terms, growth implies giving up obscurity and the autonomy that accompanies it. As we suggested in chapter 4, a single department within a large organization can often conduct its affairs without being subject to searching examination from those outside the organization. However, if that department is transformed into a separate organization, it attracts a higher level of attention and scrutiny. In terms of internal organization, rapid growth can break the tenuous ties of understanding and common concern that can develop in a small group. For both these reasons, the assumed link between increase in size and increase in achievement should be challenged continually and mercilessly.

7. Is It Time for a Turnover in Management?

Every manager harbors the suspicion that he or she is invaluable. It is difficult for any individual, let alone a "manager," to believe he or she cannot intervene to improve a course of events. Yet it may occasionally be that the most helpful intervention is an exit. When a new agency is in trouble the easiest means of easing external pressure is to remove top management. If for no other reason than the need for fresh symbolism, the managers of new bureaucracies are well advised to think of themselves as expendable and to keep their resumes up to date.[9]

General answers to these seven questions are not available. Answers depend upon a particular organization's context, strengths, and weaknesses. Moreover, even the existence of these questions is not reassuring on a crucial point: How can they be raised within an organization in a timely and forceful manner? A number of devices might be considered to foster such institutional self-examination. Retreats to conference centers, employment of outside consultants, and arrangement for internal dissenters all come to mind.[10] All these techniques are worthy of serious consideration, but it is not likely that they or any other simple techniques will insure the serious examination of these questions, for three reasons.

First, raising and debating questions of fundamental importance is time-consuming. And time is in short supply in a new organization. Dealing with day-to-day problems involves less ambiguity and leads to a more immediate sense of efficacy than does challenging the fundamental assumptions of top managers and their key external sponsors.

Second, new bureaucracies encourage the display of some attitudes and styles within the agency and suppress others. (For example, in the early days of NIE, it was appropriate to engage in intellectual debate over the goals of education, but it would have been inappropriate to bring up questions of political expediency. In the early days of the Office of Economic Opportunity, agreement with the notion of grass-roots community organization was obligatory.) Employees who fail to demonstrate the prevailing attitude and style are often perceived as having their primary loyalty elsewhere and hence are ignored or distrusted.

Third, new agencies attract personnel who are efficacious, ambitious, and optimistic. Those who choose managers for new agencies look for "winners," or people with a "good track record." The new manager who has been previously successful is likely to bring to the new organization both general feelings of personal efficacy and specific beliefs about useful techniques and procedures for handling particular problems. Past failures are perceived to be the result of incompetence in the previous generation of managers; the newcomers are convinced that they will not fall into similar traps. Not only top management but other agency personnel as well tend to be optimists.[11] They tend to believe that the existence of a problem implies the existence of a solution. They tend not to take a Tolstoyan view of bureaucratic history. Hence, they would find it difficult to consider questions such as those we raise above.

Only severe and sustained bureaucratic disappointment is likely to engender an interest in our questions. Ironically, of course, by that time it may be too late.

Conclusion

Creating organizations is an extraordinarily complex and delicate endeavor.[12] Chance occurrences and uncontrollable factors will always play a large role in the success—or failure—of any new organization. Even if the organization must overcome seemingly impossible difficulties, it may do so and succeed. That is reason for being optimistic. On the other hand, even though the organization's success may seem assured, it may fail. That is reason for tempering optimism with an understanding that success may not occur.[13]

In large part, this book is the story of how able people failed to lead an organization in the direction they sought. Yet one should not necessarily conclude that individual policymakers and managers are likely to have little positive influence upon the fate of organizations. It is the case, however, that their primary impact is likely to be upon how people feel about the agency, not upon conventional organization outcomes.

Because new organizations are usually created with optimism and ambitious expectations, disappointment is common, even in the "successful" agency. Disappointment should not lead to disillusionment, however. It should lead instead to the realization that organizations are not perfect instruments of human intention. They are, however, a means for discovering better intentions.

Appendix 1

Persons Interviewed in the Preparation of This Book

The position given is that held at the time of the interview; other relevant positions are given in parentheses. Most of the interviews were conducted during the spring and summer of 1974.

Barnes, Edward	Assistant Director, Office of Human Rights, NIE
Binswanger, Robert	Assistant Director, Experimental Schools Program, NIE
Boyan, Norman J.	Dean, School of Education, University of California at Santa Barbara (Associate Commissioner for Research, Office of Education)
Brainard, Suzanne	Program specialist, Handicapped research program, NIE (member of NIE Planning Unit)
Burchinal, Lee B.	Program Officer, NSF (Task Force Leader, NIE Dissemination Task Force; Director, National Center for Education Communication, OE)
Campbell, Ed	President, Education Development Corporation, Newton, Massachusetts
Christensen, John	Chief Budget Officer, NIE
Clemens, Tom	Acting Associate Director, Office of Dissemination, NIE
Cody, Wilmer	Superintendent of Schools, Birmingham, Alabama (Task Force Leader, Applied Studies Task Force, NIE; Senior Planner, NIE Planning Unit)
Coleman, James S.	Professor of Sociology, University of Chicago
Cross, Christopher	Staff member, House Education and Labor Committee (HEW Deputy Assistant Secretary for Legislation at time of passage of NIE legislation)

Datta, Lois-Ellen | Deputy Assistant Director, Career Education Program, NIE

Dershimer, Richard | Executive Officer, American Education Research Association, Washington, D.C.

Dirks, Harley | Chief aide, Labor–HEW Subcommittee, Senate Appropriations Committee

Doyle, Denis | Assistant Director, Education Voucher Program, NIE

Duby, Martin | Chief, Contracts and Grants Division, NIE

Duncan, Jack | Counsel, House Select Subcommittee on Education

Egermier, John | Program specialist, Office of R&D Resources, NIE

Elliott, Emerson | Deputy Director, NIE

Elmendorf, Richard | Program Associate, Office of R&D Resources, NIE

Emery, Richard | Assistant to the Associate Director, Office of Research, NIE

Falender, Andrew | Assistant Director, Office of Research Grants, NIE

Feldman, Elissa | Program specialist, Education Voucher Program, NIE

Fisher, Don | Research Assistant, Essential Skills Program, NIE

Gary, Doris | Equal Employment Opportunity Officer, NIE

Gerber, Peter | Program Analyst, Office of Planning and Management, NIE

Glennan, Thomas K., Jr. | Director, NIE (November 1972 to November 1974)

Gordon, Shana | Senior Associate, Office of Planning and Management, NIE

Gustafson, George | Advisor to the Director for External Relations, NIE

Haggerty, Patrick E. | Chairman, National Council on Education Research

Halperin, Samuel | Director, Institute for Educational Leadership, Washington, D.C.

Hansford, Byron   Executive Secretary, Council of
                                   Chief State School Officers,
                                   Washington, D.C.

Hansot, Elisabeth   Associate, Local Problem Solving
                                   Program, NIE

Haughy, Charles   Program specialist, Office of R&D
                                   Resources, NIE

Hill, Paul   Assistant Director, Policy Studies,
                                   NIE

Hodgkinson, Harold   Director, NIE (after June 1975)

Holt, Harrison   Analyst, Education Voucher
                                   Program, NIE

Kooi, Beverly   Senior Associate, System
                                   Development Corporation, Santa
                                   Monica, California (Senior planner,
                                   NIE Planning Unit)

Koshel, Patricia   Administrative Assistant to the
                                   Director, NIE

Levien, Roger   Head of Domestic Programs,
                                   Rand Corporation, Washington,
                                   D.C.

Levitin, Teri   Branch Chief, Career Education
                                   Program, NIE

Liddicoet, William   Program Assistant, Basic Studies,
                                   NIE

Lipman-Blumen, Jean   Senior Associate, Basic Studies, NIE

Lipson, Joseph   Vice Provost, University of Illinois,
                                   Chicago Circle campus (Senior
                                   Planner, NIE Planning Unit)

McDaniels, Garry   Assistant Director, Teaching
                                   and Curriculum Program, NIE

McElroy, James   Executive Director, National
                                   Committee for Educational Change,
                                   Washington, D.C.

Marland, Sidney P.   President, College Entrance
                                   Examination Board (HEW Assistant
                                   Secretary for Education, 1972–73;
                                   OE Commissioner of Education,
                                   1970–72)

Martin, Bernard   Associate Director, Office of
                                   Planning and Management, NIE

Mastrangelo, Richard	Special Assistant to Elliott Richardson
Mays, John	Science Advisor, NIE
Melmed, Arthur	Acting Associate Director, Office of Programs, NIE
Missar, Charles	Specialist, Education Reference Division, NIE
Moorman, Hunter	Analyst, Office of Planning and Management, NIE
Nicosia, Eileen	Assistant, Office of External Relations, NIE
O'Keefe, Michael	Director, Policy Analysis and Evaluation, University of Illinois, Champaign-Urbana (formerly with Office of Assistant Secretary for Planning and Evaluation, HEW)
Parker, Elizabeth	Program Assistant, Education Reference Division, NIE
Parks, Gail	Specialist, Policy Studies, NIE (member of NIE Planning Unit)
Pfluger, Fred	Staff assistant, Subcommittee on Labor–HEW, House Appropriations Committee
Phillips, Caroline	Aide to NCER, Office of Planning and Management, NIE
Phillips, Martha	Staff director, House Republican Policy Committee
Raizen, Senta	Senior Associate, Rand Corporation, Washington, D.C. (Associate Director, Office of Dissemination, NIE; Senior Planner, NIE Planning Unit)
Russell, Ernest	Associate Director, Office of Administration, NIE
Saario, Terry	Education Officer, the Ford Foundation, New York City (Assistant for Federal and Professional Affairs, American Education Research Association, Washington, D.C.)
Schiller, Jeffry	Associate, Technology Program, NIE

Selden, David   President, American Federation of
                                     Teachers, Washington, D.C.
Silberman, Harry   Professor, Graduate School of
                                     Education, University of California
                                     at Los Angeles (Director, NIE
                                     Planning Unit)
Smith, Marshall   Assistant Director, Essential Skills
                                     Program, NIE
Smith, Richard   Associate General Counsel, Senate
                                     Subcommittee on Education
Timpane, Michael   Fellow, Brookings Institution,
                                     Washington, D.C. (Education
                                     Planner, ASPE)
Tomlinson, Tom   Assistant Director, Division of
                                     Research, NIE
Tucker, Marc   Assistant Director, Local Problem
                                     Solving Program, NIE
Upp, Melinda   Public Information Officer, NIE
Ward, Spencer   Associate, Teaching and Curriculum
                                     Program, NIE
Werksman, Richard   Legal Adviser, NIE
Wexler, Stephen   Chief General Counsel, Senate
                                     Subcommittee on Education
Wheeler, Charles   Project Officer, Teaching and
                                     Curriculum Program, NIE
Williamson, John   Analyst, Office of Planning and
                                     Management, NIE
Wise, Arthur   Associate Director, Office of
                                     Research, NIE

Appendix 2

Laboratories	1966	1972
Total, all laboratories	8,658	22,743
Appalachia Educational Laboratory (AEL)	461	1,404
Center for Urban Education (CUE)	919	2,219
Central Atlantic Regional Educational Laboratory (CAREL)	—	—
Central Midwestern Regional Educational Laboratory (CEMREL)	836	2,385
Cooperative Educational Research Laboratory (CERLI)	189	—
Eastern Regional Institute for Education (ERIE)	200	—
Education Development Center (EDC)	168	—
Far West Laboratory for Educational Research and Development (FWLERD)	458	2,570
Michigan-Ohio Regional Educational Laboratory (MOREL)	184	—
Mid-Continent Regional Educational Laboratory (McREL)	759	910
National Laboratory for Higher Education (NLHE)	190	1,017
Northwest Regional Educational Laboratory (NWREL)	571	1,889
Research for Better Schools (RBS)	503	3,652
Rocky Mountain Educational Laboratory (RMEL)	411	—
South Central Regional Educational Laboratory (SCREL)	181	—
Southeastern Educational Laboratory (SEL)	503	—
Southwest Educational Development Laboratory (SWEDL)	216	2,160
Southwestern Cooperative Educational Laboratory (SWCEL)	294	1,109
Southwest Regional Laboratory for Educational Research and Development (SWRL)	957	3,428
Upper Midwest Regional Educational Laboratory (UMREL)	658	—

R&D Centers

Total, all centers	6,580	13,696
Center for Advanced Study of Educational Administration, University of Oregon	663	681
Center for Occupational Education, North Carolina State University	–	450
Center for Research and Development in Higher Education, University of California at Berkeley	316	890
Center for Research and Development in the Study of Individual Differences, Harvard University	1,112	–
Center for the Study of the Evaluation of Instructional Programs, University of California at Los Angeles	409	686
Center for Urban Education[a]	1,020	
Center for Vocational and Technical Education, Ohio State University	–	2,320
Learning Research and Development Center, University of Pittsburgh	1,042	1,811
National Center for Higher Educational Management Systems, WICHE[b]	–	926
National Program in Early Childhood Education, CEMREL[c]	–	1,560
Research and Development Center on Cognitive Learning, University of Wisconsin	808	1,803
Research and Development Center on Educational Stimulation, University of Georgia	401	–
Research and Development Center on the Social Organization of the Schools, Johns Hopkins University	–	650
Research and Development Center on Teacher Education, University of Texas	459	805
Stanford Center for Research and Development in Teaching, Stanford University	350	1,114

Source: NIE (1976, pp. 41–42).
[a]Administered in its first year as an R&D center by a consortium of New York universities, transferred to the Regional Laboratory Program in 1967.
[b]Western Interstate Commission on Higher Education.
[c]Transferred from the University of Illinois in 1970; primary contract with CEMREL terminated in 1973.

Appendix 3

"Part A—Education Division of the Department of Health, Education, and Welfare

"THE EDUCATION DIVISION

"Sec. 401. There shall be, within the Department of Health, Education, and Welfare, an Education Division which shall be composed of the Office of Education and the National Institute of Education, and shall be headed by the Assistant Secretary for Education.

"ASSISTANT SECRETARY FOR EDUCATION

"Sec. 402. (a) There shall be in the Department of Health, Education, and Welfare an Assistant Secretary for Education, who shall be appointed by the President by and with the advice and consent of the Senate. The Assistant Secretary for Education shall be compensated at the rate specified for level IV of the Executive Schedule under section 5315 of title 5, United States Code.

80 Stat. 461;
83 Stat. 864.

"(b) The Assistant Secretary shall be the principal officer in the Department to whom the Secretary shall assign responsibility for the direction and supervision of the Education Division. He shall not serve as Commissioner of Education or as Director of the National Institute of Education on either a temporary or permanent basis.

"THE OFFICE OF EDUCATION

"Sec. 403. (a) The purpose and duties of the Office of Education shall be to collect statistics and facts showing the condition and progress of education in the United States, and to disseminate such information respecting the organization and management of schools and school systems, and methods of teaching, as shall aid the people of the United States in the establishment and maintenance of efficient school systems, and otherwise promote the cause of education throughout the country. The Office of Education shall not have authority which is not expressly provided for by statute or implied therein.

"(b)(1) The management of the Office of Education, shall, subject to the direction and supervision of the Secretary, be entrusted to a Commissioner of Education, who shall be appointed by the President by and with the advice and consent of the Senate, and who shall serve at the pleasure of the President.

"(2) The Commissioner may not engage in any other business, vocation, or employment while serving in any such position; nor may he, except with the express approval of the President in writing, hold any office in, or act in any capacity for, or have a financial interest in, any organization, agency, or institution to which the Office of Education makes a grant or with which it makes a contract or other financial arrangement.

"SUPPORT FOR IMPROVEMENT OF POSTSECONDARY EDUCATION

"Sec. 404. (a) Subject to the provisions of subsection (b), the Secretary is authorized to make grants to, and contracts with, institutions of postsecondary education (including combinations of such institutions) and other public and private educational institutions and agencies (except that no grant shall be made to an educational institution or agency other than a nonprofit institution or agency) to improve postsecondary educational opportunities by providing assistance to such educational institutions and agencies for—

"(1) encouraging the reform, innovation, and improvement of postsecondary education, and providing equal educational opportunity for all;

"(2) the creation of institutions and programs involving new paths to career and professional training, and new combinations of academic and experimental learning;

"(3) the establishment of institutions and programs based on the technology of communications;

"(4) the carrying out in postsecondary educational institutions of changes in internal structure and operations designed to clarify institutional priorities and purposes;

"(5) the design and introduction of cost-effective methods of instruction and operation;

"(6) the introduction of institutional reforms designed to expand individual opportunities for entering and reentering institutions and pursuing programs of study tailored to individual needs;

"(7) the introduction of reforms in graduate education, in the structure of academic professions, and in the recruitment and retention of faculties; and

"(8) the creation of new institutions and programs for examining and awarding credentials to individuals, and the introduction of reforms in current institutional practices related thereto.

"(b) No grant shall be made or contract entered into under subsection (a) for a project or program with any institution of postsecondary education unless it has been submitted to each appropriate State Commission established under section 1202 of the Higher Education Act of 1965, and an opportunity afforded such Commission to submit its comments and recommendations to the Secretary.   Ante, p. 324.

"(c) For the purposes of this section, the authority granted to the Commissioner in part D of this Act shall apply to the Secretary.   Ante, p. 326.

"(d) The Secretary may appoint, for terms not to exceed three years, without regard to the provisions of title 5 of the United States Code governing appointments in the competitive service, not more than five technical employees to administer this section who may be paid without regard to the provisions of chapter 51 and subchapter III of chapter 53 of such title relating to classification and General Schedule pay rates.   5 USC 101 et seq.

"(e) There are authorized to be appropriated $10,000,000 for the fiscal year ending June 30, 1973, $50,000,000 for the fiscal year ending June 30, 1974, and $75,000,000 for the fiscal year ending June 30, 1975, for the purposes of this section.   5 USC 5101, 5331, 5332 note. Appropriations.

"NATIONAL INSTITUTE OF EDUCATION

"Sec. 405. (a) (1) The Congress hereby declares it to be the policy of the United States to provide to every person an equal opportunity to receive an education of high quality regardless of his race, color, religion, sex, national origin, or social class. Although the American educational system has pursued this objective, it has not yet attained that objective. Inequalities of opportunity to receive high quality education remain pronounced. To achieve quality will require far more dependable knowledge about the processes of learning and education than now exists or can be expected from present research and experimentation in this field. While the direction of the education system remains primarily the responsibility of State and local governments, the Federal Government has a clear responsibility to provide leadership in the conduct and support of scientific inquiry into the educational process.

86 STAT. 329   Pub. Law 92-318   June 23, 1972

"(2) The Congress further declares it to be the policy of the United States to—

"(i) help to solve or to alleviate the problems of, and promote the reform and renewal of American education;

"(ii) advance the practice of education, as an art, science, and profession;

"(iii) strengthen the scientific and technological foundations of education; and

"(iv) build an effective educational research and development system.

Establishment.   "(b)(1) In order to carry out the policy set forth in subsection (a), there is established the National Institute of Education (hereinafter referred to as the 'Institute') which shall consist of a National Council on Educational Research (referred to in this section as the 'Council') and a Director of the Institute (hereinafter referred to as the 'Director'). The Institute shall have only such authority as may be vested therein by this section.

"(2) The Institute shall, in accordance with the provisions of this section, seek to improve education, including career education, in the United States through—

"(A) helping to solve or to alleviate the problems of, and achieve the objectives of American education;

"(B) advancing the practice of education, as an art, science, and profession;

"(C) the strengthening of the scientific and technological foundations of education; and

"(D) building an effective educational research and development system.

Members.   "(c)(1) The Council shall consist of fifteen members appointed by the President, by and with the advice and consent of the Senate, the Director, and such other ex officio members who are officers of the United States as the President may designate. Eight members of the Council (excluding ex officio members) shall constitute a quorum. The Chairman of the Council shall be designated from among its appointed members by the President. Ex officio members shall not have a vote on the Council.

"(2) The term of office of the members of the Council (other than ex officio members) shall be three years, except that (A) the members first taking office shall serve as designated by the President, five for terms of three years, five for terms of two years, and five for terms of one year, and (B) any member appointed to fill a vacancy shall serve for the remainder of the term for which his predecessor was appointed. Any appointed member who has been a member of the Council for six consecutive years shall thereafter be ineligible for appointment to the Council during the two-year period following the expiration of such sixth year.

"(3) The Council shall—

"(A) establish general policies for, and review the conduct of, the Institute;

"(B) advise the Assistant Secretary and the Director of the Institute on development of programs to be carried out by the Institute;

"(C) present to the Assistant Secretary and the Director such recommendations as it may deem appropriate for the strengthening of educational research, the improvement of methods of collecting and disseminating the findings of educational research and of insuring the implementation of educational renewal and reform based upon the findings of educational research;

"(D) conduct such studies as may be necessary to fulfill its functions under this section;

"(E) prepare an annual report to the Assistant Secretary on the current status and needs of educational research in the United States;

"(F) submit an annual report to the President on the activities of the Institute, and on education and educational research in general, (i) which shall include such recommendations and comments as the Council may deem appropriate, and (ii) shall be submitted to the Congress not later than March 31 of each year; and

Report to President and Congress.

"(G) meet at the call of the Chairman, except that it shall meet (i) at least four times during each fiscal year, or (ii) whenever one-third of the members request in writing that a meeting be held. The Director shall make available to the Council such information and assistance as may be necessary to enable the Council to carry out its functions.

"(d)(1) The Director of the Institute shall be appointed by the President, by and with the advice and consent of the Senate, and shall serve at the pleasure of the President. The Director shall be compensated at the rate provided for level V of the Executive Schedule under section 5316 of title 5, United States Code, and shall perform such duties and exercise such powers and authorities as the Council, subject to the general supervision of the Assistant Secretary, may prescribe. The Director shall be responsible to the Assistant Secretary and shall report to the Secretary through the Assistant Secretary and not to or through any other officer of the Department of Health, Education, and Welfare. The Director shall not delegate any of his functions to any other officer who is not directly responsible to him.

Director.

80 Stat. 463;
83 Stat. 864.

"(2) There shall be a Deputy Director of the Institute (referred to in this section as the 'Deputy Director') who shall be appointed by the President and shall serve at the pleasure of the President. The Deputy Director shall be compensated at the rate provided for grade 18 of the General Schedule set forth in section 5332 of title 5, United States Code, and shall act for the Director during the absence or disability of the Director and exercise such powers and authorities as the Director may prescribe. The position created by this paragraph shall be in addition to the number of positions placed in grade 18 of the General Schedule under section 5108 of title 5, United States Code.

5 USC 5332 note.

80 Stat. 453;
84 Stat. 1955.
Research.

"(e)(1) In order to carry out the objectives of the Institute, the Director is authorized, through the Institute, to conduct educational research; collect and disseminate the findings of educational research; train individuals in educational research; assist and foster such research, collection, dissemination, or training through grants, or technical assistance to, or jointly financed cooperative arrangements with, public or private organizations, institutions, agencies, or individuals; promote the coordination of such research and research support within the Federal Government; and may construct or provide (by grant or otherwise) for such facilities as he determines may be required to accomplish such purposes. As used in this subsection, the term 'educational research' includes research (basic and applied), planning, surveys, evaluations, investigations, experiments, developments, and demonstrations in the field of education (including career education).

"(2) Not less than 90 per centum of the funds appropriated pursuant to subsection (h) for any fiscal year shall be expended to carry out this section through grants or contracts with qualified public or private agencies and individuals.

"(3) The Director may appoint, for terms not to exceed three years,

5 USC 101 et seq.

without regard to the provisions of title 5 of the United States Code governing appointment in the competitive service and may compensate without regard to the provisions of chapter 51 and subchapter III of

5 USC 5101, 5331, 5332 note.

chapter 53 of such title relating to classification and General Schedule pay rates, such technical or professional employees of the Institute as he deems necessary to accomplish its functions and also appoint and compensate without regard to such provisions not to exceed one-fifth of the number of full-time, regular technical or professional employees of the Institute.

"(f)(1) The Director, in order to carry out the provisions of this section, is authorized—

Rules and regulations.

"(A) to make, promulgate, issue, rescind, and amend rules and regulations governing the manner of operation of the Institute;

"(B) to accept unconditional gifts or donations of services, money or property, real, personal or mixed, tangible or intangible;

"(C) without regard to section 3648 of the Revised Statutes of the United States (31 U.S.C. 529), United States Code, to enter into and perform such contracts, leases, cooperative agreements or other transactions as may be necessary for the conduct of the Institute's work and on such terms as he may deem appropriate with any agency or instrumentality of the United States, or with any State, territory or possession, or with any political subdivision thereof, or with any international organization or agency, or with any firm, association, corporation or educational institution, or with any person, without regard to statutory provisions prohibiting payment of compensation to aliens;

"(D) to acquire (by purchase, lease, condemnation or otherwise), construct, improve, repair, operate and maintain laboratories, research and testing facilities, computing devices, communications networks and machinery, and such other real and personal property or interest therein as deemed necessary;

"(E) to acquire (by purchase, lease, condemnation or otherwise) and to lease to others or to sell such property in accordance with the provisions of the Federal Property and Administrative

63 Stat. 377.
40 USC 471 note.

Services Act, patents, copyrights, computing programs, theatrical and broadcast performance rights or any form of property whatsoever or any rights thereunder; and

"(F) to use the services, computation capacity, communications networks, equipment, personnel, and facilities of Federal and other agencies with their consent, with or without reimbursement. Each department and agency of the Federal Government shall cooperate fully with the Director in making its services, equipment, personnel and facilities available to the Institute.

"(2) All laborers and mechanics employed by contractors or subcontractors on all construction projects assisted under this title shall be paid wages at rates not less than those prevailing on similar construction in the locality as determined by the Secretary of Labor in accordance with the Davis-Bacon Act, as amended (40 U.S.C.

49 Stat. 1011.

276a—276a-5). The Secretary of Labor shall have with respect to the labor standards specified in this section the authority and functions set forth in Reorganization Plan Numbered 14 of 1950 (15 F.R. 3176;

64 Stat. 1267.
5 USC app.
63 Stat. 108.

5 U.S.C. 133z-15) and section 2 of the Act of June 13, 1934, as amended (40 U.S.C. 276(c)).

"(g) Where funds are advanced for a single project by more than one Federal agency for the purposes of this section, the National Institute of Education may act for all in administering the funds advanced.

June 23, 1972   **Pub. Law 92-318**   86 STAT. 332
───

"(h) There are hereby authorized to be appropriated, without fiscal year   Appropriation.
limitations, $550,000,000, in the aggregate, for the period beginning July 1,
1972, and ending June 30, 1975, to carry out the functions of the Institute.
Sums so appropriated shall, notwithstanding any other provision of law
unless enacted in express limitation of this subsection, remain available
for the purposes of this subsection until expended."

(b) (1) The amendments made by subsection (a) shall be effective after
June 30, 1972.   Effective date.

(2) (A) Effective July 1, 1972, sections 516 and 517 of the Revised Statutes of the United States (20 U.S.C. 1, 2) are repealed.   Repeals.

(B) Effective July 1, 1972, section 422 of the General Education Provisions Act is amended by striking out "(as set forth in section 516 of the
Revised Statutes (20 U.S.C. 1)" and inserting in lieu thereof "(as set forth Ante, p. 326.
in section 403(a) of this Act)".

Appendix 4

NIE Five Priorities, Announced in December 1973

WHAT DOES NIE PROPOSE TO DO?

The Institute proposes to use the $130 million requested in fiscal year 1975 to support activities in the five priority areas approved by our National Council (essential skills, productivity, education and work, local problem-solving, and diversity) and in the areas of dissemination and research. I shall describe these activities briefly.

ESSENTIAL SKILLS

We have placed priority on finding ways to teach the basic skills deemed necessary to function in our society. Our initial emphasis is on reading, probably the most fundamental skill of all. By and large, the schools know how to teach children how to read; to translate letters into sounds and words. Most children master those skills in the first three grades, and many complete the next stage: learning how to make sense out of words. But at least 10 to 15 percent of the children in the middle grades cannot master those comprehension skills, to move from understanding simple written passages to comprehending newspapers, new curricular materials, or even cookbooks or driver's license applications.

NIE plans, therefore, to conduct research over the next 5 years that will lead to development of curricula, teaching techniques, and teacher training programs that will improve children's ability to comprehend the kinds of written materials required by the fourth through eighth grades.

In addition to this major new initiative, NIE will continue existing programs that are developing more efficient curriculum materials for the early grades and are examining specific learning problems that affect a child's ability to read. A total of $11,962,000 is requested for both new initiatives and continuation of these ongoing programs.

LOCAL PROBLEM SOLVING

Several State and local education agencies—including those in Rhode Island, Florida, Maine, Texas, Oregon—have developed model programs for defining the problems faced by their schools and either devising their own solutions or adapting the solutions suggested by R. & D. or other school districts. For example, the Maine School Administrative District No. 3 is using a 4-day student week and the results are promising. Teachers and administrators now have the time to more effectively plan ways students can best achieve academic success at their own pace. Initial evaluation indicates that not only is the system saving money, but also that the achievement scores of students have improved. NIE will be able to examine this type of locally initiated innovation and to tell other districts how they might adapt it to their own needs. This type of local problem-solving capacity, however, is not widespread. And, unless local schools do have that capacity, the full potential of NIE's work cannot be realized.

In fiscal year 1974, NIE is examining the development of this capacity in large urban schools. Eight to 10 schools or clusters of schools will be given funds to extend existing programs, such as teacher centers, new governance systems, staffing and scheduling patterns, and other arrangements that provide opportunities for school staffs to improve the education they can offer their students. While the immediate beneficiaries will be those grantees, the evaluation component of this project will collect data that will be useful to all large urban school districts. Further, the evaluation contractor will be available to provide assistance to any other district that requests help.

In fiscal year 1975, NIE is requesting $8,638,000 to continue this and other fiscal year 1974 actiivties and to support 8 to 10 sites at the school district level that are developing approaches, such as research and evaluation offices or extensive staff development programs, that will strengthen their ability to improve education.

PRODUCTIVITY

Education expenditures are rising rapidly—from $9 billion in 1950 to $96 billion this year—one-third faster in these years than can be explained by inflation or increased enrollments. Taxpayers, legislators, Governors, schools boards—all are concerned with lowering the rate of increase while not diminishing educational quality. NIE will assist schools in meeting this objective.

NIE's present emphasis is on developing ways of using modern communications technologies, such as television, audio casettes, videotapes, and even a communications satellite, so that they can enhance the quality of education available while reducing its cost. For example, it has been suggested that the communications satellite can be effective in serving remote rural populations or persons in mountainous areas. NIE has sponsored development of career education materials, preschool education programs, and teacher training courses than can effectively be transmitted to Appalachia, the Rocky Mountains, and Alaska by means of a satellite expected to be launched in June. The costs of this program, and the effectiveness of these means of transmission, will be evaluated in fiscal year 1975; the results of this project will help clarify the potential of advanced communications technologies in improving the education of children. A total of $16,458,000 is requested for this and other technology programs in 1975.

EDUCATION AND WORK

Americans believe that education should advance their career and assume that education and economic success are related. In a 1972 Gallup Poll, 82 percent of those asked why they wanted their children to get an education responded either, "to get better jobs" or "to achieve financial success." At the same time, it is not clear what are, and what are not, the best ways for education to assist students in obtaining jobs in our society.

The experience-based program I mentioned earlier is developing one means of offering young people a chance to explore different career options and to prepare them with specific work skills and experience. In fiscal year 1975, NIE will explore ways that education can better prepare young people to assume the responsibilities of adult careers.

In addition, NIE will continue to support development of programs that will help adults advance in careers or to obtain worthwhile employment. Among the programs to be continued, for example, is the mountain plains residential program at Glasgow Air Force Base in Montana. In this project, NIE is exploring whether it is possible to help the hardcore unemployed by providing them work-related counseling and training, as well as by assisting their families with health services, financial counseling, and other education-related services. The project is being evaluated both in terms of the benefits to the participants, as well as in costs to the Government. The findings are preliminary, but they suggest that such a program might be cost effective. Since the project was transferred to NIE, costs have been lowered from $16,000 per family to $10,640—a sum roughly equal to what would be expended in just 5 years in welfare payments to the family in Montana. Of those who complete the program, 88 percent are employed, and they find jobs that pay 25 percent more per month than their last job before entering the program. If subsequent indications are as promising as these initial returns, R. & D. may have developed an approach to helping the hardcore unemployed that could be adopted on a wide scale.

A total of $21,293,000 is requested for these and other programs in fiscal year 1975.

DIVERSITY

Children learn in different ways. Some learn better from oral presentations, some from written materials. Some learn better in open classrooms, some in traditional settings. Some non-English speaking children learn better if taught first in their native tongue, transferring later to English, others benefit from initial instruction in English. NIE's purpose in this priority area is to assist schools in developing approaches that accommodate the diverse educational needs of a pluralistic student population.

A total of $20,343,000 is being requested for programs in the diversity area, which includes the experimental schools, education vouchers, handicapped, and bilingual activities. I think you are familiar with the experimental schools and voucher programs, but let me briefly mention what we plan to do in the bilingual and handicapped areas. First, standardized tests used to measure the achievements of non-English speaking students often are inadequate to measure their abilities or diagnose learning problems. NIE will develop better and more accurate tests. Second, the needs of minority students too often are defined by persons outside minority communities. NIE will bring together researchers and educators from these communities so they, themselves, can suggest appropriate problems on which NIE should focus its resources.

DISSEMINATION

Congress gave NIE the responsibility to assure that the products of research and development—whether they are supported by NIE or not—are transmitted to teachers, students, local school boards, and policy makers who are dealing with the day-to-day problems of American education. This dissemination function is a key activity of the Institute, for which we are requesting $12,850,000 in fiscal year 1975.

The bulk of this sum will be used to continue and improve the ERIC system, a compilation of materials relating to virtually all aspects of education and the largest information retrieval system in any of the social sciences. ERIC is used about 5 million times a year by those familiar with its operation, who have access to its materials, and who can frame their requests to receive the information they need. Despite this heavy use, ERIC needs improvement: It needs a broader base of information that is more relevant to educators, and it needs to be made more accessible to its users. NIE plans to correct both deficiencies, putting users in contact with people who can both collect data from the field and help them get information from the system.

In addition, NIE will provide funds to developers of promising educational products and practices so they can provide more useful information to schools about them. Through this program, for example, schools will be able to discover which products of the educational labs and centers are available to them and which meet their precise requirements.

RESEARCH

Many of the activities above have immediate applicability to educators. Our basic and policy studies, on the other hand, are more clearly investments in the future.

For example, there is abundant evidence that education leads to different lifetime outcomes for boys and girls. An important part of this difference appears to result from biases in the way boys and girls are counseled, in the roles men and women are assigned in textbooks, or from the expectations that teachers have for accomplishments by boys and girls. Our understanding of the sources of this bias and the relative importance of factors causing it is fragmentary, being based upon ad hoc studies. The NIE proposes to develop a more comprehensive and systematic view of sex discrimination associated with schooling with the intent of providing information to teachers and administrators as well as publishers on how to correct undesirable biases.

NIE also is making a substantial investment in the area of teaching and curriculum. Some 32 States are adopting laws requiring that teacher certification be related to an applicants' competency to teach, yet, in truth, little is known about the attributes of a competent teacher. NIE's research, thus, is focusing on determination what teacher skills are needed to improve student achievement, how those skills can be taught and improved, and how selection procedures can be designed to measure those skills. Finally, NIE is continuing the major curriculum development efforts, such as Wisconsin's individually guided education program, which I described earlier.

A total of $25,556,000 is requested for basic and policy studies and teaching and curriculum activities in fiscal year 1975.

Source: U.S. House of Representatives Appropriations Subcommittee, Appropriations Hearings for 1975, pp. 794–96.

Appendix 5

Annual Federal Budget Cycle

The following is the sequence of federal agency budget events applicable to the period covered by this study. The sequence depicts dates as they would have applied to a fiscal year 1975 budget.

Time	Event
April 1973	First request from HEW for preliminary budget information on fiscal year 1975
May to August 1973	Further development and refinement of fiscal year 1975 budget
September 1973	NIE budget, including five-year rationale, due to HEW
October 1973	HEW budget due to OMB
November 1973	OMB mark handed down
December 1973	OMB hears appeals
January 1974	Presidential budget message
February 1974	House Appropriations Subcommittee hearings, marks, and appeals
March 1974	Senate Appropriations Subcommittee hearings, marks, and appeals
May to June 1974	Congressional conference meeting and report
June 1974	Appropriations bill acted on by Congress and signed or vetoed by president
July 1974	OMB apportionment process or operation under continuing resolution.[a]

[a]If Congress does not pass an appropriations bill by the time a fiscal year begins, federal spending automatically continues under a "continuing resolution." This specifies that agencies operate as if their budget were the same as in the preceding fiscal year.

Notes

Introduction

1. The label is unfortunate, because, in Western culture, at least, rationality has become a high moral good and, by extension, so has rational decision-making. Steinbruner (1974) notes, "In common discourse the word, 'rational,' is drenched with normative connotations. It means doing that which is 'best' under the circumstances, or that which is most worthy of approval. By implication, any decision which is not held to be rational is thereby condemned" (p. 27).

2. The theme of high expectations in new organizations is explored in Sarason (1972).

3. The theory of organized anarchies is discussed in Cohen, March, and Olsen (1972), Cohen and March (1974), and March and Olsen (1976).

Chapter 1

1. See "Models of Success, Models of Failure Chronology." In each chapter we provide a chronology of the major events described in the chapter.

2. A glossary of acronyms is provided on p. 2.

3. See, for example, Lomask (1976) for a history of NSF that details some of the congressional difficulties this agency faced.

4. Much of the discussion of the federal role in science R&D is taken from Estler (1975).

5. A simple index of the strength of the relationship between science and government is the proportion of the federal budget devoted to R&D. According to the Commission on Government Procurement, "In 1972 federal R&D spending was about $15.2 billion which represented 6.4% of the federal budget. This was the eighth year of decline in the percentage of the federal budget devoted to R&D since the peak of 12.5% in 1965" (Commission on Government Procurement, December 1972, p. 5).

6. See, for example, Kuhn (1970).

7. Examples of small-scale but significant work are Clark's research on self-concepts of black and white children; Piaget's work on stages of cognitive development; and Schultz's work on education and human capital. (See Getzels 1970, for further examples.)

8. See Boyan (1969, 1974); Boyan and Mason (1968); Dershimer (1976); and Sieber (1974) for histories of this period.

9. Unless otherwise noted, the following history draws primarily upon Boyan and Mason (1968); and Boyan (1969, 1974).

10. OE was by no means the only federal agency supporting education R&D. In fiscal 1968 the federal government spent $192.3 million to support education R&D (Gideonse 1970, p. 117). OE accounted for 53% of these expenditures, with another 12% coming from NSF, 7% from OEO, 6% from NIMH, and the remainder (22%) from other agencies. State and local education agencies have traditionally been only minor contributors to research and development activities. Cronbach and Suppes (1965) estimated that states contributed only 12% of the resources devoted to education R&D and that local school districts contributed only 3% (p. 205).

11. Representatives of the laboratories and R&D centers formally organized as the Council on Educational Development and Research (CEDaR) in late 1970.

12. In 1967 the Bureau of Research had approximately 270 employees; the entire Office of Education employed 2,614 full-time personnel. The bureau's budget was $100 million; the total OE budget was more than $4 billion (House Special Subcommittee on Education 1967, pp. 37, 1, 204).

13. See Downs (1967, pp. 148–59) for a discussion of the role of monitoring agencies and staffs in controlling operating agencies such as OE and its research office.

14. Gideonse (1970) provides a summary of these studies.

15. The words "good people," heard so often by the Bureau of Research in its conversations with the Unholy Trinity, meant people who had strong reputations in the natural and social science disciplines. Such a definition tended to exclude most researchers based solely in schools of education.

16. OE's research bureau was not alone in emulating the Department of Defense in the late sixties and early seventies. All of HEW was embracing the rhetoric, if not the practice, of such Department of Defense features as program planning and budgeting systems. Warwick (1975) documents similar efforts in the Department of State.

17. Members of the Working Group on new education initiatives were: Lee DuBridge, the president's science adviser and director of OST; Daniel Moynihan, head of the Domestic Council; Chester Finn, Moynihan's deputy; Dick Nathan, associate director of OMB; Tom Glennan, director of research and evaluation in OEO; Lewis Butler, assistant secretary for planning and evaluation in HEW; and James Allen, commissioner of education. Staff assisting the working group were John Mays, assistant to the director of OST for education; and Bernard Martin, education budget officer in OMB.

18. See Finn (1974) for this story in more detail.

19. In 1958 an advisory board organized by the National Academy of Sciences–National Research Council proposed an Organization for Research in Education to conduct and sponsor educational research in a manner comparable to the National Institute of Mental Health (National Academy of Sciences 1958). The proposal fell on deaf ears (Cronbach and Suppes 1969, p. 10). Six years later new institutional arrangements for the management and dissemination of educational research were urged in a report of the Panel on Educational Research and Development of the President's Science Advisory Committee (1964). In 1967 Amitai Etzioni of Columbia University proposed the creation of "A Center for Advanced Research and Study" to be supported by OE (Etzioni 1967). In 1969 there were two separate proposals for a new educational research organization at the federal level. Both of these proposals, one by David Krathwohl, then president of the American Educational Research Association, and the other by the Commission on Instructional Technology, chaired by the former commissioner of education, Sterling McMurrin, advocated National Institutes of Education, with the plural form of "institutes" referring to a grouping of constituent organizations each addressing a separate educational problem. Krathwohl suggested that the problems of interest to each institute could be as broad as urban education or as circumscribed as the program of the existing OE Bureau of the Handicapped (Levien 1971, p. 155). The Commission on Instructional Technology specified that one constituent institute be devoted to instructional technology (Levien 1971, p. 155). The commission emphasized that a group of constituent institutes could foster a diversity in approaches to educational questions. Both proposals suggested that NIE be created outside of OE and report directly to the assistant secretary of education. Krathwohl asserted that such an arrangement would place NIE one step away from "the pressures" where it "could resolve the priorities issue of which problems have a combination of high social need and appear amenable to research attack" (Levien 1971, p. 156). The commission argued that NIE should be involved in research projects running three to five years or more in length and should have multiyear funding authority to make this feasible.

Chapter 2

1. Tom Glennan, then assistant director of OEO for planning, research, and evaluation, actually made the suggestion. Glennan and Levien had been classmates in college and both had worked for Rand. Glennan was later to be named first director of NIE.

2. Levien's plan would have created four program areas for the agency: solving major educational problems; advancing educational practice; strengthening education's foundations; and strengthening the research and development system. He suggested that the problem-solving division of NIE should receive 50% of the agency's budget to develop comprehensive national programs—"carefully designed, coherent combinations of research, development, experimentation, evaluation, and implementation activities directed at solutions of major problems" (p. 49). Levien suggested his three targets of improvement and reform (Improving Education for the Disadvantaged, Improving the Quality of Education, and Improving Resource Use in Education) as likely candidates for the problem-solving component of the new agency.

The second program area, Improving Educational Practice, would receive one-quarter of the budget. It would comprise centers for instruction, organization forms, assessment, and professional development. This unit most resembled conventional government-sponsored work in education—curriculum development projects, teacher-training institutes, and such. The third program area, to receive 10–15% of the annual budget, would sponsor basic research, primarily university-based academic work, with no short-term payoff expected. And the fourth program area, Improving the Educational R&D System, would sponsor fellowships, traineeships, and institutional support grants to improve the capability of personnel and organizations within the R&D system. (All four of these areas in fact have appeared at one time or another as organization units within NIE. Chapter 7 will attempt to trace the course of these and other organizational units over two years of reorganizations.)

3. In describing the Preliminary Plan, Levien said, "*Its primary role is to solicit the comments and reactions of concerned audiences.* Please read it carefully and consider the National Institute it portrays. What has been left out? What has been included that should not be? How might the proposed Institute be improved?" (p. 18).

4. There was a certain amount of confusion over Silberman's being named director of the Planning Unit. From January through April 1971 some members of the Unholy Trinity and others assumed Silberman would continue as head of NCERD with an outside person named to head the Planning Unit (Mays, 21 March 1974; Kooi, 28 February 1974; Cross, 20 January 1971). In fact, the first official document announcing the establishment of a Commissioner's Planning Unit for the NIE and naming Silberman as its director does not appear until 10 May 1971. Silberman, however, is emphatic that he came to Washington to head the planning effort (Silberman, 28 February 1974). As he puts it, "Marland asked me to put together a little group to oversee the birth of the new organization." Marland's recollection is consistent with this description (Marland, 22 March 1974).

5. Charter members of the NIE Planning Unit Steering Committee were Richard Darman, HEW deputy assistant secretary for policy analysis; Chris Cross, HEW deputy assistant secretary for legislation; Bernard Martin from OMB; and John Ottina, then deputy commissioner for planning, evaluation, and management in OE (Cross, 20 January 1971). According to one of its members, the Steering Committee was "fluid" in composition (Mays, 22 March 1974). At later dates some or all of the following people also attended meetings: Michael Timpane, director for education planning in ASPE; Joan Bissell, Lyle Spencer, and Robert Krughoff, members of his staff; Fred Pfluger from the HEW Comptroller's Office, and Don Davies, deputy commissioner for education renewal in OE, the person to whom Silberman reported when he first arrived at OE.

6. In the summer and early fall of 1971 four academic meetings were convened by Mays and the Planning Unit: one of psychologists chaired by George Miller of Rockefeller University; one of sociologists chaired by Burton Clark of Yale; one of people interested in education technology chaired by John Truxal of the State University of New York at Stony Brook; and one of anthropologists chaired by John Whiting of Harvard.

7. Silberman believed that one of the main reasons education innovations or products of education R&D had not been widely adopted or had had little significant impact on the education system in the past was that their developers had not focused on system characteristics; they had created add-on programs or products that in no way affected structural or process variables. He believed that, no matter what new initiatives were proposed, they had to

incorporate system incentives, information, sanctions, and agents if they were to result in significant changes.

Chapter 3

1. All references in this chapter, unless otherwise indicated, are from U.S. Congress, House, Committee on Education and Labor, Select Subcommittee on Education, *Hearings to Establish a National Institute of Education*, 92nd Cong., 1st sess., 1971.

2. He was, however, in persistent disagreement with that other recognized expert on education issues and friend of education (although not of the Office of Education), Edith Green (D–Oregon). Their relationship was not cordial. As an associate of both representatives remarked, their disagreements were "partly ideological, but personalities are a big part of it. . . . Their ideological differences wouldn't be so great if they didn't hate one another" (Jarin 1972).

3. The nature of the witnesses no doubt depended upon whom Brademas and his subcommittee staff chose to invite. It seems unlikely, however, that representatives from groups other than those represented would have been denied the opportunity to speak had they sought it.

4. He advocated the creation of fifty separate "institutes," one to be located in each of the state offices of public instruction (Bakalis, pp. 423–25).

5. There were dissenters from this common view. During the Brademas hearings several witnesses offered a modest defense of OE's R&D programs and strongly cautioned against unrealistic promises and overoptimistic expectations for NIE. The dissenters were all current or past participants in OE's R&D efforts.

6. See Cohen, March, and Olsen 1972, "A Garbage-Can Model of Organizational Choice," for a description of decisions as receptacles for assorted issues.

Chapter 4

1. Glennan had been a member of the White House group that created the NIE proposal. His recommendation led to the hiring of Roger Levien as the initial NIE architect. The process of Glennan's selection and his qualifications for the job are detailed in chapter 5.

2. The rapid pace of the nomination and confirmation process left little time for the courtesy visits to Senate committee members that presidential nominees usually make. At the time, the absence of meetings with the senators did not seem significant. Later, after NIE had begun incurring budget cuts, it was cited by Senate staff members as a problem (cited in Glennan, September 1975, p. 6).

3. The NCER nominations might have languished even longer had it not been for a feisty little watchdog group that began making trouble for NIE six months after NIE's creation. The National Committee for Educational Change (NCEC), a small group of university professors and administrators, was convinced that NIE was not living up to its mandate to promote equality of education opportunities—a mandate NCEC believed to be specified clearly in the preamble to NIE's authorizing legislation. In a desire to gain some leverage over the institute, NCEC and its executive director, James McElroy, seized upon the fact that NIE was operating without its NCER and thus, according to the NCEC analysis, was operating illegally. McElroy complained about NIE's alleged illegal activities to Brademas, who called oversight hearings on the institute in February 1973. Brademas reacted angrily to the delay in the NCER appointments:

I have certainly personally tried to work as hard as I can to insure bipartisan support [for NIE]. But I suggest to you [Glennan] that you are in flagrant violation of the law. The institute was established last summer. The question of the provision of a National Council was not a whim of the members of this committee or of Congress. . . . I suggest to you that the failure of the administration, of the White House, of President Nixon—who wrote me a very gracious personal letter thanking me for my help on [NIE]—to appoint this high level council, to simply follow the law, is jeopardizing all of the effort that has gone before in Congress. [House Select Subcommittee on Education Oversight Hearings, 6 February 1973, pp. 12, 34]

After the hearing NCEC filed a lawsuit seeking an injunction to suspend NIE operations until the council was appointed. On 24 March 1973, only a few days before the government was required to respond to the suit, Nixon announced his fifteen nominees for the NCER, the nominees that had been agreed upon three months earlier. But McElroy was not quite finished with NIE. First he had complained about the delay in naming the council. Now he proceeded to delay Senate confirmation of the council by persuading the chairman of the relevant Senate committee that before approving the nominees he should elicit from each a written statement of his or her position on equality of education opportunity (McElroy, June, 1974). Senate confirmation was indeed withheld until all statements were received; the NCER was not officially confirmed until 7 June 1973—349 days after the NIE legislation had been signed. (The merits of the NCEC's argument for equality of education opportunity aside, it is clear that the interpretation of NIE's legislation as requiring sole attention to that subject was overly narrow. A clear Congressional mandate for NIE to concentrate solely on equality of educational opportunity was never articulated—not in Brademas's 1971 hearings on the creation of NIE, in the oversight hearing, in the appropriations committees hearings, or in floor debate.) Shortly thereafter McElroy became ill; the NCEC had exhausted its meager initial funding; and it ceased operations.

4. During this period in NIE's history the federal government fiscal year ran from 1 July to 30 June. (The fiscal year date is that of the second calendar year; thus fiscal year 1973 ran from 1 July 1972 to 30 June 1973.)

5. Technically, Congress appropriated $92 million and approved an $18-million administrative transfer of funds from OE (House Appropriations Subcommittee, 9 March 1973, p. 211).

6. In this chapter we refer to NIE actions as though they were the coherent outcomes of a rational decision process. This is no more than a shorthand technique on our part. In fact, the process by which the institute made and did not make decisions was extraordinarily complicated. The nature of this process is explored in part 2, which focuses on the internal activity of the agency. Chapter 8 contains a section specifically devoted to how budget decisions were made.

7. Estimating "commitments" is an extremely arcane activity, described more fully in chapter 8. Here we need note only that the estimates the House used to decide that $142 million was necessary to support transferred programs in fiscal year 1974 ($110 million for programs transferred from OE at the beginning of the 1973 fiscal year; $8 million for programs transferred from OE and $26 million for programs transferred from OEO at the beginning of the 1974 fiscal year) were inflated (House Appropriations Subcommittee, 9 March 1973, pp. 204–9). NIE had reduced the commitments to OE programs from approximately $118 million to approximately $70 million, and the OEO programs cost closer to $6 million than to $26 million (House Appropriations Subcommittee, 27 February 1974, p. 295; Senate Appropriations Subcommittee, 7 March 1974, p. 335; Senate Appropriations Subcommittee, 6 June 1974, pp. 2887–95).

8. "Political" is a slippery word. In general, we use it in this chapter to mean NIE's relations with the legislative branch of government.

9. This exchange between Senator Magnuson and Glennan during the Senate hearings on NIE's fiscal year 1974 budget illustrates Magnuson's confusion:

Senator Magnuson: How much did you spend in 1973?

Mr. Glennan: The Institute, under my direction spent $106.5 million. . . .

M: How much did you spend in 1973, $109 million?

G: $106.5 million.

M: $106.5 million. . . .

M: It doesn't matter how it comes to us, we want to know how much you spent in 1973. The National Institute of Education spent $109.5 million, is that correct?

G: $106.5 million. . . .

M: You spent $109 million?

G: $106 million.

M: $106 million, let's get that correct. [Senate Appropriations Subcommittee Hearings, 23 October 1973, pp. 4179–81]

10. Fifty-six lines out of Congresswoman Green's total 224 lines of comments and questions in the record of the hearings were devoted to nontransferred OE activities (House Appropriations Subcommittee, 9 March 1973, pp. 188–203).

11. Forty-seven lines out of 224 total lines for Congresswoman Green in the record of the hearings were about programs transferred from OE (House Appropriations Subcommittee, 9 March 1973, pp. 188–203).

12. Seventy-six lines out of 166 total lines for Congresswoman Green in the record of hearings on the supplemental request were about OE activities (House Appropriations Subcommittee, 27 February 1974, pp. 284–92; 306–18).

13. NIE's position was not helped by the fact that in April 1973 two members of the NCER, including Chairman Haggerty, signed a newspaper advertisement from "Citizens for Control of Federal Spending" endorsing the Nixon budget (*Education USA*, 16 April 1973, p. 33).

14. In his testimony for the fiscal year 1974 budget, Glennan responded with "I don't know," or "I guess ... " or "We'll have to provide that for the record," nine times to the House subcommittee and eight times to the Senate subcommittee.

15. Glennan had reduced the number of "I don't know" and "We'll have to provide that for the record" answers. For supplemental testimony, in the House there were four such answers; in the Senate there were five. For fiscal year 1975 testimony, in the House there were six such answers; in the Senate there were two.

16. See Downs (1967, pp. 44–47) and Rourke (1969, particularly pp. 11–24 and 63–69) for a discussion of the political characteristics of government bureaucracies.

17. NIE inherited 68 projects at 23 laboratories and R&D centers costing approximately $35 million in fiscal year 1972. For fiscal year 1974 NIE proposed support for only 32 projects at 15 laboratories and R&D centers for a total expenditure of $26.6 million (Senate Appropriations Subcommittee, 6 June 1974, p. 2933).

18. The American Association of School Administrators wanted NIE to provide "a substantial amount of money ... to develop the understanding and commitment of administrators for new programs" (Paul Salmon, executive secretary AASA, quoted in Senate Appropriations Subcommittee, 6 June 1974, p. 2907). The Council of Chief State School Officers wanted NIE to increase its dissemination budget and channel those funds directly through the state education agencies. Although the Council of Chief State School Officers endorsed NIE's request for supplemental funds, it was—like CEDaR—the kind of friend that meant NIE needed no enemies. The director of the Council of Chief State School Officers observed:

> It is true that the Council is supporting NIE's supplemental budget request, but we are doing that primarily because we feel educational research is essential to improvement in education and the NIE is at present about our only hope for significant Federal involvement in this area. [*Report on Education Research*, 10 April 1974, p. 3]

Although NIE's support from administrators' groups was far from satisfactory, it was enthusiastic compared with the actions of the two powerful organizations representing teachers—the 1.5-million-member National Education Association and the 400,000-member American Federation of Teachers. Both groups were offended by NIE's support of a project transferred from OEO, the education voucher experiment, which the teacher organizations feared might lead to a decline in support for public schools. In addition, they believed NIE was not funding programs of direct usefulness to teachers or consulting teacher groups in developing its plans. After the Senate subcommittee cut NIE's fiscal year 1974 budget to $65 million, the president of the American Federation of Teachers sent Magnuson a congratulatory telegram (Selden, March 1974). The head of government relations for the National Education Association told the Senate Appropriations Subcommittee that it supported NIE's fiscal year 1975 budget request "with some reservation." It supported research on the "processes of learning and teaching . . . [and] wide dissemination of the results of research on teaching and learning through State education agencies" but opposed spending NIE funds "for demonstration of the voucher system" (Senate Appropriations Subcommittee, 17 July 1974, p. 6031). He then hinted that NIE was misspending money. "There are rumors floating around, which we cannot pin down, that there is a hell of a misuse of funds" (Senate Appropriations Subcommittee, 17 July 1974, p. 6032). At those hearings Senator Stevens (R–Alaska) warned that "subsurface opposition" from education groups was putting NIE "on the road to oblivion" (Senate Appropriations Subcommittee, 17 July 1974, pp. 6031–34).

19. The groups subscribing to the statement were the American Association of Colleges for Teacher Education, American Association of School Administrators, American Council on Education, American Educational Research Association, American Federation of Teachers, American Psychological Association, Association for Supervision and Curriculum Development, Association of Colleges and Schools of Education in State Universities and Land-Grant Colleges, Council of Chief State School Officers, Council on Educational Development and Research, Education Commission of the States, National Association of Elementary School Principals, National Association of Secondary School Principals, National Education Association and the National School Boards Association.

20. The first director of the Office of External Relations was actually the second person to have accepted the job. In December 1972 Glennan offered the position to Martha Phillips, then a staff member for the House Republican Research Committee. Although Phillips was concerned that Glennan seemed too sophisticated in speech and manner to communicate with Congress, the NIE job represented an attractive promotion and a challenging assignment that she decided to accept. But once the House Republicans learned of her decision, they offered her a higher salary and greater responsibility and finally persuaded her to rescind her acceptance of the NIE position (Phillips, March 1974).

21. Chapter 6 describes the programs included in the five priority areas. Chapter 8 describes the decision-making process that culminated in the Five Priorities.

22. An even more potent example comes not from NIE, but from NSF—one of the principal models for NIE. The NSF education division, which had sponsored the development of a number of science curricula in the sixties, was severely criticized by Congress in 1974 for its sponsorship of a fifth-grade social studies curriculum project, *Man: A Course of Study* (*Congressional Record*, 9 April 1975).

23. NIE was asking for budget increments of 50–70%. Congress usually scrutinizes requested increments much more carefully than it does the "base" figure. (See Wildavsky 1964 for a discussion of the congressional budget review process.)

Chapter 5

1. In many cases this perception was probably based not on fact, but rather on the assumption of incompetence by association—that is, if it was a part of OE, it must be bad. Even if there had been no truth at all in the assumption, the symbolic value of a complete break with OE seemed enormously important.

2. This number represents 100% of the NIE permanent staff on that date. An additional sixteen people were still employed under the NIE Planning Unit contract, and there were thirteen people—including Elliott, who was still officially an employee of OMB—on loan from other agencies.

3. Congress authorizes the number of positions every agency can fill. These positions are usually attached to specific appropriations measures and cannot be switched at will from one

spending authority to another. Technically, the only way to be hired by the federal government is to be "hired into a slot." Thus, if the slot is moved from one office to another, the person occupying the slot either must move with it or find an empty slot in the first office into which to move.

4. Participants in the lottery called it the "football draft," but that term implies greater knowledge of the players and a more intentional game plan than were evident in the process.

5. The two programs transferred intact from OE to NIE were Experimental Schools (with eight people) and the National Center for Educational Communications (twenty-six people).

6. Richardson remained secretary of HEW for only two months after Glennan took office.

7. As has been noted earlier, Glennan was a member of the White House working group that made the original NIE recommendation.

8. His work at Rand included "Evaluating Federal Manpower Programs: Notes and Observations" (1969); "Innovation and Product Quality under the Total Package Procurement Concept" (1966); and "The Usefulness of Aerospace Management Techniques in Other Sectors of the Economy" (1964).

9. Harry Silberman remained until the end of December 1972 in charge of a small group working on ideas for new NIE programs, then left to take a faculty position at the UCLA Graduate School of Education. Wilmer Cody remained for a year, leading a group that was monitoring contracts transferred from OE, then left to become superintendent of schools in Birmingham, Alabama. Lee Burchinal, who had been head of the National Center for Educational Communications in OE which was transferred intact to NIE, left NIE for NSF in February 1973.

10. Robert Binswanger was director of the Experimental Schools program until November 1974. Tom Clemens was acting director of the Dissemination program until July 1974, when an associate director was hired for that office.

11. Werksman graduated from Columbia College and Columbia law school and worked for HEW and OEO. Mays graduated from California Institute of Technology, earned his Ph.D. from Columbia University, and worked for NSF and OST.

12. Twenty-four out of twenty-five members of the NIE professional staff selected at random and interviewed in June 1974, responded affirmatively to the question, "Is there an informal organization or group of influentials apart from the top management [at NIE]?" Glennan, Elliott, and Martin also responded affirmatively to this question.

13. Academicians operate within an incentive structure that does not greatly reward government service; highly productive people are usually working on several endeavors at the same time and may find it difficult to break free from all of them at once; there was a governmentwide ceiling on salaries that meant that in several cases NIE could not match a candidate's current salary; the spirit of Nixonian Washington was uncongenial to many social scientists.

14. Under a condition of expanding resources the nature of current staff presumably need not seriously constrain the nature of future staff. It could be argued that at this point, before the first budget cut, NIE leadership was still operating under the assumption of expanding resources.

15. Glennan saw the relationship between key personnel appointments and organization structure as a "chicken-and-egg problem." In announcing one of the first organization structures, which he described as a "compromise that deals with this paradox," he said:

> Clearly, the task of intelligent personnel selection is complicated by the newness of the Institute and the absence of a structured research plan that dictates staffing requirements. On the other hand, little can be accomplished in the way of formulating the required research structure until key staff have been recruited. [Glennan, 17 May 1973, p. 1]

16. The lists of specific candidates for the Office of Programs associate directorship generated during NIE's second year also reflect the changing criteria. At one point, when it seemed that

NIE had an inadequate number of Spanish-surnamed senior staff, a number of Spanish-surnamed candidates were added to the lists. But once one was approved for another senior position,
the remainder were dropped from the list of candidates for associate director. Similarly, once a
woman was hired to fill another associate director position, all women, with the exception of one
chief state school officer and one scholar, were dropped from the Office of Programs list
(Goldman, 17 May 1974, pp. 11–12). Shortly after the budget cut and denial of the supplemental
request, six chief state school officers and the directors of three regional laboratories and R&D
centers appeared on the list. In the ten months of lists preceding this point, only one chief state
school officer and one R&D center director had been listed.

17. Of the 148 names generated and presented to the NIE leadership during the second year,
only 27 were approached. Of those 27, 17 turned down NIE: 12 were "not interested," 3 declined
for family considerations, and 2 declined for financial reasons. Of the remaining 10, only 4 were
hired (Goldman, 17 May 1974).

18. The data in this section are drawn from a questionnaire administered in June 1974, to the
entire professional staff (N = 288; response rate = 89%).

19. Approximately 60% of the university group claimed they were in the office after 6 P.M.
more than half the working days every month; approximately 30% of the OEO people and about
24% of the OE people said they often worked late. We infer from these data not that the
university group necessarily worked longer than the other groups, but simply that it worked
different hours.

20. See Simon (1953), the classic study of the Economic Cooperation Agency, for a description
of the cell-division model.

21. Had this model been employed we would expect to see a high proportion of senior
appointments with strong ties to the politically powerful education groups such as the Council of
Chief State School Officers or the National Education Association. As the beginning of NIE's
second year, out of a senior staff of fifteen (excluding the Office of Administration) only one
could have been said to have any such political credentials. Eleven had come from other federal
agencies. One had been a school superintendent, but he was not viewed as a spokesman for the
American Association of School Administrators. One had worked for two of the educational
laboratories and so might have been considered a spokesman for educational researchers. But his
work at both labs had been managerial; he was not an educational researcher and did not see
himself as their representative. Only Gustafson, the adviser for external affairs, could have been
said to be related to a political power—the chief state school officers—through his work in
California, but even that tie was tenuous.

22. Had this model been implemented, we would expect to see senior appointments in the
program areas continuing work they had begun in their previous positions or implementing
specific new plans they had brought with them. Of the seven senior program staff hired by the
beginning of the second year, only two continued work begun in a previous position (both were
heads of transferred programs), and none arrived with a specific new program to implement.

Chapter 6

1. Rapid turnover among OE monitors and uncertainties about year to year funding had
impeded careful documentation of laboratories and centers programs while they were still within
OE.

2. This does not imply that the laboratories and centers themselves were easy to fragment (or
ignore) as institutions.

3. The Experimental Schools program had $15 million in signed contracts plus an additional
$15 million in projected contracts at the end of fiscal year 1972. The actual fiscal year 1973
expenditures for this program totaled approximately $20 million.

4. This first implementation was less experimental than many would have wished. Only public
schools were eligible for voucher payments, thus severely limiting the competitive market

element of the program. On the other hand, some groups viewed the program as more experimental than they would have liked. The national teachers' organizations in particular were troubled by the possibility that teachers might be placed in unseemly competition with one another (Weiler 1974).

5. David Selden, president of the American Federation of Teachers, who sent Senator Magnuson a congratulatory telegram after the 1974 NIE budget cut, had no strong admiration for the voucher project. But even he said that the voucher project would not be so objectionable if NIE were "balancing" it with more "appropriate" work, which in his case meant funding teachers' groups or research on classroom problems (Selden, March 1974).

6. Note that the National Council on Education Research had not yet been approved. Hence, beginning any new program was somewhat problematic.

7. More than 45% of the reviewers came from ten universities: five each came from Harvard and Berkeley, four each from Stanford and Chicago, three each from Yale and Illinois, two each from Rockefeller, Michigan, Cornell, and Columbia. These figures represent assignments as of 23 February 1973. The final totals may have been slightly higher. (Field Initiated Studies, 23 February 1973).

8. The other 30% would go to basic research and dissemination.

9. In 1976 "Organization and Management for Change" and "Finance and Productivity" were combined into a single priority, "Finance, Productivity, and Management." The other three 1974 priorities were unchanged. "Dissemination" had become the fifth priority.

Chapter 7

1. In market-economy organizations, structure is related to the production technology (Ouchi and Harris 1974, pp. 115–26). Hence, structural change is often a sign of evolution in the technology. As we have noted, however, the technology for producing good education R&D is unclear. Thus NIE's reorganizations were never informed or constrained by any well-understood set of technological features.

2. Before one concludes that structural instability must be associated with organizational chaos, we note that an "announced reorganization" is a highly ambiguous event. First, because a reorganization is announced does not guarantee that it has been or will be implemented. Second, and more important, the meaning of the term "reorganization" is not at all clear (either in the way it was used at NIE, or in the literature on organizations). Some of NIE's reorganizations featured changes in reporting relationships, in the size of operating units, and in the number of hierarchical levels. However, one of the announcements involved the creation of a supplementary committee and changed virtually nothing on the organization chart. No attempt will be made here to settle the issue of what constitutes a reorganization; for our purposes it is important that NIE leadership chose to announce them regularly.

3. Note that although a number of management problems had been identified by NIE leadership by this time, they were not addressed by the reorganization.

4. Because each of the units within the Office of Programs performed its own research, one observer labeled the 25 January reorganization a hoax: "There was more research going on in the Office of Programs than there was in the Office of Research and there was more development going in the Office of Research than there was in some of the programs."

5. This committee was not a new idea. Glennan and others, including an outside management consultant, had been discussing it since at least the January 1974 reorganization, but they had been reluctant to form the committee until all associate directors had been hired. By this time Senta Raizen had agreed to take the associate directorship of the Office of Utilization and Resources, but no promising candidate had been found for the position of director of the Office of Programs. After some negotiating with the assistant directors in the office, Glennan appointed one of them acting associate director for that office.

6. Glennan had been involved in planning for this reorganization, but both he and Elliott believed the announcement should come from Elliott.

7. The Local Problem Solving group was the first new NIE initiative to reach program status. This was achieved by giving an existing group the responsibility to develop a program. The other new programs of any size (Essential Skills and Compensatory Education) required that a working unit be developed along with the substance of a program. As a result these initiatives have been slower to achieve an effort of any size (i.e., of any visibility to outsiders).

8. See Starbuck (1965) for a summary of much of the literature in this field.

9. These figures reflect people officially "on board"—that is, excluding pending appointments and consultants. We have no reliable personnel data for the period after 31 March 1974. We would estimate, however, that the roster never included very many more than the 436 persons of 31 March 1974 and, in fact, commenced a slow decline beginning in late spring of 1974.

10. One might expect to see coalitions form among some of the program managers. We saw little evidence of this.

11. This approach is inspired by the provocative writings on American political behavior by Murray Edelman (1972).

12. This is not to imply that NIE's reorganizations were conscious attempts to fool outsiders. Quite the contrary, they were serious undertakings involving much energy and inconvenience for participants.

13. One way of viewing the creation of the Executive Committee is as just such an attempt. The announcement billed this group as a virtual panacea for NIE's management woes. Yet it would not dislocate one person in any work group.

14. Reorganizations were not the only response to major crises. Two other traditional symbolic responses included the rapid fire resignations of Glennan and Haggerty. Symbolically, these moves were appropriate; in actuality they left the institute without its two most important leaders during a critical period.

15. It is ironic, in this regard, that the reorganizations in fact did little to alter the fundamental structural stability we have described above.

Chapter 8

1. The appointment calendars of Glennan and Elliott indicate that these two issues took up a considerable portion of all meeting time during the first year.

2. There are a number of other agencywide issues we might have chosen to discuss—for example, development of personnel promotion policies or development of a system to monitor communications with Congress. (Indeed, chaps. 5–7 in part convey something of the character of agencywide decision making in their discussions of personnel recruitment, program development, and reorganization announcements.) We selected the paradigm search, planning process, and budget-making for three reasons: they were of great importance as measured by the attention top management gave them; they conveyed the major themes evident across a multitude of decision processes; and the data at our disposal were most complete for these three issues.

3. The literature on R&D agendas in education consisted of the four NIE Planning Unit "team reports"; Cronbach and Suppes, *Research for Tomorrow's Schools* (1969); Gideonse, *Educational Research and Development in the United States* (1970); and Levien, *NIE: Preliminary Plan* (1971).

4. Under the sponsorship of the Carnegie Corporation, Levien and his staff at the Rand Corporation had been working on the design for a national R&D agenda for education.

5. The characteristics of this meeting and the one attended by Planning Unit and Steering Committee members to review the team reports on 2 May 1972 (see chap. 2, page 2–35) are strikingly similar.

6. See Sarason (1972, particularly pp. 97–109) for a psychologically oriented discussion of optimism and disregard of the past in new organizations.

7. The Educational Staff Seminar, sponsored primarily by the Ford Foundation, is intended to provide stimulating formats such as lectures, exhibits, workshops, and field trips within which

Washington-based people interested in education can bring themselves up to date on timely issues. This particular gathering was held at the Embassy Row Hotel on 27 October 1972; the topic was NIE.

8. The summer institute organized by Mays had been chaired by George Miller of the Institute for Advanced Study at Princeton.

9. The first criterion stemmed from Martin's observation that most agencies operated in a reactive fashion, always mounting last-minute efforts to comply with deadlines imposed by OMB and HEW. This was not to be the case at NIE. The second criterion demanded that the procedures handle all projects or programs the institute was considering or currently supporting. The gathering and sifting of ideas, the preliminary design of research, the pilot testing of research programs, the decision to move to a large-scale programmatic effort, the review of ongoing programs, the dissemination of research findings and developed products—all of these stages and the information required to make decisions relative to the shift of projects across stages were to be accommodated by the planning procedures. The criterion of openness came from Glennan, who had committed the institute to substantial interaction with the education and educational R&D communities in both public statements and internal memoranda. "I am most concerned . . . that the Institute be built on an open, participatory planning process that reflects the interests and needs of researchers, teachers and administrators, parents, policy makers, and all others concerned about education" (House Appropriations Subcommittee, 9 March 1973, pp. 140–141).

10. This model seems at least superficially consistent with our data. The promotion of two of the more articulate assistant directors, Rieder and Tucker, to associate director in late 1974 also tends to support this theory.

11. Complicating the interpretation of this analysis is the fact that expertise did exist and was respected at the program level. Most of the managers ran their own units with only limited top management supervision. Competence at the work unit level did not, however, make one an expert at the agency level.

12. The memo was sent to the leaders of Essential Skills, Experimental Schools, Career Education, the Office of Research, and the Office of Research Grants.

13. At the end of December 1973, Haggerty sent the institute a review of seven budget planning schemes used in private industry, singling out two as possibly useful for NIE. That these two approaches were closely scrutinized by those developing the planning process is virtually certain; a copy of this document was sent to each OPM staff member on 2 January 1974, under a memo from Martin that said simply: "The attached paper describes, in some detail, two major decision processes used at Texas Instruments Inc.—Zero-Based Budgeting and Objectives, Strategies and Tactics. It also discusses 'decision packages.' You should read it with some care."

14. Furthermore, by virtue of some of the controversies that developed as the fiscal year 1975 internal allocations emerged under Martin's direction, many of the more influential assistant directors became very sensitive to issues that would also appear as part of the eventual planning process.

15. Highlighting the extent to which participation in devising the planning process was changing is the fact that drafts twelve and thirteen were written by one of Elliott's circle of young management specialists while Martin's staff man was out of town.

16. The planning process stepped nimbly through this controversy: "The Associate Directors are in an important pivotal position. On the one hand they are expected to perform in every way as the senior decision-maker in each office. Thus they will generate ideas, proposals or actions; review submissions; give direction on program plans and 'decision packages,' modify or delete items, etc. They may also comment on and make recommendations for modification of target figures assigned by OPM to programs within their offices. On the other hand, they are responsible for advising the Director and Deputy Director on an institute-wide basis as to what proposals should be supported; they are viewed as judges, assessing programs in an NIE-wide context (Martin, 1 May 1974, p. 3)."

17. It is interesting to note that two groups that might have played a pivotal role in the development of this budget did not. Externally, the OMB did not exercise much of the critical oversight for which it is renowned. During the fall and winter of 1972 OMB did not have the breadth and depth of expertise in education it had had in previous years. After Martin and Elliott left that organization and their positions were not filled with people of equivalent experience, the capacity of the OMB to critically review the plans of education agencies was greatly reduced. At the same time, because of their experience within the OMB, Elliott and Martin were able to effectively manage relationships with that organization. The timing of NIE's budget development also posed difficulties for the OMB. The NIE information came late relative to established OMB deadlines, reducing the time available for its scrutiny. Also, other very much larger and more complex budget analyses were under way, including work relating to the reauthorization of the multibillion-dollar Elementary and Secondary Education Act. Because of these factors, the OMB did not influence the NIE fiscal year 1974 budget as it did that of most other agencies. Internally, the Management Task Force, or the Office of Planning and Management, did not exercise much critical oversight—for many of the same reasons that hampered OMB. As we have already noted, the Task Force did not have a full complement of staff at this time, and its capacity for critical analysis was limited. The staff who had been hired were working on issues of agencywide scope (including the paradigm search and the planning process). Although the budget affects the entire agency, a thorough, critical analysis of it would concentrate on individual programs. Under the press of other work, the Management Task Force staff simply had not been able to become familiar with the activities of every operating unit.

18. Note that the $162 million included two major programs that had not been transferred to NIE until after the fiscal year 1973 budget was approved. These are the Special Technology Program from OE and the Educational Voucher Program and the Teacher Competence Study from OEO. Combined, these programs involved an "estimated" $34 million in fiscal year 1973. As noted in chapter 4, these were inflated figures.

The fiscal year 1974 budget justification does not supply complete detail on the amount to be spent on the Voucher and Technology programs. However, based on what data is provided we can make the following estimates:

Total FY 1974 request: $162 million

Less Vouchers and Teacher Study: $22 million

Less Technology: $7 million

Totals: $133 million

This $133 million is the fiscal year 1974 budget on the same base as the $110-million fiscal year 1973 budget; on this basis, the fiscal year 1974 request was 21% above that granted in fiscal year 1973. But the more straightforward comparison of $110 million with $162 million yields an increase of 47% (House Appropriations Subcommittee, 9 March 1973, p. 209).

19. The NCER pressed for reducing the supplemental request from $50 million to $25 million.

20. The 1976 "planning process" did require substantial anticipation of the future. In May 1974, NIE units were being asked to outline activities and budgets for the period July 1975–June 1976, and this anticipation had to be carried out amid considerable uncertainty about the fiscal year 1975 budget.

21. In the face of the complaints, OPM proceeded to formulate an "official allocation" of fiscal year 1975 funds on 23 April 1974. This allocation presumed the availability of $134,500,000 for fiscal year 1975. It was to be revised downward on 14 June 1974, in the light of the House Appropriations Committee cut to $100 million. Then after the action of the full House on 28 June it had to be reduced to $80 million. Ultimately the institute would be required to develop a $70 million fiscal year 1975 budget in response to final congressional action in late 1974. Thus, as

the year progressed NIE was forced to cut into its commitment base, which had been at $90,735,000 in early June. However, the definition of "commitment" was sufficiently flexible that the $80-million budget allocation, completed on 7 August, was able to set aside $6,710,000 for new activity and only $73,290,000 for past commitments. The definition and defense of "committed" funds remained one of the unfathomable mysteries of the NIE budget process.

22. The NIE's own Equal Educational Opportunity Committee was reviewing budget documents internally and was also pressing for more explicit attention to funding for projects that involved poor and minority communities and researchers from minority groups.

23. President Ford proposed a budget of only $80 million for NIE's fiscal year 1976 budget in January 1975. The proposed budget was almost 50% less than the "low budget mark" used in the original May planning effort.

24. The list that follows is a compilation of some of the systems or procedures uncompleted by the end of the first year (indeed, most were still uncompleted by the end of the second year): contracts and grants monitoring; communicating with HEW offices; communicating with other agencies running education programs; providing descriptive statistics about contract and grant recipients; financial recording; tracking congressional correspondence; personnel evaluation and promotion; determining copyright and royalty eligibility for NIE-sponsored publications; an institutewide evaluation plan (compiled from Elliott, 11 June 1974; Martin, 14 June 1974b).

Chapter 9

1. After the period of our research ended, there continued to be external negative events: for example, a Jack Anderson newspaper column charging NIE with conflict of interest in its own contracting procedures, and a Civil Service Commission's highly critical review of NIE hiring practices.

2. This chapter makes use of NIE professional staff responses, in June 1974, to the question, "What are the major lessons to be learned from the NIE experience thus far?" (N = 288; response rate = 86%). Each staff member was assigned a code number to protect his or her identity.

3. In response to the open-ended question, "What lessons can be learned from the NIE experience thus far?" the three most frequent responses referred to congressional/external relations (41%); lack of sense of purpose (17%); and inadequate management (17%).

4. Even the agency itself could not be regarded unambiguously as only one year old. By the fall of 1973 the initial plans for the institute were already three years old.

5. Mathews and Stimson (1975) document the extent to which members of Congress are unable even to read, let alone study, all the bills they must vote upon each year. They found that a majority of members of the United States House of Representatives devote less than thirty minutes a day to legislative study outside their areas of primary interest (p. 20); a majority of members vote on up to 75% of the measures in a particular session without even having read them (p. 22). They suggest that, under these conditions, legislators often rely upon simple cues to guide their votes. It is surely the case that in floor votes about NIE, most legislators relied on such simple cues rather than on knowledge about the agency.

6. Other writers have described a different phenomenon associated with belief structure in new organizations—reduction in aspiration level (see Sarason 1972, p. 99; also see Cyert and March 1963, pp. 114–27, for a general discussion of changes in aspiration). Initially, goals are impossibly ambitious. Over time, as the goals are not achieved, aspirations are reduced to more "realistic" levels. (Sarason suggests that this reduction may well be accompanied by frustration or disillusionment on the part of organization members. Cyert and March simply suggest that participants "learn" more "reasonable" goals.) In the case of NIE, failure brought not goal reduction, but changes in the beliefs about how to achieve the goals. (Reduction in aspirations may have come later. Our continuing, informal contact with members of the institute staff indicates that, by mid-1975, at any rate, expectations about growth had been dampened.)

Chapter 10

1. Although our study provides no evidence on this point, we suspect that the tools for redirection of other low-technology federal programs in the social sector are similarly limited. Community mental health and manpower training and development, for example, share some of the characteristics of the R&D enterprise: ambiguous goals, fluid participation, and an unclear technology. One major difference may be that these programs are easier to justify on the grounds that they are "helping people" (a strategy discussed in chap. 4).

2. The analyses concerning the weak scientific base of and diffuse political support for education R&D are not new. Similar points were raised by former OE research officials at the Brademas hearings in 1971. They were largely ignored there, however. Chief among those who critically assessed the pro-NIE assumptions in 1971 were Hendrik Gideonse, former director of program planning and evaluation for NCERD; James Gallagher, former deputy assistant secretary for planning, research and evaluation in OE; and Robert Dentler, then director of the OE-supported Center for Urban Education in New York City. The conclusion of much of this testimony was that the solution lay in the massive expansion of federal education R&D budgets. For example, Gideonse urged annual expenditures in the range of $2–3 billion. Although we concur in the analysis, our conclusions differ. A similar analysis was presented by a panel of consultants convened by NIE in 1975 to advise it on funding policies for the regional laboratories and R&D centers (Campbell et al. 1975, pp. 5–8). The conclusions of this group also seemed to be founded on the axiomatic beliefs: they included a recommendation for an immediate budget increase of 100% and a more directive role for NIE staff in managing the R&D process. Again, we found ourselves in agreement with much of the analysis but not with the conclusions.

3. We use this word as Geertz (1973) uses it.

4. In social psychology, Weick (1969) has argued that a variety of experiences enhances learning and leads to goal discovery. He suggests, "Chaotic action is preferable to orderly inaction" (p. 107). A different perspective, that of computer programming, also points to the value of action. Anyone who has ever written a computer program knows that you have to try to run it before you can debug it.

5. We do not mean to imply that loose connections produce nothing but difficulties; loosely connected systems have advantages as well as disadvantages. Weick (1976) suggests seven positive attributes of loosely coupled systems, including the ability to persist, locally adapt, and seal off mistakes.

6. Each of these questions is predicated on the assumption of an environment that is either neutral or hostile. If the environment is benign, the agency will probably prosper (i.e., budgets will increase) no matter what the manager does or thinks.

7. Edelman (1972) provides an extensive discussion of symbolic leadership.

8. Selznick (1957) describes this process as the "elaboration of socially integrating myths . . . efforts to state, in the language of uplift and idealism, what is distinctive about the aims and methods of the enterprise" (p. 151).

9. It is difficult for any manager to recognize or accept failure, especially when a new enterprise has been undertaken with high hopes. However, in the event of involuntary departure, there are constructive purposes that disappointed managers can serve. These purposes are often best served by public protest rather than quiet submission. A graphic description of the political, programmatic, and organizational constraints and uncertainties that promoted failure provides some leverage for the next set of managers. The resignation in protest often causes at least a momentary relaxation of external pressure upon the new bureaucracy, thus providing the new managers with some flexibility. Further, the resignation in protest, by declaring the existence of a crisis, provides a sense that new leadership has only one direction to go—toward improvement—and thus lays the basis for a favorable evaluation of the new managers. This course of action is unlikey to be pursued by individuals who hope to be employed in the same context in the future.

Thus, managers who pursue Washington-based careers often leave federal posts quietly for fear of spoiling their future chances for high level appointment. For further discussion of the trade-offs in various forms of resignation see Hirschman (1970) and Weisband and Franck (1975).

10. See George (1972) for an exposition of multiple advocacy in foreign policy. A similar argument can be made for domestic policy.

11. Downs (1967) suggests that the new bureau attracts "zealots" or "advocates." We believe that zealots are simply a special class of optimists—optimists with an ideology.

12. Most of what we have learned about how to study organizations that are new or can be characterized by ambiguous goals, unclear technology, and fluid participation is implicit in the foregoing pages. We would like to reiterate only three points. (1) Beware of arbitrary distinctions between "organization" and "environment" that tend to obscure the ways each influences the other. We found it useful to realize that internal decision processes are more permeable to the environment than past work may have indicated. (2) Cognitive images of the organization that develop in the minds of participants and observers can have a profound influence on organization action. (See Sproull and Weiner 1976 for a more extended discussion of the function of cognitive images in creating new organizations.) Understanding what people believe and how those beliefs develop is an important task for students of organizations. (3) Conventional assumptions about tightly connected systems are not necessarily useful in understanding certain kinds of organizations. These points suggest reassessing the appropriateness of conventional methods of cross-organization questionnaire analysis. They require careful attention to what people are doing and to what else is going on at the same time. They demand that the investigator look for complicating factors, not simplifying ones, in every explanation of organization action. And they suggest that the researcher treat informant responses as projective tests as much as objective data.

13. See March (1975) for a discussion of optimism without hope in education organizations.

References

Allison, Graham. 1971. *Essence of decision: Explaining the Cuban missile crisis*. Boston: Little, Brown.

American Council on Education. 17 September 1974. Statement in support of the National Institute of Education by major educational organizations and associations. Washington, D. C.: Press release.

ASPE. 1971. Memorandum to the counselor to the department concerning NIE director.

Avery, Chester. 27 July 1972. Memorandum to S. P. Marland concerning NCERD staff response to the R&D personnel transition.

Baltimore Evening Sun. 1 October 1974.

Barnes, Edward. June 1974. Personal interview with authors.

Benson, Charles. 1971. Research priorities for R&D projects in the economics of education. Paper prepared for NIE Planning Unit, unpublished.

Bissell, Joan. 18 May 1971. Suggested format for NIE problem analyses. ASPE, unpublished.

Bowman, Mary Jean. 1971. Educational outcomes, processes, and decisions: Frontiers of economic research and development for the 1970's. Paper prepared for NIE Planning Unit, unpublished.

Boyan, Norman J. August 1974. Personal interview with authors.

———. 1969. The political realities of educational R&D. *Journal of Research and Development in Education*, vol. 2, no. 4, pp. 3–18.

Boyan, Norman J. and Ward S. Mason. 1968. Perspectives on educational R&D centers. *Journal of Research and Development in Education*, vol. 1, no. 4, pp. 190–202.

Brademas, John. 19 November 1973. Address before annual fall convention, Council for Educational Development and Research. Washington, D. C.

———. 25 March 1974. Memorandum to Tom Glennan concerning the status of the Institute.

Brainard, Suzanne. 25 June 1973. Memorandum to John Mays concerning evaluation of Office of Research Grants program. NIE, unpublished.

———. 26 March 1974. Personal interview with authors.

Burchinal, Lee B. 1973. Influence of federal initiatives upon communication in education. *Journal of Research and Development in Education*, vol. 6, no. 4, pp. 116–31.

———. 23 June 1974. Personal interview with authors.

263

Bush, Robert. 24 January 1974. Personal interview with authors.

Bush, Vannevar. 1945. *Science: The endless frontier.* Washington, D. C.: USGPO.

———. 1970. *Pieces of the action.* New York: William Morrow.

Campbell, Roald, et al. July 1975. R&D funding policies of the National Institute of Education: Review and recommendations. NIE, unpublished draft report.

Change Magazine. November 1974.

Chase, Francis. 1971. Educational research and development in the sixties: The mixed report card. In *Educational research: Prospects and priorities,* Appendix 1 to hearings on the National Institute of Education. House Select Subcommittee on Education. 92d Cong., 1st sess.

Christensen, John. March 1974. Personal interview with authors.

Chronicle of Higher Education, 19 September 1974.

Clark, Burton. 1971. Sociology and the NIE. Paper prepared for NIE Planning Unit, unpublished.

Cohen, David. 27 October 1972. How society learns from educational research and development. Speech at Embassy Row Hotel, Washington, D. C.

Cohen Michael, and March, James. 1974. *Leadership and ambiguity: The American college president.* New York: McGraw Hill.

Cohen, Michael; March, James; and Olsen, Johan. 1972. A garbage-can model of organizational choice. *Administrative Science Quarterly,* vol. 17, no. 1, pp. 1–25.

Coleman, James S., et al. 1966. *Equality of educational opportunity.* Washington, D. C.: USGPO.

Coleman, James S.. May 1975. Personal interview with authors.

Commission on Government Procurement. December 1972. *Report of the Commission on Government Procurement. Volume II: Part B—Acquisition of research and development.* Washington, D. C.: USGPO.

Congressional Record. 4 November 1971.

———. 4 October 1973.

———. 28 June 1974.

———. 16 September 1974.

———. 19 April 1975.

Cronbach, Lee and Suppes, Patrick. 1969. *Research for tomorrow's schools.* London: Macmillan.

Cross, Chris. 20 January 1971. Memorandum to Secretary Richardson. HEW, unpublished

———. March 1974. Personal interview with authors.

Cyert, Richard and March, James. 1963. *A behavioral theory of the firm.* Englewood Cliffs, N. J.: Prentice-Hall.

Datta, Lois-Ellen. June 1974. Personal interview with authors.

Davis, Robert. 1971. Improving the quality of education. Paper prepared for NIE Planning Unit, unpublished.

Dershimer, Richard. July 1974. Personal interview with authors.

————. 1976. *The federal government and educational R&D.* Lexington, Mass.: Lexington Books.

Dershimer, Richard A., and Iannacone, Laurence. 1973. Social and political influences on educational research. In *Second handbook of research on teaching*, ed. Robert Travers. Chicago: Rand McNally.

Dirks, Harley. March 1974. Personal interview with authors.

Downs, Anthony. 1967. *Inside bureaucracy.* Boston: Little, Brown.

Doyle, Denis. June 1974. Personal interview with authors.

Duby, Martin. June 1974. Personal interview with authors.

Edelman, Murray. 1972. *The symbolic uses of politics.* Urbana: University of Illinois Press.

Education Researcher. November 1973.

————. November 1974.

Education USA. 9 March 1970.

————. 9 October 1972.

————. 16 April 1973.

Elliott, Emerson. N.d. Memorandum concerning follow-up on organization plans and related documents. NIE, unpublished.

————. 22 July 1972. Personal notes on OE personnel transfer. NIE, unpublished.

————. 8 September 1972. NIE Task Force current work statement, sent as an attachment to Memo to the Secretary from Emerson Elliott through Sidney Marland concerning status report on National Institute of Education. NIE, unpublished.

————. 1973. Appointment calendar.

————. 9 July 1973. Memorandum to the Office of the Director concerning priorities. NIE, unpublished.

————. 27 July 1973. Memorandum to the Office of the Director concerning priorities for NIE policy issues. NIE, unpublished.

————. 25 November 1973. Personal interview with Susan McCarthy, NIE archivist.

————. 28 November 1973. Personal interview with Susan McCarthy, NIE archivist.

————. January 14, 1974. Personal interview with Susan McCarthy, NIE archivist.

————. 11 March 1974. Personal interview with Susan McCarthy, NIE archivist.

————. 25 March 1974. Personal interview with authors.

————. 11 June 1974. Personal interview with authors.

————. 7 November 1974. Memorandum to NIE staff concerning structure for NIE's program. NIE, unpublished.

Elmendorf, Richard. June 1974. Personal interview with authors.

Emery, Richard. March 1974. Personal interview with authors.

————. June 1974. Personal interview with authors.

Estler, Suzanne. 1975. Big science and the federal government. Stanford University, unpublished paper.

Etzioni, Amitai. 1967. A center for advanced research and study: A design by Amitai Etzioni. New York: Columbia University.

Etzioni, Amitai, et al. 1972. An NIE strategy paper. Paper prepared for NIE Planning Unit, unpublished.

Falender, Andrew. N.d. Proposed planning sequence: Version V. NIE, unpublished. Distributed 11 March 1974.

————. 13 March 1974. Note for Emerson Elliott. NIE, unpublished.

————. June 1974. Personal interview with authors.

Field Initiated Studies. 23 February 1973. Panels. NIE, unpublished.

Finn, Chester. 1974. The National Institute of Education. *Yale Review*, vol. 64, pp. 227–43.

Gallagher, James. 1971. Testimony before the House Select Subcommittee on Education. Hearings to establish a National Institute of Education. 92d Congress, 1st sess., pp. 31–48.

Geertz, Clifford. 1973. *The interpretation of cultures*. New York: Basic Books.

General Accounting Office. October 1971. *Need for improving the administration of study and evaluation contracts: Office of Education*. Washington, D. C.: USGPO.

George, Alexander. 1972. The case for multiple advocacy in foreign policy. *American Political Science Review*, vol. 66, no. 3, pp. 751–85.

Getzels, J. W. 1970. Examples of successful research related to education. University of Chicago, informal paper.

Gideonse, Hendrik. 1970. *Educational research and development in the United States*. Washington, D. C.: USGPO.

Glennan, Thomas K. Jr. N.d. Memorandum concerning dilemmas faced by the NIE. NIE, unpublished.

————. N.d. Memorandum concerning a few notes on the styles of research considered at our meeting last week. NIE, unpublished.

————. N.d. Memorandum to senior staff. NIE, unpublished.

————. 1964. The usefulness of aerospace management techniques in other sectors of the economy. Santa Monica: Rand Corporation, P–2927.

————. 1966. Innovation and product quality under the total package procurement concept. Santa Monica: Rand Corporation, RM–5097–PR.

————. 1967. New product development: Some observations based on the development of military aircraft. Ph. D. diss., Stanford University

————. 1969. Evaluating federal manpower programs: Notes and observations. Santa Monica: Rand Corporation, RM–5743–OEO.

————. 1972. Appointment calendar.

————. 18 November 1972. The status of NIE planning. Speech before the joint meeting of the state and national advisory councils on vocational education.

————. 1973. Appointment calendar.

————. 26 February 1973. NIE: A personal view. Speech before the American Educational Research Association.

————. March 1973. Personal interview with authors.

————. 17 May 1973*a*. Memorandum to NIE staff concerning organization structure. NIE, unpublished.

————. 17 May 1973*b*. Memorandum to NIE staff concerning staffing and organization. NIE, unpublished.

————. 5 October 1973. Personal interview with Susan McCarthy, NIE archivist.

————. 30 October 1973. Memorandum to the Secretary of HEW concerning NIE and the appropriations cut—information. NIE, unpublished.

————. 7 December 1973. Personal interview with Susan McCarthy, NIE archivist.

————. 25 January 1974. Memorandum concerning organization and management actions. NIE, unpublished.

————. March 1974. Personal interview with authors.

————. 6 May 1974. Memorandum to NIE staff concerning the executive committee. NIE, unpublished.

————. 21 May 1974. Memorandum to NCER concerning planning for FY 1976 budget. NIE, unpublished.

————. 13 June 1974. Personal interview with authors.

————. 24 June 1974. Memorandum to senior staff concerning FY 1975–FY 1976 planning and resource allocation. NIE, unpublished.

————. 25 June 1974. Memorandum to Emerson Elliott. NIE, unpublished.

————. 31 July 1974. Personal interview with Susan McCarthy, NIE archivist.

————. 7 August 1974. Memorandum to senior staff concerning FY 1975 planning and budget guidance. NIE, unpublished.

————. 28 August 1974. Letter to President Gerald R. Ford.

————. July 1975. Personal interview with authors.

————. September 1976. Personal communication to authors.

Goldman, Andrea. 17 May 1974. Memorandum to Emerson Elliott concerning background report on recruitment for associate director, Office of Programs. NIE, unpublished.

Greenwood, Peter and Weiler, Daniel. 1972. *Alternative models for the ERIC clearinghouse network*. Santa Monica: Rand Corporation, R–951–HEW.

Gustafson, George. March 1974. Personal interview with authors.

Haggerty, Patrick E. 1965. *Management philosophies and practices of Texas Instruments Incorporated*. Dallas: Texas Instruments Incorporated.

————. 23 November 1973. Letter to Thomas K. Glennan.

Hannaway, Jane. 1974. Educational research 1970: It was a very bad year. Stanford University, unpublished paper.

Hansot, Elisabeth. 28 November 1972. Memorandum with attachments concerning criteria for choices among R&D proposals. NIE, unpublished.

————. 29 November 1972. Memorandum concerning NIE planning meeting. NIE, unpublished.

————. 5 December 1972. Memorandum with attachment concerning summary of NIE planning meeting of November 30 and December 1. NIE, unpublished.

————. 19 December 1972. Memorandum with attachment concerning descriptive and analytic summaries of NIE planning proposals. NIE, unpublished.

————. 9 March 1973. Planning paper. NIE, unpublished.

————. 19 March 1973. Second draft. NIE, unpublished.

————. 1 March 1974. Issues. NIE, unpublished.

————. 13 June 1974. Personal interview with authors.

————. 26 December 1974. Telephone interview with authors.

Hansot, Elisabeth, and Williamson, John. 11 December 1973. Response to draft planning process: December 7. NIE, unpublished.

Hansot, Elisabeth, and Wolf, David. 23 March 1973. NIE planning: A paper for decision. NIE, unpublished.

Hansot, Elisabeth, and Wolf, David. 29 March 1973. The NIE planning process. NIE, unpublished.

Hansot, Elisabeth, and Wolf, David. 25 April 1973. NIE planning process. NIE, unpublished.

Harahan, Mary. 1972. OE Transfer Programs. NIE Planning Unit, unpublished.

Hechinger, Fred. 8 March 1970. Aim: "More education for the dollar." *New York Times*, 4:7.

Hill, Paul. June 1974. Personal interview with authors.

Hirschman, Albert. 1970. *Exit, voice, and loyalty: Responses to decline in firms, organizations, and states.* Cambridge: Harvard University Press.

House, Ernest. 1974. *The politics of educational innovation.* Berkeley: McCutchan.

Jarin, Kenneth M. 1972. John Brademas: Democratic representative from Indiana. Washington, D. C.: Ralph Nader Congress Project.

Jencks, Christopher, et al. 1972. *Inequality.* New York: Basic Books.

Kooi, Beverly. May 1971. Internal note. NIE Planning Unit, unpublished.

————. 28 February 1974. Personal interview with authors.

Kooi, Beverly et al. 1972. A research and development agenda for the National Institute of Education. NIE Planning Unit, unpublished.

Koshel, Patricia. June 1974. Personal interview with authors.

Kuhn, Thomas. 1970. *The structure of scientific revolutions.* Chicago: University of Chicago Press, 2d. ed.

Lake, Dale. 4 June 1973. National Institute of Education panel review process: Field Initiated Studies program FY 1973. NIE, unpublished.

Levien, Roger. 1971. *National Institute of Education: Preliminary plan for the proposed institute.* Santa Monica: Rand Corporation, R–657–HEW.

———. 21 March 1974. Personal interview with authors.

Lipman-Blumen, Jean. June 1974. Personal interview with authors.

Lomask, Milton. 1976. *A minor miracle: An informal history of the National Science Foundation.* Washington, D. C.: National Science Foundation.

Lynn, Larry. 24 January 1972. Memorandum to Harry Silberman. ASPE, unpublished.

———. 4 February 1972. Memorandum to Secretary Richardson concerning status of NIE Planning. ASPE, unpublished.

McDaniels, Garry. 19 March 1974. Personal interview with Susan McCarthy, NIE archivist.

McElroy, James. June 1974. Personal interview with authors.

March, James. 1975. Education and the pursuit of optimism. *Texas Tech Journal of Education,* vol. 2, no. 1, pp. 5–17.

March James, and Olsen, Johan, eds. 1976. *Ambiguity and choice in organizations.* Bergen, Norway: University Press.

March, James, and Simon, Herbert. 1958. *Organizations.* New York: Wiley.

Markley, Owen, et al. 1972. Alternative strategies and program initiatives for NIE. Paper prepared for NIE Planning Unit, unpublished.

Marland, Sidney P. 22 March 1974. Personal interview with authors.

Martin, Bernard. 29 September 1972. Memorandum concerning a reminder on assignments. NIE, unpublished.

———. 20 November 1972. Memorandum concerning NIE planning meeting. NIE, unpublished.

———. 17 May 1973. Paper on planning process. NIE, unpublished.

———. 13 November 1973. Memorandum to Thomas K. Glennan concerning senior staff comments on proposed program structure. NIE, unpublished.

———. 28 November 1973. Personal interview with Susan McCarthy, NIE archivist.

———. 2 January 1974. Memorandum to OPM staff concerning "the Texas Instrument Way." NIE, unpublished.

———. 26 March 1974. Personal interview with authors.

———. 29 March 1974*a*. Memorandum to Binswanger, McDaniels, Werksman, concerning alternative strategies work group. NIE, unpublished.

———. 29 March 1974*b*. Memorandum to Glennan concerning senior staff reaction to proposed FY 1975 budget. NIE, unpublished.

———. 1 May 1974. Memorandum to all program heads concerning FY 1976 planning process. NIE, unpublished.

———. 14 June 1974*a*. Personal interview with authors.

———. 14 June 1974*b*. Memorandum to Executive Committee concerning FY 1976 program plans. NIE, unpublished.

———. 15 October 1974. Personal interview with authors.

Mastrangelo, Richard. March 1974. Personal interview with authors.

Mathews, Donald, and Stimson, James. 1975. *Yeas and nays: Normal decision-making in the U.S. House of Representatives.* New York: Wiley.

Mays, John. 21 March 1974. Personal interview with authors.

Melmed, Arthur. June 1974. Personal interview with authors.

National Academy of Sciences–National Research Council. 1958. *A proposed organization for research in education.* Washington, D. C.: National Academy of Sciences–National Research Council.

NCER. April 1973. Minutes of the conference of nominated members of the NCER.

———. 5 November 1973. Minutes of the meeting.

New York Times. 1 March 1970. "Benign Neglect" on race is proposed by Moynihan, p. 1

New York Times. 4 March 1970. Nixon proposes re-examination of aid to schools, p. 1

New York Times. 22 October 1973. Institute of Education gets a lesson in how not to win more money from Congress, p. 64.

New York Times. 27 January 1973.

New York Times. 15 March 1973.

New York Times. 30 September 1974.

New York Times. 7 November 1974.

Nicosia, Eileen. October 1974. Personal interview with authors.

NIE. 1973. *Building capacity for renewal and reform.* Washington, D. C.: USGPO.

NIE. 30 June 1973. Personnel report. NIE, unpublished.

NIE. July 1974. NIE statistical summary: Fiscal year 1974. NIE, unpublished.

NIE. 1976. The status of education research and development in the United States—1976 databook. Washington, D. C.: USGPO.

NIE. Spring 1976. Information. Washington, D. C.: NIE.

NIE Task Force on Planning and Management. n.d. Discussion paper on staffing. NIE, unpublished.

NIE Executive Committee. Minutes of the following 1974 meetings: 3 May; 6 May; 7 May; 13 May: 20 May; 3 June; 10 June; 17 June; 1 July; 22 July.

NIE Planning Unit. 10 May 1971. Proposed work plan for the Planning Unit for period ending 30 June 1971 and 30 June 1972. NIE Planning Unit, unpublished.

———. 30 June 1971. NIE planning report. NIE Planning Unit, unpublished.

———. 6 October 1971. Status report: Planning for the National Institute of Education. NIE Planning Unit, unpublished.

———. January 1972. Year-end report. NIE Planning Unit, unpublished.

———. 1 March 1972. Interim report on organization and management. NIE Planning Unit, unpublished.

———. March 1972. Status report. NIE Planning Unit, unpublished.

———. 15 April 1972. Report on organization and management. NIE Planning Unit, unpublished.

———. 15 June 1972. Report on organization and management: An interim organization. NIE Planning Unit, unpublished.

Nixon, Richard. March 1970. Message on educational reform. Washington, D. C.: The White House.

OE. n.d. Confidential memorandum concerning personnel transfer. OE: unpublished.

———. 12 July 1972. Note on order of selection. OE, unpublished.

OECD. 1971. Educational research and development in the United States. In House Select Subcommittee on Education, *Hearings on the National Institute of Education.* 92d Cong., 1st sess., pp. 263–317.

O'Keefe, Michael. March 1974. Personal interview with authors.

OMB. 1975. *Special analyses: Budget of the United States government, fiscal year 1976.* Washington, D. C.: USGPO.

Oregonian. 20 September 1974.

Ouchi, William, and Harris, Reubin. 1974. The dynamic organization: Structure, technology and environment. In *Organization behavior: Issues and research,* ed. O. Strauss, R. Miles, and A. Tannenbaum. Madison: Industrial Relations Research Organization.

Pell, Claiborne. 30 March 1973. Letter to Thomas K. Glennan, Jr.

Pennick, James L., et al., eds. 1972. *The politics of American science.* Cambridge: M.I.T. Press.

Perkins, Dennis. 4 January 1973. Alternative organization plans for the National Institute of Education. NIE, unpublished.

Phi Delta Kappa. November 1974.

Phillips, Martha. March 1974. Personal interview with authors.

President's Science Advisory Committee Panel on Educational Research and Development. 1964. *Innovation and experiment in education.* Washington, D. C.: USGPO.

Publishers Weekly. 9 September 1974.

Raizen, Senta. 25 March 1974. Personal interview with authors.

Raizen, Senta, et al. 1972. Research and development in education: Analysis and program development. NIE Planning Unit, unpublished.

———. 1973. *Career education: An R&D plan.* Santa Monica: Rand Corporation, R–1199–HEW.

Report on education research. 10 April 1974. Washington, D. C.: Capitol Publications.

Richardson, Elliott. 30 December 1971. Research and evaluation guidance. HEW, unpublished.

Rourke, Francis. 1969. *Bureaucracy, politics, and public policy.* Boston: Little, Brown.

Russell, Ernest. 17 January 1974. Personal interview with Susan McCarthy, NIE archivist.

Saario, Terry. 22 March 1974. Personal interview with authors.

Sarason, Seymour. 1972. *The creation of settings and the future societies.* San Francisco: Jossey-Bass.

Selden, David. March 1974. Personal interview with authors.

Selznick, Philip. 1949. *TVA and the grassroots: A study in the sociology of formal organization.* Berkeley: University of California Press.

———. 1957. *Leadership in adminstration.* New York: Harper and Row.

Shafftner, Dorothy. 1969. *The National Science Foundation.* New York: Frederick A. Praeger.

Sieber, Sam D. 1974. Federal support for research and development in education and its effects. In *Uses of sociology in education,* ed. Wayne Gordon. 73d Yearbook of the National Society for the Study of Education, pp. 478–502. Chicago: National Society for the Study of Education.

Silberman, Harry. 28 February 1974. Personal interview with authors.

———. 15 May 1972. Notes on 2 May 1972 meeting (NIE programs). NIE Planning Unit: unpublished.

Simon, Herbert. 1953. Birth of an organization: The Economic Cooperation Administration. *Public Adminstration Review,* vol. 13, no. 4, pp. 227–36.

Simon, Herbert. 1964. On the concept of organization goals. *Administrative Science Quarterly,* vol. 9, no. 1, pp. 1–22.

Singell, Larry. 1971. The problem of obtaining and using resources in education: Some proposed programs for purposive change. Paper prepared for NIE Planning Unit, unpublished.

Smith, Richard. March 1974. Personal interview with authors.

Sproull, Lee, and Weiner, Stephen. 1976. Easier "seen" than done: The function of cognitive images in creating a new organization. Paper presented at annual AERA convention, San Francisco.

Starbuck, William H. 1965. Organizational growth and development. In *Handbook of organizations,* ed. James March. Chicago: Rand McNally.

Steinbruner, John. 1974. *The cybernetic theory of decision.* Princeton: Princeton University Press.

Strickland, Stephen. 1972. *Politics, science, and dread disease: A short history of the United States medical research policy.* Cambridge: Harvard University Press.

Thompson, James D. 1967. *Organizations in action.* New York: McGraw-Hill.

Timpane, Michael. 24 January 1972. Memorandum to Harry Silberman. ASPE, unpublished.

———. March 1974. Personal interview with author.

Tomlinson, Tom. 9 August 1974. Memorandum to NIE staff concerning NIE child study center. NIE, unpublished.

Tucker, Marc. March 1974. Personal interview with authors.

Tucker, Marc. 6 February 1975. Personal interview with authors.

U. S. Congress. House. 8 October 1971. Report no. 92–554. *Committee on Education and Labor Report.* 92d Cong., 1st sess.

————. 21 June 1973. Report 93–305. *Committee on Appropriations report on Labor–HEW appropriations bill, 1974.* 93d Cong., 1st sess.

————. 8 November 1973. Report 93–626. *Conference report on Labor–HEW appropriations bill, 1974.* 93d Cong., 1st sess.

————. 4 April 1974. Report 93–1997. *Committee on Appropriations report on second supplemental appropriations bill, 1974.* 93d Cong., 2d sess.

————. 29 May 1974. Report 93–1070. *Conference report on second supplemental appropriations bill, 1974.* 93d Cong., 2d sess.

————. 21 November 1974. Report 93–1489. *Conference report on Labor–HEW appropriations bill, 1975.* 93d Cong., 2d sess.

U. S. Congress. House. Appropriations Subcommittee. 1970. *Hearings on Labor–HEW appropriations bill, fiscal year 1971.* 91st Cong., 2d sess.

————. 9 March 1973. *Hearings on Labor–HEW appropriations bill, fiscal year 1974.* 93 Cong., 1st sess.

————. February 1974. *Hearings on second supplemental appropriations request.* 93d Cong., 2d sess.

————. April 1974. *Hearings on Labor–HEW approprations bill, fiscal year 1975.* 93d Cong., 2d sess.

U. S. Congress. House. Committee on Education and Labor. General Subcommittee on Education. 1969. *The needs of elementary and secondary education for the seventies.* 91st Cong., 1st sess.

U. S. Congress. House. Committee on Education and Labor. Select Subcommittee on Education. 1971. *Hearings to establish a National Institute of Education.* 92d Cong., 1st sess.

————. 6 February 1973. *Oversight hearings on the National Institute of Education.* 93d Cong., 1st sess.

U. S. Congress. House. Committee on Education and Labor. Special Subcommittee on Education. 1967. *Study of the United States Office of Education.* House document no. 193. 90th Cong., 1st sess.

U. S. Congress. House. Committee on Government Operations. Subcommittee on Research–Technical Programs. 1967. *The uses of social research in federal domestic programs.* 90th Cong., 1st sess.

U. S. Congress. Senate. 2 October 1973. Report 93–114. *Committee on Appropriations report on Labor–HEW appropriations bill, fiscal year 1974.* 93d Cong., 1st sess.

————. 11 September 1974. Report 93–1146. *Committee on Appropriations report on Labor–HEW appropriations bill, fiscal year 1975.* 93d Cong., 2d sess.

U. S. Congress. Senate. Hearings. 1974. *Senate hearing before the Committee on Appropriations: Second supplemental appropriations for FY 1974.* 93d Cong., 2d sess., part 1.

U. S. Congress. Senate. Appropriations Subcommittee. 23 July 1973. *Hearings on Labor–HEW appropriations bill, fiscal year 1974.* 93d Cong., 1st sess.

————. 7 March 1974. *Hearings on second supplemental appropriations request*. 93d Cong., 2d sess.

————. 6 June 1974. *Hearings on Labor–HEW appropriations bill, fiscal year 1975*. 93d Cong., 2d sess.

————. 17–18 July 1974. *Hearings on Labor–HEW appropriations bill, fiscal year 1975: Non-departmental witnesses*. 93d Cong., 2d sess.

U. S. Congress. Senate. Committee on Labor and Public Welfare. Subcommittee on Education. 21 April 1971. *Hearings on education amendments of 1971, part 2*. 92d Cong., 1st sess.

Upp, Melinda. 27 March 1974. Personal interview with authors.

Wall Street Journal. 28 June 1973. Researchers under fire: Lack of political clout in Congress threatens once-glamorous National Institute of Education, p. 36.

Wall Street Journal. 8 July 1974.

Ward, Spencer. 24 November 1972. Memo to Glennan and Mays concerning alternative organizational structures. NIE, unpublished.

Warwick, Donald. 1975. *A theory of public bureaucracy: Politics, personality, and organization in the State Department*. Cambridge: Harvard University Press.

Weick, Karl. 1969. *The social psychology of organizing*. Reading, Mass.: Addison-Wesley.

————. 1976. Educational organizations as loosely-coupled systems. *Administrative Science Quarterly*, vol. 21, no. 1, pp. 1–19.

Weiler, Daniel. 1974. *A public school voucher demonstration: The first year at Alum Rock*. Santa Monica: Rand Corporation, R–1495–NIE.

————. 1975. Personal communication with the authors.

Weisband, Edward, and Frank, Thomas M. 1975. *Resignation in protest: Political and ethical choices between loyalty to team and loyalty to conscience in American public life*. New York: Grossman/Viking.

Werksman, Richard. June 1974. Personal interview with authors.

Werksman, Richard; Binswanger, Robert; and McDaniels, Garry. 15 April 1974. Memorandum to Martin concerning strategies. NIE, unpublished.

Westinghouse Learning Corporation. 1969. *The impact of Head Start: An evaluation of the effects of Head Start on children's cognitive and affective development*. Bladensburg, Md.: PB184328.

Wexler, Stephen. March 1974. Personal interview with authors.

White, Sheldon. 27 October 1972. Speech at Embassy Row Hotel. Washington.

Wildavsky, Aaron. 1964. *The politics of the budgetary process*. Boston: Little, Brown.

Williamson, John. n.d. Letter to Elisabeth Hansot.

————. 7 September 1973. Outline of planning sequence. NIE, unpublished.

————. 13 December 1973. Draft criteria. NIE, unpublished.

————. 25 February 1974. Proposed planning sequence. NIE, unpublished.

————. 28 February 1974. Proposed planning sequence: Draft 2. NIE, unpublished.

————. 4 March 1974*a*. Issues. NIE, unpublished.

————. 4 March 1974*b*. Feasibility of priority ranking decision packages. NIE, unpublished.

————. 4 March 1974*c*. The interdependence of the commitment base and new activity categories. NIE, unpublished.

————. 4 March 1974*d*. Need for policy planning at the institute level. NIE, unpublished.

————. 4 March 1974*e*. The role of OPM. NIE, unpublished.

————. 5 March 1974. The role of the council. NIE, unpublished.

————. 7 March 1974. What is a decision package? NIE, unpublished.

————. 8 March 1974. Memorandum to Martin and Elliott concerning the planning process. NIE, unpublished.

Williamson, John, and Hansot, Elisabeth. 24 September 1973. Planning process paper. NIE, unpublished.

————. 5 December 1973. Structuring FY 1975 planning in the priority areas: Some preliminary thoughts. NIE, unpublished.

Williamson, John, and Young, Emily. 1 March 1974. Short form decision packages. NIE, unpublished.

Wirt, John. 1972. *Alternative designs for the National Institute of Education.* Washington, D. C.: Rand Corporation.

Wirt, John, et al. 1972. Organization for innovation. Santa Monica: Rand Corporation. Preliminary report.

Wolf, David. January 1973. Notes on tasks from December 1972.

————. 25 January 1973. Memorandum concerning things which Leni Rosenfield might help out with. NIE, unpublished.

————. 7 February 1973. Memorandum concerning current tasks before me. NIE, unpublished.

————. 22 February 1973. NIE planning: A paper for discussion. NIE, unpublished.

————. 21 May 1973. Tasks for week of May 21. NIE, unpublished.

————. 7 June 1973. Memorandum concerning current tasks before me. NIE, unpublished.

Young, Emily. 27 February 1974. Possible planning process. NIE, unpublished.

Index

Accidents, as source of NIE problems, 209–10
Action, in new organizations, 221–22
AERA. *See* American Educational Research Association
AFGE. *See* American Federation of Government Employees
Allen, James, 32, 38
Ambiguity: in new organizations, 107–8; in NIE mandate, 71
American Association of School Administrators (AASA), 69
American Educational Research Association (AERA), 94–95
American Federation of Government Employees (AFGE), 113
Appropriations for NIE. *See* Budgets for NIE
Ashbrook, John (Representative, R–Ohio), 70, 81–82
ASPE. *See* Assistant Secretary for Planning and Evaluation
Assessment of NIE: external, 206–9; internal, 209–15; speed with which reached, 215–16. *See also* Belief
Assistant Secretary for Planning and Evaluation (ASPE): as member of "Unholy Trinity," 28; and NIE directorship, 115–16; reaction to Planning Unit work, 50–52; reviews Bureau of Research policy, 26; reviews HEW education R&D activities, 30; and transfer of OE employees to NIE, 113

Baker, William, 73
Bayh, Birch (Senator, D–Indiana), 85
Beall, J. Glenn (Senator, R–Maryland), 79
Belief: axioms of progress and management, 203–4; and external events, 205–6; influencing, 224–25; model of development of, 203
Belief about NIE, 202–16; and experienced managers, 213–14; by insiders, 209–15;

and plan of action, 214; and relations with Congress, 213
Big Six Education Association, 69
Binswanger, Robert, 132
Bissell, Joan, 52
Brademas, John (Representative, D–Indiana): and appointment of NCER, 85; assesses NIE, 208; background of, 68; as chairman of House Select Subcommittee on Education, 67–68; on congressional perceptions of education R&D, 68; as defender of NIE legislation, 69; and education lobbies, 95; and Five Priorities, 172
Brooke, Edward (Senator, R–Massachusetts), 79
Budgets for NIE: fiscal year 1973, 73, 76; fiscal year 1974, 76–80, 85–86, 185–90; supplemental fiscal year 1974, 80–81, 87–89, 190–92; fiscal year 1975, 81–84, 86, 192–99; and annual federal budget cycle, 245; compared with total federal spending on education, 95; in context of total Nixon administration budgets, 91–92; difficulties in applying proved strategies for support of, 104–5; failure to achieve fiscal-year exemptions, 74; impact of deadlines on, 193–94; and problems with accidents and mistakes, 84–88; and problems with bureaucracy, 88–91; and problems with politics, 91–98; and problems with programs, 98–103; summary of congressional reaction to, 104–5
Burchinal, Lee, 132–33
Bureaucracy, NIE problems with, 88–91
Bureau of Research: attacks upon, 28, 29; budgets of, 20; budget reductions of 1969, 30; inadequacies of, 25–26; management problems of, 24; and NIE's rational approach, 168; reorganization of 1965, 26; reorientation of 1969, 31; reviewed by various agencies, 26; studies of, 29–31; summary of problems of, 31. *See also*

INSTITUTE FOR RESEARCH ON
TEACHING INFORMATION CENTER
238 Erickson Hall